T R A V E L E R ' S

JAPAN

C O M P A N I O N

The 1998–1999 Traveler's Companions

ARGENTINA • AUSTRALIA • BALI • CALIFORNIA • CANADA • CHINA • COSTA RICA • CUBA • EASTERN CANADA • ECUADOR • FLORIDA • HAWAII • HONG KONG • INDIA • INDONESIA • JAPAN • KENYA • MALAYSIA & SINGAPORE • MEDITERRANEAN FRANCE • MEXICO • NEPAL • NEW ENGLAND • NEW ZEALAND • PERU • PHILIPPINES • PORTUGAL • RUSSIA • SPAIN • THAILAND • TURKEY • VENEZUELA • VIETNAM, LAOS AND CAMBODIA • WESTERN CANADA

Traveler's JAPAN Companion

First Published 1998
The Globe Pequot Press
6 Business Park Road, P.O. Box 833,
Old Saybrook, CT 06475-0833
www.globe.pequot.com

ISBN: 0-7627-0253-2

By arrangement with Kümmerly+Frey AG, Switzerland
© 1998 Kümmerly+Frey AG, Switzerland

Created, edited and produced by
Allan Amsel Publishing, 53 rue Beaudouin,
27700 Les Andelys, France. E-mail: Allan.Amsel@wanadoo.fr
Editor in Chief: Allan Amsel
Editor: Fiona Nichols
Original design concept: Hon Bing-wah
Picture editor and designer: Fiona Nichols

CREDIT
Photo of Cinderella's Castle, Tokyo Disneyland on page 142
© Walt Disney Productions Inc. Photo by Tim Porter.

Printed by Samhwa Printing Co. Ltd., Seoul, Korea

TRAVELER'S JAPAN COMPANION

by Peter Popham and Bradley Winterton

Photographed by Nik Wheeler

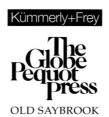

Kümmerly+Frey

The
Globe
Pequot
Press

OLD SAYBROOK

Contents

TRAVELER'S JAPAN COMPANION

N

KYUSHU · Kagoshima

EAST CHINA SEA

NANSEI ISLANDS

Okinawa Island
· Naha

Iriomote National Park
Ishigaki Island

HONSHU

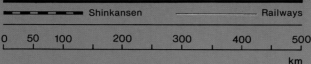

ISHIKAWA
· Hakui
· Kanazawa
TOYAMA
Chubu-Sangaku National Park

· Masuda
SHIMANE
TOTTORI
· Hagi
· Tsuwano
Ogori YAMAGUCHI
· Tottori
Miyazu Bay
· Fukui
FUKUI
· Takayama

Shimonoseki
Hiroshima
CHUGOKU
Amanohashidate
· Tsuruga
CHUBU
NAG

Fukuoka (Hakata)
Kitakyushu
FUKUOKA
HIROSHIMA
OKAYAMA
HYOGO
SHIGA
· Gifu
GIFU

SAGA
Miyajima
Onomichi Okayama Kurashiki
KYOTO
Lake Biwa

Imabari Inland Sea Shodo Island
Himeji
Mt. Rokko
· Kyoto
· Nagoya

NAGASAKI
OITA
Matsuyama
Marugame Takamatsu
Kobe
AICHI

Nagasaki
Beppu
EHIME
Kotohira KAGAWA
Osaka
· Nara
SHIZ

Unzen-Amakusa National Park
Kumamoto · Aso
KOCHI
TOKUSHIMA
NARA MIE
· Ise
· Hamamatsu

Amakusa Islands
Mt. Aso
Uwajima
· Tokushima
KINKI
· Toba

KUMAMOTO
· Kochi
WAKAYAMA
Kii Peninsula

KAGOSHIMA MIYAZAKI · Hyuga
SHIKOKU

Kagoshima
Mt. Takachino
KYUSHU

Sakurajima Island · Shibushi
· Miyazaki

Ibusuki
Mt. Kaimon

HOKKAIDO

Daisetsuzan
National Park

Akan National Park

Shikotsu-Toya
National Park
Noboribetsu Spa
Lake Toya

● Sapporo

● Akankokan
Lake Kutcharo
Lake Akan

Lake Shikotsu

● Tomakomai

Noboribetsu

SEA OF JAPAN

● Aomori

AOMORI

AKITA   IWATE

Akita ●   TOHOKU

● Morioka

YAMAGATA

▲ Mt. Haguro

Sado Island

▲ Mt. Gasson

MIYAGI
Ayukawa
● Ojika Peninsula

Niigata ●

Matsushima
Sendai ●

Kinkazan
Island

NIIGATA

▲ Mt. Bandai

● Fukushima

GUMMA

Nikko●

FUKUSHIMA

Matsumoto

Lake Chuzenji

Chichibu-Tama
National Park

TOCHIGI

● Mashiko

SAITAMA

● Tsukuba

KANTO   IBARAKI

▲ Mt. Mitake

es

-Izu

Tokyo ◉

● Narita

k

Hakone

Kawasaki ●

● Yokohama

CHIBA

dawara

Atami ●

Kamakura

imoda

● Ito

eninsula

KANAGAWA

Oshima
Island

PACIFIC OCEAN

TOP SPOTS

Meditate in Kyoto

I FIRST SAW KYOTO ON AN AUTUMN DAY OF INCOMPARABLE SPLENDOR — SILENT, WINDLESS AND SERENE. I have returned to the city many times since, and whatever the season it has always held me in its grasp.

It's a fabulous place, endlessly fascinating, and no trip to Japan could possibly be complete without a visit. Like Venice, it's one of the cultural treasure-houses of the world. But if a poetic image to represent Venice were a young girl with her hair spread out on the water, for Kyoto it would a middle-aged woman, bound tight in a kimono, setting out yellow chrysanthemums in a temple on a blue October morning.

Kyoto is in so many different ways Japan's past. The appalling damage done to the country's major cities by

the American fire-bombing in the last phase of World War II didn't extend to Kyoto, and as a result it is a unique repository of pre-modern Japanese culture.

It's also a demurely prosperous place. Even the monks and Shinto luminaries standing in the streets holding their begging bowls are decked out in their immaculate, neatly pressed best.

Kyoto's temples that are the heart of the place. There are 1,500 — an almost unbelievable figure. It's hardly surprising, then, that you can find yourself almost alone in many of them, watched only by the odd astute cat.

But when I first came out of that railway station — since 1997 enlarged into a structure of considerable grandeur — I was confronted, as you still are today, not with a temple or a lake overhung with cherry blossom, but with a multicolored Viewing Tower that would be more appropriate in Disneyland than in Japan's most venerable city.

You can't miss the Tourist Information Center of the Japan National Tourist Organization — it's at street level right at the tower's base. Nearer the top is a Viewing Platform, and on the way there you can inspect scenes of old Kyoto life (including executions, fortunately performed only by costumed robots).

Go up to that **Viewing Platform**. From it you can see spread out before you the whole city, symmetrically laid-out and

In Kyoto ABOVE a local woman dresses for the geisha parade. LEFT: Autumn paints the trees of Kyoto with an entrancing beauty.

surrounded by hills. Immediately below the tower you'll notice a large old temple, and you can peer right down into its lovingly-raked courtyards.

But most of the temples (and smaller shrines) are just on the edge of town, basking among luminous red leaves in the clear light of autumn, or gaunt and heroic between the bare branches of winter.

You don't have to go far from the station to find some of the finest temples of all. Quite a few are ten minutes away, on the other side of the river in the Higashiyama-ku district.

Every time I go to Kyoto I always make a point of going straight to the wonderful and very famous **Kiyomizu Temple**. Wooden and unpainted, it juts out from a Higashiyama-ku hillside and overlooks the town. There's an excess of curio shops on the stone steps leading up there, but, like everything else in Kyoto, it's organized with such restraint and good taste you'll scarcely notice them if you don't want to. It's useful to know the structure dates from 798 AD, even though most of what you see today was constructed in the seventeenth century.

The orange and green **Yasuka Shrine** nearby also shouldn't be missed. Few visitors go there, and I'm always undisturbed, sometimes for near on half an hour. It gives you the other half of Kyoto's magic formula — a meditative quiet as opposed to Kiyomizu's display of spiritual authority and grandeur.

In the centre of the city is **Nijo Castle**, set behind a moat in beautiful grounds. Unexpectedly for a castle, it's built entirely of wood.

But this isn't all. Kyoto has a vigorous modern life as well.

The old and new, hand-in-hand, can be experienced in the marvelous **Toei Movieland** (*Toei Uzamasa Eigamura*). It's a working film studio for films featuring old Japan — samurai epics a specialty — and you can not only watch but dress up and (almost) take part.

You're unlikely to be offered a part in a movie on the spot. But the place does combine genuine filmmaking with a

unique experience for tourists. The entire site is an assembly of Edo-era locations, from inns to "pleasure quarters", period streets to a special effects area.

Don't expect just to stand on the sidelines and watch the professionals. The campus is as much laid out for tourists as it is for filming (and bad weather may mean there's none of the latter going on the day you show up, though there are indoor studios as well).

This is a really unique attraction, something only the Japanese could have dreamed up. There's a Costume Photo Studio, for instance, where you can dress up as samurai or geisha and be filmed for the astonishment of the folks back home.

Or you can simply play with remote-control boats in their Miniature Model Corner. And there might be something important being filmed in the Special Effects Pool, or in the Simulated Live Film Studio. You never know your luck.

I was also charmed by the house of the famous Japanese potter and wood-carver, **Kawai Kanjiro**. He was the friend of, and his work deeply influenced by, the celebrated British ceramicist Bernard Leach. When Leach came to Japan for a second time, in 1934, they worked together at Kawai Kanjiro's kiln. A lover of the simple and the natural in all things,

Ryoan-ji LEFT, Temple of the Peaceful Dragon. The graceful clean lines ABOVE of traditional Japanese roofs.

he structured the house deliberately to be in the style of a traditional Japanese rural cottage.

If you fancy a quiet walk around with a Japanese English-speaking guide, try one of the morning walking tours in the company of Johnnie Hillwalker (Japanese name: Hajime Hirooka). Groups in the past have averaged only three or four people per day so there should be plenty of opportunity to pose questions on nature and the local environment.

After your walk no doubt you'll fancy some lunch. Try **Honke Owariya** ℂ (075) 231-3446 — it's the oldest noodle house in Kyoto and very famous. It was founded in 1465 and is still in business! The most it will set you back is around ¥1,600. It's on the street called Kurumayacho, one block east of Oike subway station (leave by Exit Nº 1). The restaurant is on the left as you walk up the street, going northwards towards the Imperial Palace. The decor, incidentally, is traditional, and worth looking at in its own right.

Lastly, note that the *butoh* theater company **Byakkosha** (literally White Tiger Brigade) is based in Kyoto (see THE PLEASURES OF JAPAN, page 112 for more on *butoh*). I've never been lucky enough to catch them on their home ground, and if by any chance they're performing when you're in town, move heaven and earth to make sure you get a ticket.

Land a 747 Aircraft

TOKYO'S UENO PARK IS HOME TO A CLUTCH OF MUSEUMS. Some, like the Tokyo National Museum, are frankly only of interest to specialists — long, high exhibition halls that appear not to have changed in decades, and certainly don't give so much as a nod in the direction of the principle of hands-on accessibility and user-friendliness.

The **National Science Museum** nearby, however, is much more congenial.

The story of the meteorite that fell at Kokubunji, in Kagawa Prefecture, in 1986, for example, is told in vivid style, with a holograph angel from outer space listening to documentary filmed testimony from locals who saw — and heard — it abruptly come to a halt after its long journey, no one knows from where, into their back gardens.

There are other attractive exhibits, and there's usually a high-profile temporary exhibition in addition (though you will have to pay extra for admission to this). But the highlight of my visit to the museum was taking my seat in the **flight simulator** and piloting a Boeing 747 jet aircraft in to land at Tokyo's Haneda Airport.

It doesn't cost anything; a trip in the simulator is included in the regular price of admission to the museum, currently ¥400. But you do need to book a place. There are only a dozen seats, and it's a popular attraction. I'd had it recommended to me so went to the unit and booked my place as soon as I arrived in the museum, and you should do the same.

First you're shown how the control joystick works. Then you're led, along with the others in your group, into the imitation aircraft cabin. Once inside you

strap yourself in and wait. An attendant explains the procedure in Japanese, with the key phrases in other languages for the benefit of foreigners.

When you were waiting to go in you'll probably watch the module rocking up and down, and tilting slightly from side to side. It actually doesn't move very much at all, and in many ways it's a consolation to know this in advance, because once you are inside, with film of the landscape below Haneda Airport projected around you, your brain quickly becomes convinced you are actually in the air. The cabin rocks gently, the "landscape" disappears as you climb into cloud, and you wait with just the faintest hint of apprehension for your turn to take over the controls to come round.

You don't change seats. Every seat has a control joystick on its right hand side. The plane circles the airport, and though you know from watching the module from outside it is only tilting slightly, you nevertheless can't help hoping you're going to be OK. And so the plane descends to land at Haneda. When I was on it the runway was slightly to the left of where we were heading, but the first "pilot" adjusted our angle of descent to

line up with it, accompanied by cheers from his friends, and we all but "landed." Just as we were about to touch down, however, the plane turned its nose up and round we went again, ready for the next candidate to have a try. One candidate deliberately "crashed" the plane. The wraparound screen displays simply the surface of the runway and the otherwise urbane attendant frowned disapprovingly. And that's about it. The whole "trip" takes some 25 minutes.

But it's a real experience. These simulators are simplified versions of what are used in training real aircraft pilots, and the feeling of being airborne is genuine. For some few people it might be a touch too real. If this is the case with you, you only have to glance at the narrow black strip dividing the wraparound screen into its individual rectangular sections to quickly regain a sense of reality, and to remember you're only in a metal box being gently jogged up and down a few feet from the museum floor.

ABOVE: A reaction to the "pilots" trying out the National Science Museum's flight simulator? These three monkeys wisely keep their distance in Nikko.

Climb a Small Mountain

WELL, WHAT'S SMALL, OF COURSE, DEPENDS ON THE VIEWPOINT OF THE CLIMBER. But as a valley location **Kamikochi** is so beautiful, so sequestered and so quiet, surrounded on all sides by high peaks that it's difficult, and for some impossible, not to be tempted to climb at least one of them.

Kamikochi is five hours from Tokyo's labyrinthine Shinjuku Station. Bullet trains *(shinkanzen)* to Matsumoto depart 36 times during the day. The journey is a revelation in itself, climbing up through wooded hills to reveal the Japan Alps themselves glistening (if you're lucky) in the mid-morning sun.

You change at Matsumoto (Platform Nº 7) for the local train to Shin-Shimashima. From there a bus takes you for the even more wonderful ride to Kamikochi itself. Kamikochi is the end of the road, but the starting point for mountain trails — upwards, of course, in all directions. It's the finest center for mountain-walking in the country.

Stay at one of the splendid mountain lodges. I opted for the reasonably-priced **Nishi-ito-ya sanso** (¥8,000 upwards), but there's also the fine **Imperial Hotel** at around ¥26,000. There are also some small budget-priced places a short walk up the valley from the bus terminal.

Most people, it's true, content themselves in Kamikochi with pottering along by the river and taking photos of each other against the backdrop of the positively celestial mountains. There's nothing wrong with that. Kamikochi is one of Japan's special places, with a pristine freshness to its water and the air, ensured by a scrupulous conservation policy. Not only is there no litter, there aren't even any litter-bins! And no private cars are allowed within half an hour's drive of the place.

If you feel called to climb a few hours and see the spectacle of the great mountains from a more exalted viewpoint, then you could do a lot worse than make

for the modest summit called **Doppyo**, a day's reasonably strenuous hike there and back from Kamikochi. June, however, is the first month when this route is clear of snow — and even in June it's wise to confirm this with your hotel before you set out. I did it in May and found the old snowdrifts higher up difficult to negotiate. If you have doubts, ask at the Nishi-ityo-ya where the manager is a Himalayan climber and speaks English.

Doppyo is on the southern ridge of the major summit of **Mt. Nishihotaka** *(Nishihotaka-dake)*. This peak is beyond your reach in a day, and anyway a more difficult proposition. But Doppyo can be done by any reasonably strong walker equipped with mountain boots, though there's no denying you'll be tired when you get back. Yet for me it was the best experience in Japan, though I wish I'd done it in summer rather than in spring. Allow eight to nine hours for the round trip.

Walk downstream from the hotels for 10 minutes until you reach the bridge (known as **Tashiro Bridge**). Don't cross it, but take the trail that leads off into the woods and is signposted "To Mount Nishihotaka".

The path climbs through giant conifers, with the stream roaring far below you in its dark gorge. After a little over an hour you'll reach an area of stark dead trees, standing white in the silence. Here the trail turns upwards to the right, and the going begins to get ever so slightly tough.

The way is clear of snow in summer, but in spring great banks of old snow stand in your way, with the ground steep underneath them. Before June the walk should not be attempted by the inexperienced.

Should you lose your way, however, there are red ribbons tied to the branches of the trees to show the route up. These ribbons are primarily for the benefit of mountaineers going up in winter when the trail is entirely hidden under snow, and sometimes they follow a slightly different route from the summer path.

Beautiful vistas LEFT and RIGHT are easily within the reach of hikers setting out from Kamikochi to explore the Japanese Alps.

the ascent. From the lodge, follow your footsteps all the way down again to Kamikochi. But if there is still snow left, take extra care, and proceed at snail's pace.

This is a wonderful climb, with an appropriate reward in the view from Doppyo (always assuming conditions are clear). You'll have climbed over 1,000 m (3,334 ft) from Kamikochi. But because Kamikochi itself is already over a 1,000 m (3,334 ft) above sea level, your highest point will have been nearer 2,500 m (8,334 ft), no mean altitude for a mere walker. Congratulations!

See Nikko

NIKKO IS ONE OF JAPAN'S GREAT SACRED PLACES, AND IT HAS BEEN THIS FOR WELL OVER A THOUSAND YEARS.

You won't be in Tokyo long before you realize that Nikko is within easy striking distance. Everyone else seemed to be going there by conducted tour, so I decided to get there on my own, by train. You should, too.

When I arrived at this ancient religious center snug in the mountains I immediately understood that a trip there combined natural splendors with magnificent and historic shrines. The other great attraction of Nikko is that all its shrines and temples are in one elaborate complex, 20 minutes' walk from the station. Situated on a thickly wooded slope and surrounded by a massive stone wall, the buildings blend Shinto and Buddhist elements, as if in homage to a place of near-incomparable peace and beauty in a fold of the hills.

It can, however, sometimes be difficult to appreciate the calm sanctity that the place undoubtedly once had on account of the large numbers of tourists who are attracted there virtually every day.

So I took my courage in both hands and, having passed through the very splendid **Yomeiman Gate** into the upper compound, escaped over the massive wall and up into the woods, no doubt breaking every regulation in the book in the process.

But they will be of great help if you get lost, and will lead you safely to the mountain lodge. Yes, there's a lodge at the point where the trail reaches the ridge! You can even stay there if you want, and you can certainly have hot coffee and a bowl of noodles as a reward for your efforts, served up by the friendly young staff (some of whom also speak a few words of English).

From here, you can see the ridge extending northwards, climbing gently all the time. It isn't hard, and Doppyo is around an hour from the mountain lodge. You'll know when you've got there. The trail winds up the side of the rocky outcrop, and from the top you get your first unimpeded view of the highest summits of the Japan Alps, beautiful **Mt. Okuhotaka** (*Okuhotaka-dake*) on the left of the view — at 3,190 m (16,340 ft) the highest of all, and second only in Japan to Mt. Fuji — and **Mt. Maehotaka** (*Maehotaka-dake*) on the right.

The walk back to the mountain lodge is more of an amble after the exertions of

ABOVE: The Grand Spring Festival of Toshogu Shrine at Nikko and RIGHT the spectacular parade leading up to the Shrine.

From this quiet vantage point I could look down onto the various gabled roofs and courtyards and see the temples and monks' quarters much as they must have originally appeared to devotees in olden times, arriving after week-long treks through the mountains.

I had lunch at the **Nikko Kanaya Hotel**, just on the outskirts of Nikko — and it's almost as interesting as the **Five Storied Pagoda** and the **Futarasan Shrine**. It epitomizes the luxurious Western styles that first arrived in Japan at the end of the last century, though it was later brought up to date in the style of the 1930s.

While the other guests were having their coffee, I nipped out and took a walk along the corridors that run alongside the restaurant. There I discovered framed bills and guest-register entries testifying to the visits in the twenties and thirties of the British Prince of Wales (later to be briefly King Edward VIII before he abdicated in order to marry the American Wallace Simpson), German-born physicist

Albert Einstein, and English historian Arnold Toynbee.

Nikko, I suddenly realized, may now be a place anyone can visit, and easily. But 60 years ago it was somewhere only the very rich and very famous found solitude and inspiration. Or, in Edward's case, probably a round of golf. He is reputed to have been partly responsible for popularizing golf in Japan, a country that is about as far as you can get from St. Andrews, but where today golf is enormously popular.

In the afternoon, I went up into the mountains. That means going, via innumerable vertiginous hairpin bends, to **Lake Chuzenji**. If you opt to visit Nikko on an organized tour, as most visitors do, you will almost certainly be taken there.

On arrival at one of the temples that dot the shoreline I was greeted by a troupe of dancers who performed a ceremonious dance, meticulously performed even though they must have gone through the routine many times before on that day alone.

Chuzenji is a volcanic lake surrounded by a variety of peaks of modest height. In summer you can hire a boat, and go out on the lake and visit some of the waterside temples. It's also magnificent country to

ABOVE: Fabulous period costumes create much of the intoxicating ambiance during the Grand Spring Festival at Nikko.

explore on foot, though if you plan to do this you'll have to have left Tokyo by an early train, and made certain of your transport back to Nikko in the evening.

There are various recommended trails — five hours round-trip to **Mt. Hangetsu** from Akechidaira (see below), four and a half hours round-trip from the **Ryuzu Falls** — accessible by road half way along the north shore of the lake — to **Lake Sainoko**, and so on. Hikes along the lake shore, or some way up into the hills, can naturally be as long or as short as you choose.

The water leaves the lake via the **Kegon Falls**, a 100-m (330-ft) drop over a precipice. I descended to inspect it in a lift constructed inside the cliff face — a typical piece of Japanese engineering ingenuity. The Kegon waterfall actually freezes over in very cold weather, a spectacle well worth making the whole trip to Nikko specially to see.

Another couple of things you can do in the vicinity are to go up by cablecar to **Akechidaira**, a plateau commanding a fine view, or via another cablecar from Chuzenji Station into the scenic **Chanokibaira Hills**.

Nikko is attractive because it has such a long history, but also because of its variety. It's true there are crowds, but I found that with a little ingenuity you can get away from them. Together with Hakone, Kamakura and the Mt. Fuji Five Lakes region, it provides a relatively quick escape from often claustrophobic Tokyo.

Be Charmed by Karuizawa

THE OFFICIAL GUIDE CALLS IT "THE OLDEST UPLAND RESORT TOWN IN JAPAN." It may be that but what it is today is a combination of the very chic, the very exclusive, and the very charming.

Rural life was, and is, what Karuizawa is all about. It's picturesque, not in itself at all challenging, but with fine views up to an active volcano on the skyline.

It's two hours from Tokyo's Ueno Station by JR's Shin-etsu Line. The one-

way fare (if you haven't got a JR Pass) is just under ¥5,000.

It's both quiet enough for a rather large number of foreigners and important Japanese to have their homes there, and accessible enough to be crowded with fashionable boutiques and restaurants during the summer season.

The little handbook put out by the town authorities is totally unlike anything to be found anywhere else in Japan. Whereas all other places produce glossy brochures luring you with dazzling photos of ancient temples, gaudy festivals, sun-soaked beaches, and snowy mountains framed by blossom, Karuizawa offers a little hand-illustrated booklet that is more in the nature of a country parson's nature diary, waiting to be filled in, while you shelter from a spring shower underneath a Japanese larch.

Walking and cycling are the usual, recommended ways of getting about (though no hiking is allowed within four kilometers of the crater of the active volcano, **Mt. Asama**). There's a bird-watching forest (some 120 species make Karuizawa their home at one time of year or another), and at night foxes prowl the lanes and fields. It all sounds very gentle and peaceful, a sort of privileged artists' retreat. This is, surely, the perfect place to relax and be alone. The only surprise comes when you see the statistics.

Karuizawa is indeed a charming place, but it's country life made available to all comers. There are 10,000 self-catering holiday chalets here, five hundred shops and restaurants on the main street alone, and every year eight million people visit this site of pastoral idyll.

It was certainly once an exclusive hidey-hole, the favorite hangout of English missionaries, retired diplomats, and Japanese poets. Today it has the same attractions, but with rather more people enjoying them. Prices are high, and it's very fashionable indeed to enjoy the country air here.

Even so, it's restful, which Tokyo, whatever else it is, is not. Even as a foreigner you won't have any problems fixing up somewhere to stay for as long or as short as you like. And despite it being a mere two hours from the capital, this is a place you will probably want to stay more than a few hours in.

At an altitude of 900 m (3,000 ft) it's cool in summer, and a veritable winter wonderland in winter. It may prove too popular for your tastes, but it has the advantages of its limitations. There is everything you could wish for in the way of accommodation, shops and restaurants. And if it does prove not quite sequestered enough, then Japan holds plenty of remoter, quieter places for your delectation. Next time, you could try somewhere like Tohoku.

Savor Hakone

HAKONE IS TOKYO'S GARDEN, PLAYGROUND AND GATEWAY TO THE GREAT BEYOND, ALL ROLLED IN ONE. It is, needless to say for an area so huge, a place of contrasts. Some of the most exclusive hotels in the land (such as the Hakone Prince) are there. But so are great expanses of rocky hills and flowery lakeside gardens. As befits a place that's in a very real sense Tokyo's biggest public park, there's something for everyone.

I love it because even a day-trip there involves, or can involve, so many different forms of transport, and hence so many different kinds of feeling.

To begin with you are hurtled there by *shinkansen*, Japan's famous bullet train. Then you climb into the mountains on the entirely different Tozan Line train, only to be winched up (to **Owakudani**) by cablecar, and then down, also by cablecar, to **Lake Ashinoko**. After all these excitements, it is a form of heaven to cruise calmly across the surface of the lake by tranquil and unhurried boat.

Hakone is big, so crowds — except in the areas directly accessible by public

OPPOSITE: Lake Ashinoko, in the Hakone region, with the ever-present Mt. Fuji. Because of its proximity to the capital, Hakone is Japan's favorite retreat for relaxation and leisure activities.

transport — can easily be avoided. One tip: if you've got a Japan Rail Pass, you'll find that it isn't valid beyond Odawara, the stop where you leave your Japan Rail bullet train and set off up the smaller Tozan Line. Help is at hand, however. There is a special Hakone Free Pass available, giving you "free" travel in the area for four full days. You can get one that's valid all the way from Tokyo's Shinjuku Station. But you can also get one, for less money, valid from Odawara — exactly what you want if you hold a JR Pass that you can use up to that point. The current price is ¥4,050 (¥2,030 for children).

Hakone is a playground in another sense. You can flee the hard realities of modern Japanese urban life there. With a Free Pass that lasts four days, you can relax, and while away time by lake and mountain, wallow in sulfurous water at elegant spas, or just admire the azaleas from hillsides. And yet, because it's so near Tokyo, all the facilities you might require are at hand. With views of Mt. Fuji out of the window, you can sample dishes that have never tasted so good as they do here, out in the fresh air. With the savings you make on your four-day pass, you might treat yourself, for example, to a meal at the famous Hakone Hotel, close to the Barrier Guardhouse and the ferry piers on the lake.

Many Tokyoites have happy memories that have been molded at Hakone. You can add yours too, and the place will still not have been exhausted of its potential for giving pleasure, which is all but unlimited.

Stay in a *Ryokan*

JAPAN'S ESSENCE IS OFTEN DESCRIBED AS ELUSIVE, AND, WHEN YOU FIND IT (WHATEVER "IT" IS), THEN ALL TOO OFTEN IT'S MINIMAL AND TRANSIENT. Stay in a traditional Japanese inn, or *ryokan*, however, and you have time to rest, and contemplate the transience of all things.

Ryokan can be found anywhere — the Japan National Tourist Office publishes a useful *Japan Ryokan Guide*, covering much of the country. It includes information on how to make reservations, and what to expect. And there are many more not listed in this guide book.

The first thing to note is that the service in a *ryokan* is more personal than in a Western-style "business hotel." Because the staff bring you tea — and maybe your meals too — in your room, because you wash in a communal *furo* (bathroom), and because the whole style is one that follows traditional Japanese custom (in which hospitality to guests plays an important part), you will be known to the management in a way you rarely are in other kinds of accommodation, excepting the stay-with-the-family *minshuku*.

When writer David Price, in his *Travels in Japan* (see FURTHER READING, page 257), decides to spend a Christmas alone in a *ryokan* in Nara, he describes his encounter with the hotel's owner. He relates how she bows low, kneeling on the *tatami* matting to deposit the tea tray, shows him how to use the TV and the heater, asks him where he has come from, and discusses the cold. In this he detects a simple human warmth combined with discretion. She has no intention of making herself at home, nor would she expect him to come and sit in her kitchen. The two of them simply exchange the knowledge that they are alive, and neither is demeaned by this. The institution itself somehow implies an equality of spirit.

And it's true. There is a blend of friendliness and discretion in almost any *ryokan* that is typical of the places, and indeed of much of Japan.

The formality begins the moment you arrive — it's normal to take off your shoes even before you walk over from the front door to the reception desk. So take them off, place them on the rack where everyone else's outdoor shoes are stacked, and put on a pair of the slippers that will be laid out in a line across your path. Then you can approach the receptionist like an old hand.

A maid or the mistress will then take you to your room. If you find beauty in simplicity, then your room will probably be your chief delight. Green tea will be placed on the table shortly after you check in. If the *ryokan* is traditional, the door to your room will be a sliding one made of paper and flimsy wood, and there will, if the place is a really traditional one, be no lock. There is no need to worry about the safety of your belongings — the honesty of the Japanese is one of the most relaxing things about their country — but, if you worry all the same, leave valuables with the maid. Nowadays some *ryokan* rooms are equipped with safes.

The floor of the room will be covered with blocks of tatami flooring (see HOW DO THEY LIVE?, page 100 for a description), so leave your slippers outside. In the room's *tokonoma* (alcove) will be displayed a painting or a piece of calligraphy and an arrangement of freshly cut flowers. There will be a low table in the room with *zabuton* (seating pads) around it; in winter the table will be replaced with a *kotatsu*, a table with an electric heat-ring element underneath, covered with a quilt under which guests toast their feet.

There will be a mirror, mysteriously shrouded in a cloth, and there will be a hand-basin. In a full-length fitted cupboard you will discover your bedding. In the room there will be a *yakuta* or cotton dressing-gown, and maybe *geta* (wooden clogs). You can wear these anywhere inside the *ryokan* — indeed, it's usual to do so, less usual — but not impolite, not to.

In the bigger *ryokan* you'll probably be asked where you would like to eat. Dinner and breakfast are invariably provided under the room-charge in a *ryokan*. You can in theory ask for them not to be provided, in which case the overnight charge will be slightly reduced; but this will be considered unusual, and even possibly a slight on the *ryokan* as a whole. All in all, it's best — and more fun — to eat in if you possibly can. Meal times are usually flexible, and besides, eating in the communal dining-room will give you a chance to meet and talk with some of your fellow guests.

Rooms often have names, and you should take a look at yours before going down to eat for the first time as it may well be displayed on a little wooden place-marker to indicate where you are expected to sit. This is important in so far as guests often receive — mysteriously — different meals. The reason for this is usually no more mysterious than the desire not to give you a repeat of what you had for breakfast. Japanese breakfasts and dinners are for the most part very similar in their general makeup. Not all *ryokan* have dining-rooms, however, and if yours doesn't then service will be in your room.

You may be offered Western food but would be wise to reject this firmly: say "Washoku kudasai," "Japanese food, please."

Before supper you will generally be invited to take a bath. This is often a large one used by all the guests, and if your *ryokan* is in a hot spring area this may be the high point of your stay.

After supper the maid will clear away the table and spread out the *futon* (mattress), quilt and pillow which are stored in the room's closet. The pillow may be filled with rice husks and rather harder than what you are used to. It will, however, help to keep your head cool. Cool head, warm feet: that's the healthy way, the Japanese believe.

In the morning the bed-making procedure will be reversed and you will eat breakfast in your room. Two meals are generally included in the *ryokan*'s tariff. Checkout is by 10 or 11 AM.

Many writers have considered traditional *ryokan* Japanese rooms to be an expression of spiritual virtues. The simplicity is itself monastic, and its simple, lightweight adaptability an emblem of the Buddhist sense of the transience of all things. Many Japanese feel happy staying in a *ryokan* because it reminds them of their roots, and gives a peace that the Western-style comforts of a business hotel do not convey.

When you come to take your bath, this sense of the continuity of Japanese life, despite the manifest modernity of existence in so many other parts of the country, will be reinforced.

There will be two completely separate communal baths, one for men and one for women. Leave your slippers outside the door when you go in. How many other pairs are standing outside the door will tell you exactly how many of your fellow guests are already inside.

Once inside, undress and leave your clothes in one of the compartments provided. Note that these will not have a key. Then go through into the main room, the one where the bath is situated.

Don't get straight into the bath — that would be very bad form. Go to one of the showers attached to the walls and sit down in front of it on one of the tiny stools you'll find there. This is where you may wash.

Wash yourself using the soap and shampoos provided, though of course you can bring your own if you wish. There will probably be disposable toothbrushes and razors for your use if you so choose.

Once scrubbed clean, you can prepare to enter the bath.

The pool itself is, according to the taste of the bather, either an endurance test or a place for meditation. It will be hot, so enter carefully. If you have a heart condition it may be better not to use it at all. Sit in it — the water will come up to your chest. Loll so as to raise the level up to your neck if you like, but note that it isn't considered right to submerge your head, and may well be dangerous into the bargain. Put your miniature towel, folded up, onto your head so as to be able to submerge both hands. It is nothing short of bliss (for more on baths see under JAPANESE BATH, page 121).

The lady of the house welcomes guests to her mellow, elegant, 100-year-old *ryokan* in Narai.

Consider Hiroshima

AN AMERICAN VOICE IN THE PUBLIC BUS (Nº 13 OR 24 FROM THE TRAIN STATION) TELLS YOU THAT YOU ARE BOUND FOR THE PEACE MEMORIAL PARK.

You pass a Sogo Department Store and a Creative Life Store, and you're there in no time (in reality, something between 10 and 15 minutes).

Hiroshima today has been seen by some as a characterless, even drab, city but it shares in the prosperity in which the whole of Japan now basks. To the rest of the world, though, it's remembered for only the one thing.

Not that the Japanese don't remember it, too. August 6, 1945 is a date every schoolchild knows, the day when an American plane called the Enola Gay set out from the United States Air Force Base on Tinian Island in the Pacific and, at 8:15 AM, released what the military called "a new kind of bomb", curiously given a name ("Little Boy"), that exploded moments later 580 m (1,934 ft) above the city.

Was it the grim opening act of the modern era, or the end of an earlier one? Either way you should go there, if only to pay your respects.

The mayors of Hiroshima have sent telegrams protesting against every nuclear test ever since, and their protests line the walls of the main exhibition hall of the **Peace Memorial Museum**, addressed to the responsible heads of state. Hiroshima has become a world peace site, and the Museum (entrance a mere ¥50) is not so much a memorial to that 1945 blast as an active protest against modern nuclear weapon stockpiles.

Nevertheless, there are sufficient reminders and more of the unspeakable horrors suffered. Somehow the existence of a special word for those who suffered, *hibakusha*, and their characteristic understated self-description "I met with the A-bomb" is terribly harrowing. Those who still survive are getting old now, and the world has far worse weapons.

Photographs of eminent figures being shown round are on display. They all look grim — Gorbachev, Pope John-Paul II, Mother Theresa — as does every member of the big crowd always to be found there. Outside, everything in the sky suddenly seems ominous, including the birds.

The really sobering thought is that today we are mildly surprised that the damage was so limited. A twisted bicycle is on display — how come it survived at all, we wonder. A model of the actual bomb hangs against a wall. Again, we are surprised how small it was — about four times bigger than a man, perhaps, though many times heavier.

And at the edge of the park, on the banks of the Motoyasu river, the ruin of the Hiroshima Prefecture **Industrial Promotion Hall** stands unrepaired as a memorial. It could have been in any of Japan's flattened, fire-bombed cities in 1945.

Nevertheless, you should not fail to go there. Hiroshima is easily accessible on the main *shinkansen* line between Kyoto and Fukuoka (always referred to by Japan rail as Hakata). The countryside behind the city — it's not far across Honshu here to the northwest coast — is especially attractive, and Hiroshima port faces mountainous **Shikoku**, the large island that forms the other side of the Inland Sea.

And, by way of contrast, when you get back to Tokyo you might make a point of visiting the inner sanctum of Japanese expansionist patriotism, the **Yasukuni Shrine** in Kudan. It's a kind of opposite pole to Hiroshima, defiant and chauvinistic. But you need to see both places if you are to begin to understand that exceptionally complex, uniquely distinct phenomenon: the modern Japanese experience.

Preserved as it survived the atomic explosion, the former Industry Promotion Hall, now named the Atomic Bomb Dome, is Hiroshima's memorial to the catastrophe.

Relish *Bunraku*

THE SECOND AUDITORIUM AT TOKYO'S
NATIONAL THEATER IS A MEDIUM-SIZED ONE,
CONTAINING AROUND 450 SEATS, AND THE
PERFORMANCE IS TO BE BUNRAKU, OR CLASSIC
JAPANESE PUPPET THEATER.

It is performed here only in May, September and December, for three weeks each time. But at other times of the year you can see the company, Japan's finest, at their home theater, the Asahi-za, in Osaka.

Entrance here in Tokyo is ¥5,800 for the five-hour show, or ¥4,800 for a seat in the back row: a set of folding chairs and not recommended if you plan to stay for the whole performance. The simultaneous-commentary device you can — and should — rent (for ¥650, English and Japanese versions only, with a ¥1,000 deposit) works like a radio and is keyed to the action as it is performed.

The stage is as large as the width of the auditorium allows and before the action begins it is hidden by a dramatic striped curtain in stylish red, green and black.

The time is 4 PM, and the hard-working company (or perhaps different members of it) have already performed a different show, itself lasting four and a half hours, earlier in the day, ending a mere 20 minutes ago.

Now it is to be one of the great classics of the *bunraku* stage, "Yoshitsune and the Thousand Cherry Trees," a play dating from 1747.

The narrator, who is also the speaker of all the characters' lines, plus an instrumentalist (a *shamisen* player), sit to the right of the stage.

The scene is a stretch of countryside where there's an inn, and a large tree center-stage. The imagined time is the late twelfth century.

The figures, entirely shrouded in black, who manipulate the half to two-thirds-size puppets look like Ku Klux Klan members of an unorthodox sect. Gradually you realize that they are

standing slightly below stage level, in a two-foot "trench." But before long you're so engrossed in the action you hardly notice them at all.

After one cycle of action, the floor on which the narrator and *shamisen* player are sitting moves. They are in fact on a miniature revolving stage and are spun out of sight as two new performers are whirled into view.

You soon discover the show is in reality a form of straightforward story-telling by the narrator, made visually present by the silent puppets who mine the drama. It's a tale of love and betrayal, of rogues along the highway who prey on a defeated noble family as it flees the retribution of the victorious political party.

When the narrator and instrumentalist are replaced once again by a third pair, the scene also changes. Now it's a forest at night, and the tale will soon present a strong man's death. There are, you soon notice, additional musicians in the wings, behind a grill let into the scenery, as in *kabuki*.

Suddenly there is a hand-to-hand fight, not unlike the fights in traditional Sicilian puppet theater, also an old dramatic form still flourishing in the modern age. But whereas in Sicily the audience is almost entirely made up of tourists, here in Japan it's almost wholly made up of Japanese.

The radio commentary is subdued, with many silent passages. You can adjust the volume, and you listen via a single earplug. And just as the narrator and *shamisen* player change yet again, so the radio commentator changes too, the retiring one announcing his name just as he had given the narrators' and instrumentalists' names when they first appeared.

The play itself is full of an irony that implies a sceptical realism in its attitude to life. The Sicilian puppets, by contrast, are playful, given wherever possible to sensation and fun. These Japanese stories have more in common with the sagas of Iceland than with the Italian stories of Ariosto that are used by the Sicilians. Though these Oriental tales are more comprehensive, with women playing a much more important role, they nevertheless share a grim realism with the Icelandic sagas, a scepticism about the victory of the good, and about the attainability of happiness. Evil is eradicable in human life, and the generally somber nature of the accompanying music reinforces the implicit injunction not to expect too much from existence.

The narrator, when speaking the words the characters utter, as he does most of the time, is a collaborator with the master puppeteer of that particular puppet. Sound and image come from some way apart, but they are synchronized perfectly.

Sometimes, you think, *bunraku* looks like a large group of somberly-dressed old men wrestling with a small number of colorfully-attired pygmies. Suspicious guests, deceptions along the road, old feuds: all are typical of heroic-era literature in all cultures, as is the universal belief that a desire for money is always the basest of motives.

The audience is expectantly attentive, and you remember how many people in the Tokyo subway trains were reading books. This is a well-educated and cultured society, with strong roots down to its past. Theater is a thriving culture here, certainly in the major cities, and despite all the electronic entertainment available. And traditional Japanese theater, of which *bunraku* is a part, is one of the great performing art traditions of the world.

The narrator's role is almost that of an operatic soloist; he intones his words, and all but sings the important guffaws and sounds of amazement that are such a feature of these plays. The single narrator provides the voices of all the characters, young and old, men and women.

One of the assumptions lying behind these dramas appears to be that no one has a monopoly on the truth, or of right. Just when our sympathies have been extensively focused on the wife who has been left alone, but now meets her husband accidentally at the country inn,

suddenly the *sushi*-shop girl, who has been about to embark on an affair with the husband, takes center stage and, in the climax of this whole section of the drama, speaks at length of *her* dreams, and her now-dashed hopes.

The reversal of fortunes so characteristic of ancient Greek tragedy becomes what the Japanese in these *bunraku* dramas call the "return", the moment when a character repents of his evil deeds. No one has a monopoly, either, on goodness or on evil.

After an hour or so, these little puppets come to take on all the profundity of human-sized drama, but the very fact that they are mere large dolls actually adds to the pathos of the ancient tales. Even the narratives early on in the plays revealing what occurred in the past are a feature, too, of Greek drama. "How strange are the workings of destiny!" is a characteristic comment in both these ancient kinds of theater.

When you go to *bunraku*, as at *kabuki*, you should familiarize yourself with the small number of names of the main characters involved. The plays begin with simple events, but the twists of fate become rather complex. Even at the start of these extraordinary stories, all is not as it seems.

Japanese *bunraku* is an insight into the Japanese soul. It has an extraordinarily broad scope, despite its restricted physical size. This is one of the world's major theatrical cultures, just as Japan has for a long time been, and continues to be, one of the world's great civilizations. Its art, as its life, has seriousness and depth, and is adult in the most real sense.

Artists elsewhere have always recognized this about Japan, and not only in theater but in the visual arts, and also in literature and the cinema (what other Asian nation can begin to match the Japanese film industry, or the Japanese achievement in the modern novel?). The truth is that the finest Japanese artists remain aristocrats of the spirit in an often crass democratic world. *Bunraku* is as clear an example of this as you are likely to find.

Cross the Alps

IT DOESN'T COME CHEAP (¥10,320 AT THE TIME OF WRITING), BUT THIS ROUTE OVER JAPAN'S HIGHEST MOUNTAIN RANGE IS A WONDERFUL EXPERIENCE. Its main virtue is that it opens up the spectacle of the high mountains to those who are unable or unwilling to undertake the lengthy and frequently strenuous walking getting there on foot involves.

The Tateyama Kurobe Alpine Route has been pieced together using a variety of means of transport — bus, train, cable railway, cablecar and trolleycar.

The entire 90-km (53-mile) traverse in the Omachi district of the Japan Alps involves only one 10-minute walk, across the top of the dam that blocks off a high-level lake. But it takes you right across the impressive 3,015 m (10,005 ft) Tateyama mountain range.

You can, however, take a break from the schedule and go off on your own side-excursions on foot, and then rejoin the Alpine Route later. Naturally in this case you'll have to make an early start and have the times of the remaining sections of the Alpine Route (or those back to where you started) to hand.

The Alpine Route runs from **Shinano Omachi** station (Japan Rail, and therefore accessible on your JR Rail Pass) to Toyama City, also on the JR system. You can also, of course, do the trip in the reverse direction.

From Shinano Omachi, the Alpine Route begins with a 40-minute bus ride to **Ogisawa**, at an altitude of 1,433 m (4,800 ft). This is followed by a 16-minute trip on a trolley bus to the dam at Kurobe, only a few meters higher but on the other side of 2,678 m (8,927 ft) **Mt. Harinoke** (*Harinoke-dake;* in Japanese *dake* means "mountain"). It's the tallest dam of this design in the country, 186 m (620 ft) from top to bottom, and took seven years to complete in the 1960s.

After the short walk across the dam you take the cable-railway for a quick (five minute) lift up to Kurobedaira at

1,828 m (6,094 ft). Here there's a restaurant, no doubt welcome. From there, you're whisked across an upland valley by cablecar to **Daikenbo**, site of another restaurant and approaching the summit of your excursion.

The scenery here is particularly magnificent, with flowery slopes and aquamarine lakes on show when the skies are clear. (It is, needless to say, important to choose a day with good weather for this entire cross-mountain excursion).

From Daikanbo you travel by bus through the tunnel that runs under the ridge that extends south of the summit of **Mt. Tateyama** itself (3,015 m or 10,050 ft), a mere 10-minute trip.

Now you are at **Murodo** Terminal, at 2,450 m (8,017 ft) the highest point of the

Alpine Route. Here there's not only a hotel, the Hotel Tateyama, but many interesting sights to visit on foot if you are prepared to take a break for a time from wheeled transport. A five-minute amble, for example, will bring you to Mikuriga-ike Pond, occupying a volcanic crater 15 m (50 ft) deep and 600 m (2,000 ft) in circumference.

The really energetic and ambitious, however, will want to make it to the Summit Sanctuary of the **Oyama Shrine**, at the peak of Mt. Tateyama itself. This is possible if you are reasonably fit and give yourself three hours for the round trip from the terminal at Murodo.

Tateyama is one of the three sacred mountains of Japan (the others are Fuji and Hakusan), and was at the heart of the old Tateyama religion. This extraordinary belief-system venerated mountains as sacred sites and dates from as far back as the eighth century.

Another destination from Murodo for keen walkers is the **Jigoku-dani Valley** where steam spouts from numerous vents — inquire at the terminal for directions and hiking times.

From Murodo it's downwards all the way, one hour by bus to **Bijodaira** (977 m or 3,257 ft) with its hotel and restaurants. You're still among fine upland scenery, however, and the upper reach of this road, known as Otani, is where buses

Okuhotaka-dake, the summit of the Japanese Alps. The climb is not too strenuous and is certainly very rewarding to the reasonably fit hiker.

often have to drive between high walls of snow in the first weeks of the season.

A sign that excitement and dramatic scenery are not yet over is that you next take another cable railway down to Tateyama Station, a mere seven minutes, before boarding the train for Toyama City, 34 km (21 miles) and 45 minutes away.

From Tatayama Station there's another side-trip available. You can take a bus (20 minutes) and then walk (half an hour) and get to Japan's biggest waterfall, the **Shomyo-daki Falls**, 350 m (1,070 ft) from top to bottom.

None of this need be done in one go. You can use any part of this route as a quick way to get to a high destination, hike off from there, and then later in the day return to the point where you began.

Note, however, that the Tateyama Kurobe Alpine Route is not open in winter, when the heavy snowfalls close the roads. It is normally operative between April 25 and November 30, though late winter conditions in any particular year might delay the opening of some sections by a few days. The last section to open is usually the one on the west-facing flank of the range, linking Murodo and Tateyama — the opening of this section is on occasion delayed until early May.

All in all, though, it's a fine trip. Though designed to give non-walkers — or those who would rather not take the trouble — the experience of the high mountains, it also provides the rest with a lift up to points from which to take their more energetic excursions.

Train to Kawaguchiko

IF YOU WANT TO SEE UNSPOILED JAPANESE COUNTRYSIDE ON A SHORT TRIP OUT OF TOKYO, THE BRANCH LINE THAT ENDS AT KAWAGUCHIKO WILL DELIGHT YOU. The scenes along the way are charming, and Kawaguchiko itself is the very epitom of a local vacation spot, with scarcely another foreign visitor in sight.

Kawaguchiko is one of the celebrated **Five Lakes** of Mt. Fuji. You look up the relevant brochure, arrive at Shinjuku Station, and in no time are leaving on the first train for Otsuki (pronounced Ots'ki) via Takao on the Chuo Line, northwards and out of the city.

Remarkably quickly for Japan you're out in the country. Now everyone's smiling, or chattering, or sitting contentedly snoozing, on their sunny day off. The train is extraordinary, too. The upholstery is soft and tastefully designed, and apparently new. The train company, you feel, must be constantly upgrading and replacing its interior furnishings.

The network of trains in the circumference around Tokyo is like the finest of spider's webs. You can set your watch by the departure times, and station personnel gesture you on board with their white-gloved hands as if nothing was remarkable about the phenomenal intricacy and meticulous accuracy of it all.

You change trains onto the private Fujikyuko Line. It's not covered by your Rail Pass, but the ¥1,100 fare seems modest enough for such another sleekly immaculate marvel, with not a hint of graffiti in sight.

And outside the nettles are moving quietly in the midday sunlight. You're not sure what it is you're going to see, but the pleasure of getting there, of going somewhere new on your Rail Pass, is simply delicious.

The conductor, resplendent in his royal blue uniform, enters and makes a little speech to the passengers — no doubt apologizing for his intrusion — before inspecting and punching the tickets.

Shinjuku to Kawaguchiko in the end takes just under two hours. You don't get off at Fujiyoshida, incidentally, though it looks as if it's the end of the line; the train backs out again and takes the short branch to Kawaguchiko via Fujikyu Highland Station, 829 m (2,764 ft) above sea level. Each stop on the Fujikyuko Line has its altitude marked in meters on the main platform, and you notice the train has been climbing slowly but steadily for some while.

Nearer Kawaguchiko the landscape is one of wooded hills in every direction, with country people planting out their onions, or standing looking at cow-parsley, or contemplating the beauty of irises, blue and yellow in the spring sunlight. (Admiring irises, you later learn, is a Japanese springtime tradition). And peeping over the hills is the summit of great **Fuji** itself.

No tour groups will crowd you in Kawaguchiko. The lake commands fine views of Fuji, and you can rent boats of various kinds, or just cruise, as I did, on one of the big ones, one looking like a whale, another like a space rocket.

Or take a trip on the "**ropeway** " (Japanese for cable car). It takes you up into the wooded hills where there are tranquil walks, plus spectacular and quite different views of the majestic mountain itself.

Kawaguchiko is Japan as only the Japanese know it, but only a couple of hours from central Tokyo. The Japanese go there to escape the heat of summer. But at any time it's astonishingly quiet and intimate for so crowded a country, yet with grand views of the nation's major emblem, stunning Mt. Fuji.

Give it a try. It's a taste of "Unknown Japan." Savor it, and you'll quickly get an appetite for more.

Climb aboard the Kawaguchiko sightseeing bus ABOVE and explore this intimate resort town and its surrounding countryside.

YOUR CHOICE

The Great Outdoors

The Japanese work hard, but they play hard too. And this means there are almost always highly developed facilities for outdoor activities that the visitor can take part in.

Japan is an outdoor country, perhaps more than anything else. To begin with, it mainly consists of mountains. Hokkaido is practically nothing else. Honshu, Japan's most urbanized and industrialized island, still has mountains covering a huge swathe of its land area. Little Shikoku bordering the inland sea is extremely mountainous. And southerly Kyushu is both hilly, and contains dramatic, active and impressive, volcanoes.

In addition, Kyushu and Okinawa boast semitropical beaches where, because this is Japan, facilities for swimming, surfing and other beach activities are highly developed.

And this is only the beginning. The Japanese are nothing if not keenly appreciative of the possibilities of their own landscape. Every opportunity appears to have been noticed. Whether it's cycling, trekking, skiing, swimming or mountaineering, there's scarcely a possibility that hasn't been taken advantage of, and is now popular.

Camping can be enjoyed virtually everywhere, and it's almost always the case that you can hire the tents, sleeping bags and other equipment on the spot.

Near Tokyo, for instance, by Tokyo Harbor, there's **Wakasu Kaihin Koen Campjo** ((03) 5569-6701 and it's open all the year round. Tents can be rented during the summer (July through September), and there's room for 130 of them. Golf and yachting are nearby (but no cars — or pets — are allowed). Charges are ¥200 (adults), ¥100 (children). Three days is the maximum time you are permitted stay. The address is Wakasu 1, Koto-ku.

In the same area is the smaller Jonanshima **Kaihin Koen Campjo** ((03) 3799-6402 to check space as they

---

OPPOSITE: Cherry blossoms, a symbol of Japan, at Lake Okutama, west of Tokyo. Their evanescence is part of their appeal. ABOVE: A brilliant burst of flowers in the Japanese Alps.

only have a 30-tent capacity. Tents can be rented. Overnight charges: ¥400 (adult), ¥200 (child). No cars. Address: 4-2-2 Jonanshima, Ota-ku.

Situated in forested country inland is Yama no Furusatomura, in **Chichibu-Tama National Park** (*Kokuritsu Koen*). Rental is available — a five-person tent, for example, costs ¥2,000 a night. Again, no cars are allowed. Charges: ¥200 (adult), ¥100 (child).

Rather more substantial — it has lodges for rent, tennis courts, a golf course and swimming pool — is **Roman no Mori Auto Camp Toyofusa** ((0439) 38-2211. You can take a car there and it's open all the year round. Mountains are nearby. Charges are naturally higher: ¥5,000 per car (and/or two people), lodges ¥10,000 to 25,000. The address is Toyofusa, Kimitsu-shi, Chiba-ken with reservations on ((03) 3388-4111.

See the ever-excellent *Tokyo Journal* for more camping listings in the area in and around the capital.

You can camp in thousands of other places, from Okinawa to Hokkaido. The Tottori region, little visited by foreigners, alone has 27 official campsites. Just ring the local Tourist Information Centers of the place you're in, or that you plan to visit, for recommendations (many phone numbers of Information Centers (ICs) are in the OFF THE BEATEN TRACK and THE BROAD HIGHWAY sections). All camping grounds in Japan have check-in and checkout times — confirm these too when you call.

Summer swimming and **winter skiing** is a combination that characterizes these temperate but mountainous islands. There may not be snow in the plains where almost everyone lives, but Japan's hills are so numerous there's snow accessible from just about anywhere. And if there's steam rising from sulphur-vents, so much more typical of these fascinating islands.

A sure indication of the high quality of skiing facilities in Japan was the selection of Nagano Prefecture in the Japan Alps as the location for the very successful 1998 Winter Olympics.

You too can ski here. **Nomugitoge**, **Norikura Kogen** (one of Japan's premier skiing sites) and **Sun Alpina Kashimayari** are all resorts in easy reach of Matsumoto, under three hours by Japan rail from Tokyo's Shinjuku Station. There's even helicopter access to a 14 km (just over eight miles) long downhill course at Tsugaike Kogen Ski Resort in the north of the Japan Alps region (at Otari).

You can ski in innumerable places in Hokkaido at any time during the winter — at popular **Niseko Kokusai Hirafu** — with its 21 ski-lifts; at **Niseko Annupuri Kokusai**, two and a half hours from Sapporo; or at **Alpha Resort Tomamu** or **Ski Resort Furano**, each two hours from Sapporo by JR and bus respectively.

Less far north, in the Tohoku region of northern Honshu, there are an extra-ordinary 37 important skiing resorts, while cross-country skiing is possible in very many places in this rugged, remote part of the country.

Typical prices are: ¥3,500 to 4,500 for a day-pass to lifts (cheaper at night); equipment hire (skis, boots and sticks) ¥3,000 to 5,000; and a helicopter to the summit, when on offer, ¥19,000 and more.

While equipment is everywhere available for hire, you should note that ski boots in sizes of 26.6 cm (11 inches) and above are hard to find. You'd be wise to phone in advance to confirm if they are available if you take these sizes.

The Christmas and New Year period tends to be very busy at ski resorts as major public holidays occur at this time. Fine weekends, too, can see long queues and fully-booked accommodation. If you're on vacation in Japan you will probably be free to visit these resorts outside these times. You'd be advised to make good use of this advantage.

Japan's Tourist Information Center publishes a mini-guide (№ MG-082) to skiing in Japan.

Or you can **skate**, at Kowaki-en and Hakone-en, both in **Hakone** just outside Tokyo, or at **Shiozawa Lakeland** and Karuizawa Skate Center — with roller-skating at the latter in summer — in **Karuizawa**, to name a few out of many examples.

As for **beaches**, you can't go wrong down in **Okinawa** in all but the absolute midwinter months. **Kyushu** has almost as long a season. **Honshu** has a very long, very unspoiled north coast where

bathing is fine from July to September. And you can swim outdoors almost anywhere in Japan during these months.

And Japan's hilly terrain often means you can swim and clamber up a small peak all in the same day, though most people will probably opt to enjoy these pleasures in the reverse order. At **Hagi**, for example, you can trot to the top of Mt. Shizuki (only a hill really at 143 m or 480 ft) and then swim at the nearby Kikugahama Beach, and there are very many comparable juxtapositions in these islands.

Climbing mountains for their own sake is naturally highly popular too. At 3,776 m (12,587 ft) Mt. Fuji takes precedence during its open season of July and August, followed by the Japan Alps (for professionals only in winter, but for almost everyone in summer). See CLIMBING MT. FUJI, page 212 in OFF THE BEATEN TRACK, for the former, and CLIMB A SMALL MOUNTAIN, page 16, and CROSS THE ALPS, page 32 in TOP SPOTS for the latter.

With sweeping curves, the wood and stone Kintai Bridge at Irakuni ABOVE spans the river.

Next in popularity are probably **Mts. Haguro**, **Yudono** and **Gassan** in Tohoku, followed by the often frozen volcanic heights of Hokkaido. But there are 1,000 and 2,000 m (3,334 ft and 6,668 ft) peaks the whole length of the country (excepting only Okinawa). There is Mt. Tsukuba, north of Tsukuba City, with the usual shrines, cablecars, ropeways, interesting-looking rocks and hiking trails, Mt. Daisen, north of Hiroshima in Tottori Prefecture, and hundreds more, mostly little known outside their locality, but well-known and well-loved locally.

If mountains are your passion, you won't be disappointed in Japan. And you can hike everywhere from main-island **Honshu** to diminutive **Sado**. Unspoiled tropical forests in Okinawa's **Yaeyama Islands** will be humid but lush, while **Hokkaido**'s forested uplands will be coolly beautiful at any time of year. And there's every possible choice in between.

Hot springs? Far too numerous to list. From the huge, ornate spas at Kyushu's **Beppu**, the sheer fecundity at Hokkaido's **Noboribetsu**, to the stumbled-on springs around Honshu's **Karuizawa**, they're everywhere. The earth's crust is thin in the Japan region, and the result is earthquakes (which we could do without), volcanoes (wonderful if you keep your distance) and hot springs, (and unalloyed blessing).

Life doesn't offer many more wonderful things than outdoor life in temperate climates. Japan has some of the best of it, and in abundance.

Sporting Spree

It wouldn't be unreasonable to believe that the Japanese are sports-crazy. The truth is more likely that so many of them live in cities, and so many of them earn good salaries and wages, that facilities for physical exercise and the skilled deployment of the body generally are everywhere available.

Take **golf**. You might think the sport wouldn't really suit the country, given its generally mountainous terrain (though the game's origins in hilly Scotland might induce you to think again). Be that as it may, the Japanese are generally golf mad. The game's virtually obligatory for aspiring executives, and netted practice areas are found all over urban areas.

The game proper doesn't come cheap, and the Japanese are known to jet away to Hawaii in order to indulge their passion for the game at more affordable rates. Nevertheless you can slice into the little white ball all over Japan if you've a mind to.

In Hakone, for instance, Tokyo's great playground and communal garden, there's the Fujiya Hotel Sengoku Golf Course, the Kurakake Golf Course, the Yunohana Golf Course and the Hakone-en Golf Course. Enough for you? No? Then how about Hokkaido, very Scottish in climate. There you can golf at Noboribetsu Golf Course ((0143) 84-2195 or the Royal Classic Toya Golf Course ((0142) 75-2475, just to give two examples. Phone them and enquire about their green fees to get some idea of the price of golfing in the country generally.

The truth is you can play golf anywhere in Japan if your budget is sufficiently elastic. There were said to be 1,700 courses in the country at the last count.

Tennis is less popular, but nevertheless available. There's little point in mentioning particular sites, but it's worth noting that in Tokyo the problem of space has made the game a rarity. In the 46 hotels in the city listed by the Japan Hotel Association, including all the capital's finest, there is not a single one that boasts a tennis court.

In more rural areas, however, they're not hard to find. Taken virtually at random, there are courts at Hakone's Hakone Prince Hotel ((0460) 3-1111, Hakone Highland Hotel ((0460) 4-8541, Palace Hotel Hakone ((0460) 4-8501, and Hotel de Yama ((0460) 3-6321 and Hakone is readily accessible from the capital. In Hokkaido you can play at Lake Toya, in the Memorial Park of Volcanic Eruption ((0142) 75-3332, or in Kitayuzawa Onsen Green Village ((0142) 68-6321. And you can play at

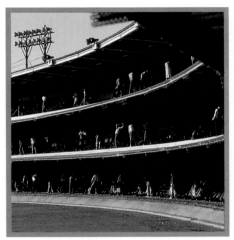

Tatsunokuchi Hills Park ((0761) 51-4166, near Kanazawa in Ishikawa Prefecture… Ask and you'll (probably) find.

But generally speaking swimming pools are much more common than tennis-courts. At Kasumigaura Park, for instance, on Lake Kasumigaura, near Tsuchiura (an hour north of Tokyo by JR), there's a pool that claims to be able to hold 10,000 people! It might be worth making the day-trip just to see that.

Swimming and sunning yourself by the sea are available for more and more of the year the further south you go, with Okinawa having the longest season. On Honshu the season is late May to mid-September. Sailing is naturally popular in so affluent a country with such a long coastline. Marinas are everywhere. Even in relatively quiet Tottori Prefecture, for example, on Honshu's north coast and not far from Hiroshima, there are four of them. **Windsurfing** can be found just about everywhere there's sailing, too.

As for **scuba diving**, Okinawa is the place to head for, and particularly the smaller Okinawan islands of **Miyako** and **Ishigaki**. Sea Friends ((09808) 20863 is one of several diving centers on Ishigaki. On Miyako you could try Twenty-Four North ((09807) 23107.

In overcrowded Japan, the chance to take to the hills OPPOSITE is very tempting, and fast transport ensures that nature is never too far away. ABOVE: For golf lovers, limited space means that a driving range has to be shared with many other enthusiasts.

And **hang-gliding** takes place at, among other places, Kurumayama Heights in the Japan Alps.

Soccer is relatively new to Japan, but its popularity is increasing very fast, especially among the young. The "J League" was established in 1993, and its aim was to encourage and then maintain a high level of professionalism in the sport. It is now watched with enthusiasm by an increasing number of fans. Indeed, due to media coverage which has generated an unprecedented interest in the sport, soccer's 2002 World Cup is to be held in the country. All of which is certain to result in a growing number of soccer pitches for amateurs in the country as a whole, but at the time of writing facilities are limited.

The Western ball-game that is best established in Japan is without doubt baseball. Almost all schools, colleges, universities and commercial companies maintain a team or teams. See BLACK BELT BASKETBALL, page 97 in THE CULTURE OF JAPAN for more details.

The baroque mysteries of sumo are involved enough to sustain a lifetime's curiosity. ABOVE: The elegantly coiffed hair of a wrestler. OPPOSITE and PREVIOUS PAGES: Wrestlers at Yasukuni Shrine.

You can also get close to traditional Japanese sports such as *aikido*, judo, karate and *kendo* on your trip.

Visitors can watch **aikido** adherents practising at four major centers, for instance; in Tokyo: at the Aikikai Hombu Dojo in Shinjuku ((03) 3203-9236, the Ki-no-Kenkyukai Headquarters, also in Shinjuku ((03) 3353-3461, and the Sobukan Hombu Dojo in Shibuya ((03) 3468-3944; and in Osaka at the Tenshin Dojo at Yodogawa-ku ((06) 304-8710. Ring in advance for times and days of the week.

For **judo**, the Dojo Kodokan, in Tokyo's Bunkyo-ku district, has a spectators' gallery which is open to visitors free of charge. ((03) 3818-4172.

For **karate**, the Japan Karate Association's International Headquarters in central Tokyo ((03) 3440-1415 would be the place to enquire about training sessions. They point out that no English is spoken, however, so you should have a Japanese speaker by your side when you phone.

For **kendo**, ring the All Japan Kendo Federation on ((03) 3211-5804 for information, and for **kyudo**, ring the All Nippon Kyudo Federation on ((03) 3481-2387; again, it's recommended you have a Japanese speaker standing by to help with your call. Kyudo is as popular with women as with men in Japan, incidentally.

Sumo is altogether less accessible, and reserved more for public display. See page 98 in THE CULTURE OF JAPAN for details of where and when to watch this highly specialized sport.

The Tourist Information Center publishes a mini-guide to *Traditional Sports* (MG-088), with fuller information, useful addresses, and additional telephone numbers.

The Open Road

Japan drives on the left. If you have a valid international driving licence (International Driver's Permit) you can rent a car, from **Nippon Rent-a-Car**

(affiliated with Hertz), **Japaren,** or one of several other companies. (Note, however, that some countries like Germany and Switzerland have not in the recent past had a reciprocal agreement with Japan to honor an international driver's licence — check before leaving home to ensure the latest facts).

It is a very good idea to take a Japanese-speaking companion along with you, at least as far as the office: the clerks are not obliged to be able to speak English and will explain the details of liability in the case of accident and so on in Japanese. If you can take your Japanese companion along for the whole trip, so much the better. Almost all road signs are in Japanese only (the one consistent exception, a completely useless one, is the names of rivers) and if you can't read the name of your destination and the various places en route in Chinese characters you stand a good chance of getting lost. If you are bent on traveling without native assistance get hold of two maps, one in Japanese, one in your language, and memorize the necessary characters in advance.

But even if you do your homework properly you will find that driving in Japan is an experience full of excitement and tension. Roads in the boondocks are astonishingly narrow, and the placing of road signs is uniformly haphazard. Furthermore, there are far too many cars crowding onto far too few decent roads, and away from the splendid expressways the traffic often crawls along.

Representative price ranges for rented vehicles are officially quoted as follows: 1000 to 1300 cc. — ¥9,000 to 14,000 a day; 1500 to 1800 cc. — ¥13,000 to 20,000 a day; 2000 cc. — ¥21,000 to 35,000 a day; 3000 cc. — ¥27,000 to 38,000 a day.

On the other hand we found one outfit offering a compact Honda City for ¥7,800 per day, while for ¥30,100 per day you got a ten-seater van. So call around.

Nippon and Toyota car rental companies both have desks at Narita Airport. Nippon's phone number in Tokyo is ((03) 3469-0919; Toyota's is ((03) 3264-2834, and Japaren's ((03) 5397-8911, with

FAX on (03) 5397-8817. Japaren have a branch close to Exit C7 of the Shinjuku-Sanchome subway station.

So, you've got your vehicle and you're ready to set out. Where to go?

Hokkaido is ideal for driving because the roads are so comparatively empty. That many of them will be closed off through impossible snowfalls for much of the winter is a small price to pay for an emptiness that in Japan is a delight. Maybe you prefer to hire your wagon once you're there. In that case you can rent a car in Sapporo from Nissan Rent-A-Car ((011) 717-4123, Nippon Rent-A-Car ((011) 251-0919, Mitsubishi Rent-A-Car ((011) 521-1311 or Orix Rent-A-Car ((011) 241-0543, among others. And off you go, into the wildness, between the massive sweet-corn fields and through the windy, forested spaces, and you might imagine that you are in Canada — until you come across another *onsen* (hot-spring) or see, smoking away on the horizon, another snow-capped volcano.

You can drive right to the northern-most tip and stare across the ocean to where Siberia broods, vast and with roads leading all the way to Paris (and rails leading nowadays even to the north coast of Scotland). One day there may even be a tunnel linking Hokkaido to Sakhalin in Siberia. Who knows? But today Hokkaido's relative isolation remains an almost unqualified blessing.

Honshu's roads are more crowded, but not in **Tohoku**. Here conditions approach Hokkaido's, and driving should be a relative pleasure. The same applies to Honshu's north coast, and to take the northern coast road via **Toyama**, **Masuda** and **Hagi** rather than the southern route through the major cities (Kyoto, Osaka, Kobe, Hiroshima and so on) would be to opt for a more pleasant, albeit slower, journey westwards.

Kyushu is quieter altogether, though in no way the back of beyond. But if you want to drive in **Okinawa**, you'll have to rent yourself a vehicle all over again once you get there. But the traffic will, again, be comparatively light. Three of Okinawa's car-renting outfits are:

X Rent-a-Car Ryukyu ((098) 868-3741, Budget Rent-a-Car ((098) 869-1432, both in Naha, and Mazda Rent-a-Lease ((098) 858-1536 at Naha Airport.

Backpacking

The first step to budget travel in Japan would appear, on first sight, to be to acquire a booklet issued by the Japan National Tourist Organization. It's called *Japan for the Budget Traveler* and it's updated every year. It doesn't cover all options, however. And unfortunately it only covers Tokyo and the Kansai region (Kobe, Osaka, Nara and Kyoto) but even so it's reasonably useful.

The booklet is clearly a product of the government tourism-promotion organization's perception that Japan is routinely seen as very expensive by foreign visitors, and notably by prospective visitors who, having examined its prices, decide to go elsewhere. 'We're not too bad!' is what the publication implicitly proclaims.

A quick look at the section dealing with accommodation will show you the booklet's strengths and limitations. Accommodation is the central problem anywhere in the world for people seeking to cut costs. Here it's recommended in three categories — ¥15,000 to 10,000 (hardly budget by any standards), ¥9,999 to 6,000 (more than you need to pay), and finally what most people who pick up a booklet with a title like this will be looking for, less than ¥6,000.

Here there are half a dozen to a dozen places listed in each city. Useful, but far from definitive.

What it leaves out, for instance, are the **capsule hotels** (*capseru hoteru*) — there's a photo of one on page 241 in TRAVELERS' TIPS. Perhaps JNTO deems them an insult to the national self-image. But many budget travelers and backpackers will value their prices (¥3,500 to 4,500 a night) as do many Japanese business men on low, or lowish, traveling expenses.

Capsule hotels in the Tokyo area can be found in the free information magazine *Tokyo Finder.* They're not places to be too casual about your belongings in. But if you're security conscious, you should be all right.

Next are the **youth hostels**. Two booklets available from TICs are vital — *Youth Hostels Map of Japan* and *Public Youth Hostels.* The former does indeed contain a map, but equally important are the addresses and phone numbers of all Japan's non-public hostels printed on the reverse. The latter, a slimmer product, also contains a map of sorts plus all the addresses and contact details.

Rates are ¥1,500 to 2,500 a night (for public hostels) and ¥3,100 a night (for private hostels).

While picking up the above printed information, get hold at the same time of a copy of the small catalog of the *Japanese Inn Group.* This group is an organization representing usually small and always reasonably priced *ryokan.* Overnight rates are generally between ¥4,000 and 6,000 a night. For details of what to expect in one of these traditional Japanese *ryokan* see STAY IN A RYOKAN, page 24 in TOP SPOTS.

Another option is to camp — much easier in Japan than in many other countries because virtually all formally organized campsites have equipment, including tents and sleeping bags, for hire. See the GREAT OUTDOORS, above for more details.

As for travel, a **Japan Rail Pass** has to be the number one recommendation, assuming you can afford one. If you aren't intending to travel enough to justify getting a Rail Pass, then long-distance buses are probably your next-best option. Once you arrive at your destination, bicycles are available for hire just about everywhere.

Hitchhiking isn't very common in Japan, but it's possible. Proceed as in other countries. A bold sign with the name of your destination (in Chinese characters) is a great aid. Hitchhiking is not popular even with young people in Japan as it conflicts with the pervasive belief that a debt incurred should be repaid — and it is difficult for a hitchhiker

to repay his debt. But hitchers in Japan often find they are overwhelmed with kindness, with drivers going miles and even days out of their way.

One last point. The Japanese may seem aloof and remote on first contact, but this impression is usually the result of a fear of having to speak another language. If you can master even a few phrases in Japanese, just enough to break the ice, you will soon find that the overwhelming majority of them are surprisingly friendly.

So pick up your pack and head out into the unknown. In all probability you'll marvel at how quickly the landscape becomes pleasantly familiar.

Living it Up

Hotels are the key to fine living when you're away from home, and Japan boasts as many of the finest hotels and hotel restaurants, as anywhere else in Asia.

A prime example is the **Park Hyatt Tokyo** ((03) 5322-1234 FAX (03) 5322-1288 — in west Shinjuku. It opened in 1994, and two years later its **New York Grill** was voted one of the ten best hotel restaurants in the world (in *Hotels* magazine, August 1996).

And everything about the Grill is indeed extraordinary. To begin with, it's located on the hotel's 52nd floor (but then the main lobby is on the 41st!), and it follows that up with having all four of its walls made of glass. Somehow the restaurant manages to incorporate four massive paintings by the Italian artist Valerio Adami as well — you'll have to go there to see just how they do it.

The cuisine is a combination of Asian and Western, pioneered by their celebrated Japanese-speaking Scottish chef Edward Crawford. You have to choose between watching him at work in the restaurant's open-style kitchen and admiring stunning views of Mount Fuji and Tokyo through the glass walls. Specialties at the time of writing included prime quality Japanese beef, fresh seafood, and roast duck.

This highly prestigious hotel naturally also has a Japanese restaurant, **Kozue**, on two floors, and next to that a fully European-style restaurant, **Girandole**, featuring a montage of black-and-white photos of people dining in the famous cafés of Europe.

Other superclass hotels in Tokyo are the renowned **Akasaka Prince Hotel** ℂ (03) 3234-1111 a masterpiece of light and space by architect Kenzo Tange. With no less than 12 restaurants, this luxurious establishment will meet the requirements of even the most discerning gourmet. Then there is the very famous, and nowadays venerable, **Okura Tokyo** ℂ (03) 3582-0111 where the understated atmosphere of refined good taste and sophistication continues to cosset the well-heeled. It has lured diplomats and travel connoisseurs for decades. Don't miss the Okura Art Museum in the hotel's grounds. If you fancy being pampered — and who doesn't? — not to mention having a personal assistant on hand to sort out your business errands, then the **Seiyo Ginza** ℂ (03) 3535-1111 is for you. Its prestigious location in the heart of the Ginza goes some ways in justifying its very expensive rates.

Flagship of the increasingly large and popular All Nippon Airways, ANA hotel group, is the **ANA Hotel Tokyo** ℂ (03) 3505-1111. With 900 airy rooms and its fine views from the top floor Astral Lounge, the ANA Hotel is also a good choice.

The finest restaurant in Tokyo? Impossible to answer. **Shunju** ℂ (03) 5561-0009, however, would rank among most connoisseurs' top few. Housed in an underground room, it's rather like a traditional baronial hall, but Japanese-style. So exclusive is it that normally you need an introduction to get in at all. But if you get your hotel to ring them (ask for Miyashita-san) you might be lucky. The advice of long-standing devotees is to let the manager choose what you eat — all you need to do it tell him how much you have to spend. Located in Akasaka-ku, it is open for dinner only. Closed Sundays and public holidays.

More people would agree, though, that **Requiem** ℂ (03) 5485-1426 is Tokyo's premier wine-bar. You can eat here too, but the main attraction is wine from every grape-growing corner of the world, including some of rarest French chateau vintages. It is located in Shibuya-ku and the manager's name

Luxury is the byword OPPOSITE LEFT and ABOVE RIGHT in the Westin Osaka Hotel while traditional simplicity is key in the Obuge *ryokan* OPPOSITE RIGHT. Stark modernity ABOVE LEFT characterizes the Akasaka Prince Hotel in Tokyo.

is Mr. Tamaoki. Open 6 PM to midnight, later on Saturdays. Closed Sundays and holidays.

Another recommendation is **Inakaya** ((03) 3408-5040 in Roppongi. This is a *robatayaki* restaurant and one of the finest in Tokyo.

Extremely fine French food can be found at **Belle France** ((03) 3564-3925, located in the Ginza Kanebo Building. Natural ingredients combine with elegance, traditional recipes with low-calorie dishes.

Just outside Tokyo, at Tokyo Bay (Urayasu), the **Tokyo Bay Hilton** ((0473) 555500, overlooks Disneyland Park. Its **Ma Maison** restaurant is popular with the elite, this time for specifically French food. It's the kind of place affluent couples choose for their fashionable wedding receptions, being up-to-date in its decor as well as serving distinctive modern versions of old-established French dishes.

Within easy reach of Tokyo is the famous **Hakone Prince Hotel** ((0460) 31111. Set in the Tokyo region's premier leisure district, this is its finest hotel.

Meanwhile Kyoto, the city that is itself the hallmark of exclusivity, boasts the **Miyako** ((075) 771-7111, the **Kyoto Hotel** ((075) 211-5111, and the smaller **Kyoto Brighton Hotel** ((075) 441-4411, each 15 minutes by car from the station. Another fine address is the most famous of Kyoto's inns, **Tawaraya** ((075) 211-2204 which has a history of over 300 years of hostelry. You'll be in good company here for it has welcomed kings and queens, princes and presidents over the centuries. Rooms feature antiques and it is best if a Japanese acquaintance makes the reservation for you. For elegance and luxury, the **Hiragiya** ((075) 221-1136 in central Kyoto and the **Takaragaike Prince** ((075) 712-1111 (with its own teahouse in the grounds), some 30 minutes from the center on the northern side of town, are the city's best addresses. Dining out, take your friends to **Yagenbori** ((075) 551-3331, if you want to impress them. It is in the heart of the geisha district and just a stone's throw from the pretty Shira River. Reservations advised.

Further afield, Hyatt have another exceptionally fine "Grand" hotel in Kyushu, at Fukuoka (also known as Hakata) at the end of the *shinkansen* line running south from Tokyo. There the most famous restaurant is **China** ((92) 282-1234 renowned throughout southern Japan for its Cantonese food, with Chinese wines, of course, also on offer.

But you could spend a lifetime going round Japan staying in sumptuous hotels. They range from the expensive to the very expensive, internationally renowned names to one-off local splendors. Some of the finest hotels in the world, in which assured quality combines with Asian service, are to be found in this country.

TRAVEL IN STYLE
As for getting about the country in style, Japan has domestic air routes that are second to none. On the other hand, *shinkansen* trains are sometimes faster once you consider the time taken to get to and from an airport. The best ploy is probably to travel by *shinkansen* between Tokyo and Morioka or Niigata in northern Honshu, and Tokyo and Kyoto (perhaps even as far as Hakata/Fukuoka on the northernmost tip of Kyushu), and by plane over longer distances.

Both systems have special arrangements for First Class passengers. *Shinkansen* have their Green Cars (sometimes called A-type coaches). These are extremely comfortable, and can be reserved in compartments containing only four seats, arranged around a table.

In addition, you can opt to travel on the super-expresses called *nozomi*. All seats in these are reserved, and they are not available on a Japan Rail Pass, even if you have bought your Pass in the superior Green Car category.

And on domestic flights, Japan Airlines and All Nippon Airways offer Super Seat tickets, available in the B747 cabins of both airlines, and in the B767, B747, DC10 and MD11 cabins of Japan Airlines.

Ready for the annual Hollyhock Festival, in Kyoto, this young girl is dressed in her best festival wear.

Family Fun

There is an amazing amount for children to do in Japan. This is because it's such a highly organized place. No one is left out, and certainly not children.

Many of the ideas featured in THE GREAT OUTDOORS on page 37 are a kids' paradise. Hiking near a volcano is an experience they'll never forget, and the beaches — of Honshu's north coast, for instance — are a child's paradise, as are the woods and fields, low hills and cable railways inland of them. Nature is a child's natural playground, and despite the urban nature of so much of the country, so much more is gloriously rough and unspoiled. What an experience for a young teenager a week in the snows of Hokkaido would be!

But often you have to be in the city, and your kids have to be there with you. It's then that Japan's super-organization really comes into its own.

In Tokyo, for example, a really wonderful place is **Children's Land** ((045) 961-2111 (*Komodo no Kuni*). It consists of a farm, zoo, playgrounds, cycling, all set in woods and fields. All kinds of activities are organized, involving such things as milking cows, a magic rope tournament, baton twirling, a Ninja Haunted House maze, drum concerts, hikes, and much more. Whole families can stay overnight for

¥5,000 a head (adults), ¥4,500 (children). Otherwise entry is ¥600, 400, 200 or 100, depending on how full a day's program is offered. The youngest kids get in free. It's closed Mondays. Children's Land is at Tsurukawa Station on the Odakyu Line, then by bus to Komodo no Kuni.

The **National Children's Castle** ((03) 3797-5666 had varied activities and an indoor swimming-pool. Again, it's closed Mondays. Entrance ¥500 and under. It's on Aoyama Dori, Omotesando subway station (Exit B2) on the Ginza Line.

The **Tokyo Metropolitan Children's Museum** ((03) 3409-6361 (Tokyo-to *Jido Kaikan*) has an athletics corner, opportunities to make stained-glass, pottery, and paper flowers, and a library. It's at Shibuya — ring for directions and details of its irregular closing days.

Then why not try the **Puk Puppet Theater** (*Ningyo Gekidan Puk*) ((03) 3370-3371/2. It's a 15-minute walk from the South Exit of Shinjuku Station. Call them for directions. Entrance ¥3,000.

Tokyo Zoo is at Ueno Park (Ueno JR and subway stations). It's strangely arranged, on two sides of a road with a monorail train linking the two parts. As zoos go it's no great shakes, but on a sunny day the kids will probably enjoy it.

Near Tokyo, at Yokohama, there's **Wild Blue Yokohama** ((045) 511-2323. A range of activities for kids takes place Saturdays, Sundays and Public Holidays. Ring them to check before you go. To get there, take the Keihin Kyuko Line train to Tsurumi or Kawasaki stations, and then it's 10 minutes on the bus. Entrance is adults ¥2,900; children ¥2,300 and ¥1,600.

There's also a **Doll Museum** in Yokohama (*Yokohama-ningo-no-ie*) — see page 209 for details.

At Hakone, Tokyo's back garden, there's a **Children's Village**. To get here, alight from the Hakone Tozan Line train (see page 158) at Kowakudani station.

Further afield, **Shirone Odako Museum** has the world's largest collection of kites. You can make your own kite there, with advice from an expert, and then test in an "Aerodynamics Tunnel."

There are kites from Japan and from all over the world on display, and all the different regions of Japan have their own distinctive kite styles and designs. And in early June a kite-battle takes place where giant kites, each 28 sq m (288 sq ft), attempt to ensnare and bring down those of the opposing team by glass and knives attached to their kite strings. The teams are from the neighboring — and rival — cities of Shirone and Ajikata, situated on either side of an 80-m (250-ft) wide river, and the battle takes place with the teams facing each other from the opposite banks.

For details and dates (they vary each year) contact the Shirone Kite Museum ((025) 372-0314 FAX (025) 372-1316.

Similar Battles of the Kites take place elsewhere in Japan in the summer, so keep your eyes and ears open, and don't miss it if one is happening near where you are. (And note that there's another Kite Museum in Tokyo. See page 142 for details).

In Kyoto, **Toei Movieland** (it's called *Toei Uzumasa Eigamura*) is a real film studio where scenes for real samurai movies are shot, and at the same time a tourist attraction. It's a haven for kids as much as for adults, with remote controlled boats, sense-around movie screenings, and numerous other attractions certain to appeal to youngsters. For more details see under MEDITATE IN KYOTO in TOP SPOTS, page 11.

Lastly, did someone say "**Disneyland**"? Yes? Well, it's doubtful if, as parents, you will be able to escape taking the children along just the once. There's so much to see it's hard to select what to mention. MicroAdventure and Professor Szalinski? Fantillusion? Toontown? Why not study your options in advance via the Internet? Tokyo Disneyland's home page is http://www.tokyodisneyland.co.jp.

Cultural Kicks

Japan is a cultural paradise, and particularly if you're interested in either theater or temples. But it's more than that. It's also the home of some of the

most ingenious and skillful people on earth, so that even relatively ordinary objects — the plastic replicas of meals on offer places in restaurant windows, for instance — sometimes assume the status of works of art.

In the first rank are the **temples** of Kyoto. They're of world-heritage standard and shouldn't on any account be missed. The ancient buildings of nearby Nara also constitute a major cultural and historical highlight in a different way.

Theater is still very important to millions of Japanese, and more accessible to visitors than Japanese films (seen in Japan these will have no subtitles). *Kabuki*, *bunraku* and *noh* performances will probably have radio-translations and commentaries available; you rent a set and plug the phone into your ear for the duration of the show. Modern *butoh* won't have this, but the attractions of this form are so specifically visual your failure to understand the occasional yelled phrase won't really matter. *Kabuki*

OPPOSITE: Kids, young and old, are seduced by Disneyland. ABOVE: Dressed for the New Year's acrobatic display, this Tokyo fireman awaits his turn.

and *butoh* can be seen most easily in Tokyo, *bunraku* in Osaka, and *noh* almost everywhere (though in many places only during festivals).

In Kyoto several other traditional theater (and musical) forms: "Japanese harp, ancient court music and dance, classical comic theater, Kyoto-style dance and puppet plays" according to their publicity, can be tasted in small doses at the Gion Corner Theater ((075) 561-1119. An hour-long program is put on twice-nightly (at 7:40 and 8:40 PM). Tickets are ¥2,800 from major hotels.

Anyone looking at the press will soon realize that Western **classical music** is big-time in Japan. The number of really famous international classical artists playing or being advertised in Tokyo at any one time is truly awesome (a phenomenon presumably explained by the high fees they can command there). Ticket prices are correspondingly high, of course, but most people can usually afford a seat somewhere in the building. Check *Tokyo Journal* for the fullest listings of upcoming performances.

The same applies to jazz and popular music — *Tokyo Journal* is indispensable.

For Kyoto, Japan's second city as far as most tourists are concerned, the monthly *Kyoto Visitors' Guide* is the place to look for details of musical — and theatrical — events. It's a valuable source of information for visitors and available free of charge at the Kyoto TIC.

Many of Japan's best **museums** are dealt with in the text of this book. Tokyo's Ueno Park is the location of several of them, most notably the **Fine Art Museum** and the **National Science Museum** (see LAND A 747 AIRCRAFT, page 14 in TOP SPOTS for more details). Tokyo's **National Museum of Modern Art** is in Kitanomaru Park. In Kyoto there's the **Costume Museum**, and Kobe has its **Fashion Museum**, out on Rokko Island. But Japan is awash with museums. Your best bet is to get hold of the Japan National Tourist Organization's mini-guide to Museums and Art Galleries (MG-081) and see what suits your tastes. Ask for it at any TIC.

The Japanese enthusiasm for copying anything from a bowl of spaghetti to an entire house in the most meticulous detail can only be admired. Should you be anxious to see William Shakespeare's Japanese birthplace, for instance, your interest can be indulged. But be prepared to make a longish day of it, and take some compelling reading for the epic train trip.

The exact replica of the building, which opened in 1997, is lovingly perfect, and is located in Rosemary Park in deepest Chiba Prefecture. From Tokyo JR station, take the train that's goes to

Narita Airport (the Yokosuka Line/Sobu Line) as far as Chiba. From Chiba, take JR's Uchibo Line all the way to distant Minamihara station — another two or so hours. From there the park is a 25-minute walk, or five minutes in a taxi. The object of your loyal pilgrimage is open daily from 9 AM to 5 PM. If in difficulty, phone the park at ((0470) 462882. In the office responsible for this shrine to the greatest master of the language the world has ever produced, you might just find someone who speaks a few words of English.

Shop till You Drop

At first sight, shopping might not seem one of Japan's outstanding attractions owing to the high cost of living generally experienced by visitors not earning in yen.

However, foreign tourists are allowed tax-free privileges on a range of goods, including cameras, audio and other electrical equipment, watches and pearls. This means a discount of between 10 and 20 percent. A number of shops with the tourist in mind specialize in tax-free goods. These include the shopping arcades in the **Imperial** and **Palace**

Hotels and the **Sukiyabashi Shopping Center** in Ginza.

In Kyoto the **Kyoto Handicrafts Center** is a special duty-free shop, with English-speaking assistants and a shipping service. It's at Marutamachi, north of the Heian Shrine ((075) 761-5080.

When you're shopping tax-free remember to take your passport, and remind the assistant about the discount. Retain copies of the documents he gives you as you will have to surrender them to Customs on leaving Japan. Customs may also demand to see your purchases, or, failing that, mailing receipts to prove you have sent them on.

Discounts are only available on fairly pricey items but there are many other Japanese souvenirs the folks back home would appreciate: *tabi, geta, zori, jikatabi* (footwear), kimono and *obi* (sash), *jimbei* (two-piece summer lounging wear), silk, pottery, dolls, woodblock prints, paper umbrellas, bamboo ware, lacquerware, tea-ceremony equipment, swords, knives, geisha wigs... .

Certain districts in Tokyo specialize in certain types of goods. Among these

OPPOSITE: Souvenir fans tempt tourists while the bright lights of Osaka's Dotomburi ABOVE constantly remind the visitor of Japan's best buys.

are: Shinjuku (west side) and Ikebukuro (east side) for **cameras** and **audiovisual** equipment; Akihabara for **electrical goods**, and Harajuku (the Oriental Bazaar) for traditional **Japanese items**.

In addition there are the **antique fairs** and **flea-markets**. The biweekly or monthly ones are: at Togo Shrine (Harajuku station on the JR Yamanote Line) first and fourth Sundays of the month; at Nogi Shrine (Nogizaka subway station) second Sunday of the month; at Sunshine City Alpha (B1 shopping arcade of Sunshine City; Higashi-Ikebukuro subway station) every third Saturday and Sunday of the month; and in front of the Iidabashi Central Plaza Building (east exit of Iidabashi station on JR Chuo Line or Yurakucho subway station) on the first Saturday of each month.

Then for three days, five times a year, there's the **Tokyo Antiques Fair** ((03) 3980-8228, with over 200 dealers. It's usually held in March, May, June, September and December. Phone for exact dates.

For your everyday needs use the many department stores. Foreign foods of all sorts are available at supermarkets such as the **Olympia Foodliner** in Roppongi and **Kinokuniya** in Aoyama. In Kyoto the biggest one is the **Daimaru Tyoto** ((075) 211-8111 on Shijo, west of Takakura. At these stores Western foods are invariably catered for; Japanese bread, for instance, has improved enormously in the past decades.

Getting hold of **foreign books** can be a problem in Japan. If it's English books you're after, and if you're staying in the country for some time, it might be worth considering mail order from the USA. The **New York Bookshop** ((075) 254-3374 FAX (075) 254-3375 has an outlet in Kyoto (4/F Nakanishi Building, Higashinoto in Nijoagaru, Nakagyo-ko, and a catalog on the Internet at http://www.bookshop.co.jp.

Otherwise check out **Tower Records** ((03) 3496-3661 on Jinnan Street in Tokyo's Shibuya district and **Maruzen** ((075) 241-2169 on Kyoto's Kawaramachi street. Both are recommended.

Kyoto and Nara are not surprisingly famous for their kimonos and handicrafts, and also for special cakes and other traditional foods. In Osaka head for **Denden Town** for electronics and cameras, and to **Matsuyamachi-suji** for toys and dolls. Among Kobe's shopping malls is **Kobe Harborland**, near the station.

Short Breaks

The extraordinary efficiency of Japan's transport systems, together with the sheer variety of its landscapes, together mean that the country is an ideal place for short to medium-length trips. The railway network penetrates everywhere and is extremely punctual (though far from cheap unless you have a Japan Rail Pass). It is augmented by a range of services — short and-long-distance buses, trams, cablecars, ropeways, ferries, rickshaws, rentable bicycles — which make Japan a veritable feast of transportation. There are always places to stay, from impersonal but convenient business hotels to elegant *ryokan* to temple youth hostels. Even in the countryside many people speak enough English to be helpful — if pushed. Armed with the advice in TRAVELERS' TIPS you can hardly go wrong.

Here are some suggested itineraries for visitors who want to get as much out of a brief stay as they can:

TWO DAYS:
Day one: Nikko. Sightseeing at **Toshogu Shrine** in the morning. Then in the afternoon a bus or taxi to **Chuzenji Temple** and **Kegon waterfall**.
Day two: Tokyo. In the morning visit **Imperial Palace East Garden** and **Hibiya Park**; then shopping in nearby **Ginza**. After an early lunch take the Ginza line subway to eastern terminus, **Asakusa**; sightseeing at temple and market, then to **Ueno** (three stops back on Ginza line) for park, temple, museums, zoo. Next stop: **Akihabara**, two stops from Ueno on Yamanote line, for cheap electrical goods. Quite a day!

FOUR DAYS:
Day one: Nikko (as first day of two-day itinerary). Day two: *shinkansen* from Tokyo to **Kyoto**. Call in at the Kyoto TIC for maps and help in booking a room. In the afternoon see **Kyoto's temples** and shrines; then traditional **Japanese art show** at Gion Corner. Day three: Nara and Kyoto. Sightseeing in **Nara** in the morning; return to Kyoto, then take sleeping train (*shindaisha*) to Tokyo.

Day four: **Tokyo**. Sightseeing as for second day of two-day schedule. Or skip Ueno and fit in an early evening trip to the **Kabuki-za** (pre-book).

SIX DAYS:
Day one: Tokyo (as second day of two-day itinerary). Day two: Nikko. Day three: Kyoto. Day four: Nara and Kyoto. Day five: *shinkansen* from Kyoto to **Hiroshima**; visit Peace Park and Museum. Then as quick as you can to **Miyajima Island**, then return to Kyoto. Day six: back to Tokyo in the morning; then **Meiji Shrine/Harajuku** or **Akihabara**.

EIGHT DAYS:
As six-day tour, but for day seven visit **Kamakura**, Gora. To Kamakura in the morning, taxi to **Daibutsu** (Great Buddha), **Zeniarai Benten** and back to station; in the afternoon Kamakura to Ofuna (Yokosuka line), change to Tokaido line Tokkyu (special express) travel to Odawara, gateway to Hakone;

OPPOSITE: Hamamatsu's Kite Festival. ABOVE: The familiar silhouette of the Great Torii at Miyajima, a feature on longer trips from the capital.

Odawara to **Gora** by Tozan line, stay at Gora Hotel or Suikokan (*ryokan*) ℂ (0460) 2-3351 — book before leaving Tokyo. Day eight: **Hakone**. Explore the Hakone area all day, winding up at Hakone–Yumoto. Take Romance Car of Odakyu line to Shinjuku in central **Tokyo** (NB The last Romance Car leaves in the early evening: check the time as soon as you arrive).

EXTRA-LUXURIOUS SHORT BREAKS

If you really want to indulge yourself, for two or four days, we suggest the following:

TWO DAYS:

One night at the **Akasaka Prince Hotel** in central Tokyo. Eat in the hotel. In the evening, take yourself along to a night club recommended by the hotel or try the new, super-luxurious **Velfarre Club** ℂ (03) 3402-8000 and discotheque. It is slated to become one of the best in town.

Next day move out of town to the **Hakone Prince Hotel**, an hour away by car. Again, dine in the hotel. The restaurants are top notch. Here you can swim in their pool or play tennis, go for a round of golf at the Fujiya Hotel close by, or take a trip on the lake.

FOUR DAYS:

First two days as above. Then transfer to **Kyoto** and check in at the Miyako Hotel or the Kyoto Hotel (totally reconstructed and reopened in 1994). Or you might prefer the smaller, more mellow Kyoto Brighton Hotel. Whichever you choose to stay in, eat dinner one night at one of the others, and take a lunch in the third.

During one day see Kyoto's temples, and sample traditional *noh* drama. The other day, take the short trip to **Nara**, coming back to your Kyoto hotel in the afternoon.

A uniquely Japanese four days!

Festive Flings

Christmas is the time when most foreigners in Japan tend to get homesick. The festival is only observed by the tiny minority of Christians and by the department stores. The Japanese calendar is spotted with so many festivals full of resonance and seasonal cheer that one more is not really necessary.

For a start, there is **O-shogatsu**, the New Year holiday when nearly all shops and offices close for several days and Japanese people swarm by the million to popular shrines such as Meiji in Tokyo to pray for a good year. Special food is eaten — all prepared, in theory, before January 1, so Mom can take a rest, too. Kites are flown, and an ancient form of battledore, or shuttlecock, is enjoyed. Around midnight on New Year's Eve the bells of Buddhist temples boom out 108 times across cities, towns and villages and people everywhere gulp bowls of *soba* (buckwheat noodles).

The day for spotting the more colorful kimonos is January 15, when girls and boys who have reached the age of 20 during the previous 365 days celebrate the event with shrine-visiting and parties. This is **Seijin-no-hi**, or Coming-of-Age Day.

Boys and girls both have their special days, girls on March 3, **Hina Matsuri**, and boys on May 5, a festival called **Tango-no-sekku**. In both cases traditional dolls are dusted off and admired. You know the boy's festival is coming up by the huge, brightly colored windsock carp flying from high poles in many gardens. Boys are exhorted to be as brave as the carp, which fights its way upstream.

The spring and autumn equinoxes, *higan*, have a significance they have long lost in the West. At these times the sun sets dead in the west, which is the location of the heavenly Pure Land according to one school of Buddhism, so at *higan* graves are visited and prayers offered for the repose of the dead.

The biggest festival in honor of ancestors, however, occurs in August and is called **O-bon**. This is the year's second major holiday, after O-shogatsu, and many millions of Japanese with roots in the

Kyoto's Spring Boat Festival commemorates the frequent trips down the Oi River made by the Heian emperor and his court.

countryside go back home at this time. The spirits of the dead are welcomed back into the home, the family taking lanterns to the graveyard to light their way. As part of the general party, made lively by the *bon-odori* dancing, small portions of the dead ones' preferred foods are set aside for them, and on the last night of the holiday, paper lantern boats are set afloat on local streams and rivers to light the spirits' way back to the celestial world.

Beauties of the season are admired at fitting times — cherry blossoms in April, the moon in September. Both are occasions of more carousing than poetry.

Another good occasion for kimono-viewing is the **Shichi-go-san** (Seven-five-three) festival on November 15. On this day, girls of seven, boys of five and three-year-olds of either sex are dressed up in finery — at vast expense — and taken to visit local shrines.

Finally, two festivals which are not marked on the calendar, and are generally celebrated by a trip to the bank, occur in June and December: the days when a *sarariman* receives his twice-yearly bonus. This may amount to as much as six times his monthly salary, so it's certainly something to celebrate.

The lifestyle of the average Japanese may seem rather bleak in Western terms: cramped living conditions, few holidays, a dogged dedication to work. But the wealth of annual festivals, each with its special atmosphere and its special treats, does a lot to even the balance.

Then there are *matsuri*, street festivals. Large and small, magnificent and humble, these erupt across Japan at all times of the year.

Sometimes it is the simplest festivals which are the most memorable. Take the ubiquitous neighborhood festivals, for example.

It is the local shrine which, all over Japan, is the focus of such festivals. There, locked away behind heavy doors, are the *o-mikoshi*, the miniature portable shrines in which the shrine's deity is said to reside for the duration of its day out. Supervised by an aged priest, the young blades of the area, looking their most macho in sweat bands, *happi* coats and straw sandals, heave the weighty shrine aloft on poles and begin their long, cheerful and grueling parade around the neighborhood. The often mean and tatty streets are transformed by it.

Watch as one approaches. On the shoulders of one of the men preceding the shrine is a little girl whose elfin face has been whitened with powder, her lips painted crimson, red dots put in the corners of her eyes, mauve shadow spread on her lids and a vivid white gash marked down the bridge of her nose — she looks supernatural. She carries a baton in either hand and waves them extravagantly, conducting the movements of the *o-mikoshi* in perfect time.

And here it comes — the shrine itself. The way it lurches from one side of the street to the other, comes to a dead halt, leaps suddenly forward, while all the time bobbing up and down in time with the bearers' hoarse cries —"*Wasshoi! Wasshoi!*" — it seems imbued with life. The big golden phoenix on the summit sparkles as it rears from side to side, the bells on the roof jangle.

The bearers, 20 or more of them, heave and strain, sweating freely, all the time keeping up a comic pigeon-toed, knee-jerking dance that goes on all day. Two men stay by the hinged handles on both sides of the shrine, banging them down in time with the cries, and at the back,

hanging on for dear life to the two twisted cotton ties which are attached to the ends of the bearers' poles, are the two helmsmen who keep it on course.

In a few minutes it's gone, but if you wait an hour or two it will be back. The parade goes on all day, rain or shine, spectators or no spectators, till the bearers are dazed with exhaustion and they have tied their town in knots like a cat with a ball of wool, reaffirming the solidarity and strength of their community. That's what the festival is really about.

Every visitor to Japan should try to experience at least one festival, both for the sake of your camera and to get some inkling of the ancient ties of effort and brotherhood which keep Japanese communities together. A comprehensive list of Japanese festivals appears under the PLEASURES OF JAPAN, page 113.

OPPOSITE LEFT: The great mound of flowers carried aloft forms part of Kyoto's Aoi Matsuri, the Hollyhock Festival. Clad in colorful uniforms OPPOSITE RIGHT a group of firemen wait for a parade. The finishing touches ABOVE are applied to the finery worn for the New Year's holiday.

Galloping Gourmets

"Like being bitten to death by butterflies", the reaction of one Westerner to *kabuki*, might apply equally to a first experience with Japanese food. At its classical best it is extremely pretty, like *kabuki*, and consists of a large number of different tiny dishes which all appear on the table, properly a low one on *tatami* mats, at the same time. The visitor doesn't have a clue where to begin. Mouthful by dainty mouthful there's a lot of food there, but does it amount to a full meal?

The answer, frankly, is no. Just as the English word "meal" also means the edible part of a grain, the Japanese word *gohan* also means rice — strictly "honorable rice." Until very recently most Japanese ate rice three times a day, and it is still the basis of their diet. Boiled until the grains, while still distinct, stick together so that it can be easily eaten with chopsticks, it is served absolutely plain — no salt, no butter, nothing. When one newcomer poured soy sauce over his rice in a Tokyo restaurant the waitress took it away and brought him another bowl, assuming he had done so by mistake.

Despite its plainness it is not a lowly food. The peasant who was so poor he had to eat a substitute such as nourishing and delicious sweet potatoes was considered pitiable indeed. Rice is the food of emperors, as the paddy field in the grounds of the Imperial Palace, ceremoniously planted by the emperor each year, attests.

The basic Japanese meal consists of rice, soup (either *miso shiru*, made of fermented soybean paste, or a consommé type), and *kazu*. *Kazu* translates inadequately as "side dishes," and it means everything which is neither rice nor soup. If one of these elements is missing, it's not a real meal.

The guest surveys the many weird and wonderful dishes spread out on the table in front of him but finds to his perplexity neither rice nor soup. The reason is that, like the lengthy and complicated rituals that precede the wrestling in a sumo bout, these *kazu* are only a prelude to the real business of the meal.

Once his eye has been charmed and his palate teased and tickled by the preparations of raw tuna, wild mountain vegetables, deep-fried pumpkin and lotus root, chilled *tofu* with ginger and *shiso* leaf, mushrooms and shrimp set in custard, once his head has been fired by good *sake*, then at last it is time for his stomach to assert itself. The strong drink is cleared away and replaced by tea and in come the rice and soup and a bowl of pickled vegetables.

He can fill up with as many bowlfuls of rice as he likes, and the soup will be replenished at the same time.

The ideal life, according to Japanese folk-wisdom, consists of eating Chinese food in a French house attended by a Japanese wife. Many people, including visitors from abroad who have eaten their way through the initial difficulties, would gladly substitute Japanese food for Chinese. Bland it is, certainly when compared with the fiery flavors of southern Asia. Tasteless it is not. Low in cholesterol and animal fats, it is at its best, and with reservations (see below), very healthy food. And its variety is mind-boggling.

The very best place to sample a meal of the type described above is at the home of a reasonably traditional and reasonably affluent Japanese family.

Failing that, *kaiseki-ryori* restaurants offer Japanese cuisine at its grandest and most elaborate. The food will generally be served on trays in a private *tatami* room, and the bill will be high.

The Oriental Carnivore

Sukiyaki (pronounced "ski-yaki') and *shabu-shabu* are the Japanese dishes most commonly offered to foreign visitors. They are delicious but much meatier than traditional Japanese cuisine. Buddhist tradition and the lack of pasture land meant that until recent times the only meat the Japanese ate in any quantity was whale; they obtained most of their protein from fish and from soybean foods such as *tofu* and *miso*. In 1872 the Meiji emperor first tasted beef and pronounced it fine, and attitudes have been changing steadily ever since. Meat is nonetheless very expensive.

Sukiyaki consists of thinly sliced beef cooked at the table with onions, mushrooms and other vegetables, jellylike *konnyaku* or *shirataki* and *tofu*, in a delicious broth of stock, soy sauce and sweet *sake*. *Shabu-shabu* is similarly thin-sliced beef cooked by each individual diner by dipping it for a few moments in a pan of boiling water then dunking it in a soy-based dipping sauce before eating. Finally, *udon* — wheat flour noodles — are cooked in the boiling water and similarly dunked, in place of rice. *Shabu-shabu* is an onomatopoeic word which is supposed to suggest the sound of the beef hitting the boiling water — "slap-slap."

Seryna in Roppongi ((03) 3403-6211, is renowned for its *shabu-shabu*.

Frying Tonight

Tempura, another favorite with visitors, is the Japanese answer to fish and chips, minus the chips. The basic idea arrived with the Portuguese in the sixteenth century and has been Japanized into a crisp, deep-fried delicacy. Items which drop, fresh and battered, into the deep fat include aubergines, *shiso* leaves, slices of lotus root and carrot, as well as shrimp, *kisu* and many other types of fish. Presented to the customer on absorbent paper which soaks up the

---

OPPOSITE: A pile of colorful *sake* tubs, decoratively labeled and tied together with straw, await delivery.
ABOVE: The intimate *Dengkaru*, in Kamakura, where *tofu*, fish and vegetables are grilled over charcoal.

grease, it is dipped in a soy-based broth before eating.

An expensive but highly recommended tempura restaurant is **Ten-Ichi Honten** ((03) 3571-1949 in Ginza. A much cheaper place, also recommended, is **Tsuruoka** ((03) 3408-4061 in Shibuya-ku.

The Raw Reality

As an island country, fish has been central to the Japanese diet for centuries, and when you enter a *sushi* shop you are in one of the most popular shrines of the national culture. Due to the recent spread of Japanese restaurants around the world, raw fish is not the object of shock and horror that it once was. As with many alien foods — frogs' legs, snails — most of the difficulty is in the mind. Once the first sliver of really good *maguro* (tuna) has melted on your tongue and slithered down your gullet, objections will evaporate in the sweet smell of *sake*.

Sashimi is raw fish plain and simple, dipped in soy sauce flavored with *wasabi* (fiery-flavored Japanese horseradish). *Nigirizushi* are slices of raw fish, shellfish, shrimp or sweet Japanese omelet, laid on thumb-sized portions of sweetened, vinegared rice and presented in pairs. Similarly dunked — it's okay to use your fingers — it is eaten in one bite, then the mouth is freshened in preparation for the next pair with a slice of ginger. Oversized mugs of green tea accompany your *sashimi* or *sushi*, unless you are drinking

sake or beer, in which case the tea will come at the end.

Sushi shops come in all grades of varying quality from brilliant to rotten. There are even shops, not recommended, where the food comes round on a little conveyer belt and you take what you fancy. For the first experience it's wise to blow some money to avoid the possibility of disappointment.

Japanese Roulette

One fish eaten *sashimi*-style, though only at restaurants which specialize in it, is *fugu* or blowfish. The liver and ovaries of *fugu* contain a deadly poison, one ounce of which could kill a man in minutes. Nowadays *fugu* chefs are all licensed by the government and deaths are rare. Has this done away with the fun? Some gourmets say so, maintaining that the slightly mouth-numbing effect of the poison (taken presumably in very small quantities) is part of the pleasure. *Fugu* is at its best — and safest — in the winter months, and is also eaten *nabe*-style, as part of a delicious stew. A good place to try it is **Ashibé** ((03) 3543-3540 in Tsukiji, near Tokyo's fish market; they also serve turtle cuisine (*suppon*). As the *fugu* here is fresh it is only served between the end of October and March.

Brown Grains

One of the reservations about the healthiness of Japanese food derives from the fact that, in common with other Asians, the Japanese polish the raw grains of rice until they are gleaming white, removing in the process all the vital Vitamin B. Poignant evidence of the national fixation with "pure", "clean" white rice is to be found in Ibuse Masuji's great novel about Hiroshima after the bomb, *Black Rain*, in which the protagonists, although practically on the verge of starvation, meticulously polish their miserable rice ration grain by grain as a way of maintaining their dignity.

The inviting door OPPOSITE to a popular Tokyo restaurant. LEFT: The classic Japanese breakfast.

Modern Japanese know that brown rice is good for the health but the great majority still shun it.

The other reservation about the healthiness of traditional Japanese food is that it contains too much salt, and this is supposed to be responsible for the high incidence of cerebral hemorrhage as a cause of death. If you are worried about this, avoid eating too many pickles and splashing soy sauce on everything.

A Tokyo restaurant specializing in healthy food is **Home** ((03) 3406-6409, situated on floor B2 in Crayon House, 3-8-15 Kita Aoyama, Minato-ku: prices ¥2,500 to 5,000.

Unblemished Bean
Tofu — soybean curd — is a food which has had an enormous impact in the West during the past decades. Served chilled in summer, stewed in winter, deep-fried, stuffed or diced in soups, it is a vital part of the Japanese diet, and much more highly regarded by gourmets than its low price (and the rather "infradig" things that get done to it in the West) would have you suppose.

Nothing To Do With Cats!
Visit the kitchen to check if you like — *tonkatsu* has nothing to do with cats. *Ton* means "pork" and *katsu* is a contraction of "cutlet". *Tonkatsu* is deep-fried pork cutlet, served either on a bed of rice *domburi*-style or as part of a *teishoku* (set meal) with raw cabbage, slices of lemon, *miso* soup and rice. At a good shop, it's great.

Other cheap and popular *domburi*-style dishes are *oyakodon* (literally "parent-and-child" *domburi*, a mixture of chicken and egg) and *unaju* (broiled eel). Prepared well, eel is a great (and expensive) delicacy. Try out **Nodaiwa** ((03) 3583-7852 in Higashi-Azabu, for the best in eel cuisine.

At the Sign of the Red Lantern
A red paper lantern hanging outside a restaurant — or outside a little cart — means *nomi-ya*, "drinking shop". But the Japanese never drink without eating at

the same time, and that doesn't mean just peanuts. *Tsumami* is the word for an appetizer accompanying beer or *sake* — be careful not to say *"tsunami"* which is a tidal wave caused by an earthquake — and they come in all shapes and sizes.

At the **Nombe** chain, for example, which has numerous branches in Tokyo, appetizers include *atsuage* (deep-fried *tofu*), *nikuzume* (green peppers stuffed with meat) and *wakame-su* (vinegared sea weed salads). Add such items as fried chicken *kawa-ebi* (fried shrimp) and *nabe-mono* (stew-like foods, marvelously warming in winter) and it's easy to see that your appetizer can swell into a fullblown meal.

If this happens, you may feel like finishing up with *o-chazuke*, boiled rice

with pickled sour plum, *nori* (sea weed) and peppery spices, with hot green tea poured over the whole lot. This dish is customarily prepared by long-suffering wives to help their tipsy husbands sober up, but you can enjoy it just as well in a restaurant.

Yakitori is a rough delicacy you will also find at the sign of the red lantern. *Yakitori-ya* restaurants, found by the dozen close to major railway stations in office areas such as Shibuya, Shinjuku and Yurakucho, are perhaps the closest Japanese equivalent to the English pub: down-to-earth, noisy, cheerful and relatively cheap.

Yakitori are bits of chicken and other fowl such as quail, duck and sparrow, often taken from highly improbable parts of the bird's body, spitted on a stick, dipped in sauce and barbecued.

No particular *yakitori-ya* cries out to be recommended and phone numbers are beside the point. Just head for that friendly looking joint crowded with flush-faced "salarymen" and find a seat. Pointing to likely looking items being devoured by the people around you is a quite acceptable way to order.

Another cheap and cheerful dish worth knowing about is *okonomiyaki*, a favorite with students. It is a sort of do-it-yourself filled omelette. The waiter

Colorful lanterns invite hungry Tokyoites to dine in this neighborhood restaurant. No menus, the price of each dish is hung up on the walls behind.

brings the ingredients of the meal, which might include cuttlefish and vegetables as well as egg, and the diners cook for themselves on the hotplate built into the table.

Ye Olde Farmhouse

The atmosphere of an old country farmhouse in the middle of Tokyo — that's what the popular *robata-yaki* restaurants offer. Surrounded by tasteful reminders of country life — straw raincoats, bamboo snowshoes, old farming implements — the diners sit at a counter or around an old wooden hearth. Like the hostelries described above, the focus of interest at *robata-yaki* is drinking, but the *tsumami* at the *robata* (grill) are varied and appetizing and may include whale steaks, shellfish, *miso*-topped aubergines and bamboo shoots. All the evening's ingredients are displayed at the counter (as in a *sushi* shop) so if you sit there you can order merely by pointing. And after it has been cooked, the dish of your choice may arrive on the end of a paddle with an immensely long handle. In most modern *robata-yaki* the grill is gas-fired.

The inviting lights BELOW of a Japanese food store. ABOVE: Many Japanese dishes are "do-it-yourself" requiring a certain adeptness with chopsticks. OPPOSITE TOP: *Sake* is the national drink though beer and whisky are also very popular. So too, the world of American fast food OPPOSITE BOTTOM such as burgers at McDonald's.

Setting 'Em Up

Whatever the *nomi-ya* you wind up in, an embarrassment of choice is not going to be one of your problems, at least not in the matter of drink. Beer, *sake* and whisky — these are the three options, wherever you go.

Beer means the excellent Japanese-made lager which has been going down the hatch here for 100 years and more. All brands are drinkable but Kirin is the most popular, while Yebisu is probably the best. Some firms market draft beer in bottles, a paradox which has confounded even the most subtle of Japanologists.

Sake is the national drink: Chinese who visited Japan nearly two millennia ago noted that the Japanese were getting drunk on it even then. In those days the fermentation was set in motion by having shrine virgins chew mouthfuls of rice then spit the mushy result into casks, where the enzyme in human saliva set to work. Conditions of hygiene have improved a lot since then, but the price has gone up too. The protection offered, for political reasons, to Japanese farmers means that Japanese rice is three times the price it

best is fine, and contains a considerable proportion of malt whisky, imported in bulk from Scotland. Most Japanese drink it as *mizuwari* with ice and lots of water. Many pubs and "snacks" operate a keep-bottle system: the customer buys a bottle of whisky and writes his name on the label, and can come back and tipple from it whenever he likes, paying only for ice and appetizers.

A Bowl of Surprises

Your first glimpse of a bowl of *oden* may set you wondering all over again about that famed aesthetic sense of the Japanese. It's the funniest collection of things — triangles of gray jelly, long, hollow, fleshy tubes, hard-boiled eggs and bundles of seaweed — presented in a thin soup with a smear of mustard on the side of the bowl. It is in effect a vegetarian- (or semi-) stew, and the least you can say for it is that it warms you up.

Kamaboko, a bland, usually white, "fish sausage", is behind several of the specialties, including the tubes (*chikuwa*) mentioned above. The gray jelly is *konnyaku*, a nutritious food made from a sort of powdered arrowroot. Another treat is *takarabukuro*, "treasure bags" made from deep-fried *tofu* and filled with translucent noodles and other surprises.

Probably the best and indeed most appropriate place to try *oden* is in one of those tiny, portable, tent-like bars which

is anywhere else in the world, and *sake* is as a result a good deal more expensive than beer, which is mostly made from imported barley.

It's a splendid tipple all the same. Taken hot in the winter it is wonderfully warming, though the best-quality *sake* may be drunk cold in all seasons. If you don't mix it with other drinks, it should leave you with an uncannily clear head the next morning.

If it doesn't, you were probably drinking in a cheap place where the *sake* is cut, quite legally, with industrial alcohol and other additives to reduce the price. *Sake* made with rice and nothing else accounts for only one percent of national production, and most of that is made in small breweries in the country.

Sake sold in liquor stores in large *issh-o* bottles containing about half a gallon comes in three grades of quality: *tokkyu* (special class), *ikkyu* (first class) and *nikyu* (second class). Sweet *sake* is called *amakuchi*: the dry variety which most Westerners prefer is called *karakuchi*. If you are keen to try 100 percent rice *sake* ask for *kome hyaku-pa-cento*.

The history of Japanese whisky goes back to the beginning of this century. The

are to be found in the streets near mainline stations in busy parts of Tokyo and elsewhere. Make your selection from the bubbling pans of *oden* by pointing and wash it down with beer or cheap, hot *sake*. Relish the fragile coziness of the place as the world buzzes about its business just the other side of the cotton walls.

An *oden-ya* (*oden* shop) with the great bonus of an illustrated menu with English and romanized captions is to be found in the Dotonbori section of Osaka. See OSAKA, page 179 in JAPAN: THE BROAD HIGHWAY for more details.

Noodles Fat and Thin

Noodles are Japan's very own fast food. The infamous instant Cup Noodle has wormed its way onto supermarket shelves all over the West, but don't let that prejudice you. There are many more palatable variants.

Soba are gray-colored buckwheat noodles made with a base of buckwheat flour. Handmade and with a high proportion of buckwheat, they transcend the fast-food category, and some of the restaurants that specialize in *soba* are quite fancy. *Udon* are fat white noodles made from wheat flour. *Ramen* are fine yellow Chinese-derived noodles.

The common way of eating all three types is in large bowls of steaming stock with trimmings such as fish or shrimp *tempura* or slices of beef.

Slurping is *de rigueur* and makes the noodles taste better. In summer, *soba* is often served cold on a bamboo screen, to be dunked into a cold sauce before eating, and similar treatment befalls a type of very fine white noodle called *somen*. The cloudy liquid in that lacquerware teapot which arrives with the cold *soba* is the water it was boiled in. When you've finished eating, pour this hot water into what remains of your dunking sauce and quaff it. It's good.

Snack time at the Asakusa Kannon Temple in Tokyo. Small sticks of grilled meat and fish balls bridge the gap between meals.

Eating On the Move

A special treat unique to Japan is the *eki-ben* or station lunchbox. Japanese food fits the lunchbox format well: small quantities of a variety of different things agreeably presented. *Makunouchi-bento* is the version most commonly found nationwide and typically consists of small pieces of fried chicken and seafood, *kamaboko* (fish paste sausage), *shumai* (Chinese-style meat dumplings), boiled or vinegared vegetables, pickles and a field of boiled rice with a pickled plum (*umeboshi*) dead center, suggesting the Japanese flag.

But many other types are encountered when traveling, some presented in charming wooden cases or ceramic pots. Just ask for *bento* on the platform of any large station, study the photographs of the contents on display and try your luck. It's the cheapest and arguably the best way of eating on the move.

Note, too, that *bento* are also available from supermarkets, department stores, and even from stalls on the street. It's not necessary, in other words, to be traveling to enjoy them.

Problems

The only serious problem for the adventurous gourmet out and about in Japan is language. Many is the time the grateful visitor has opened a menu, on the cover of which the restaurant's name and the word MENU are boldly printed in flawless English, only to find that the dishes themselves are described only in flawless Japanese.

There is usually a way out of this fix. A great many restaurants have wax or plastic replicas of the food on offer displayed in the window. Just take the waitress out to the front and point. Pointing, this time at the ingredients themselves, is also recommended in *sushi* shops and *robata-yaki* (though in the former there may also be models of set dinners to help you). Sit at the counter as close as possible to the man in charge.

If there is nothing to point at and no one is willing to help you out, retire with dignity and, if it smells as if it's worth it

and there are plenty of satisfied customers, resolve to return to fight again another day with your own secret weapon — a Japanese-speaking companion.

However warm and helpful the service, don't leave a tip on the table: more than likely your waiter will come running down the street after you to return it. Tipping is not the custom in Japan.

Special Interests

It's interesting but not all that strange when you come to think about it, how so many of the minority interests that visitors bring with them to Japan find their counterpart, and resolution, not in Tokyo, but in Kyoto.

The reason this is not really so very strange is that Kyoto is Japan's biggest traditional city, and one that is still largely intact. And specialty interests are for the most part concerned with Japanese arts, crafts, and other traditionalist pursuits which keep this city so traditional.

Ceramics are a case in point, though also in some ways an exception. Potters'

kilns are indeed to be found in Kyoto, but they're also found in great numbers in many other parts of central and southern Japan as well.

Ceramics have been important in Japan since the introduction of the skills needed to make them from China in the thirteenth century. Today potters and their kilns are everywhere in central and western Honshu, and in Kyushu, and Japanese ceramics are prized worldwide.

In Kyoto there is a Potters' Village, Kiyomizu-yaki, 15 minutes by taxi from Kyoto Station. The other important areas in Kyoto are the Gojozaka and Sennyuji districts in Higashiyama, 10 minutes by bus from Kyoto station. Here there's a Pottery Center (*Kyoto Tojiki Kaikan*), ((075) 541-1102, where articles are on display and for sale.

For the famous **Echizenware** (see page 220 in OFF THE BEATEN TRACK for more on Echizen), take a bus bound for Echizen Kaigan (via Hatta) from Takefu Station on the Hokuriku Line. Get off at Togeimura-irigichi. At Togeimura there's the Fukei Prefectural Ceramics Hall ((0778) 32-2174 (closed Mondays), and the Furukawa Toen Workshop ((0778) 32-2176 (closed Sundays). There's also an annual Pottery Fair at Togeimura on the last Saturday and Sunday of May.

Hagi (see page 195 in JAPAN: THE BROAD HIGHWAY) also has its own renowned pottery style.

There's much more, notably in Kyushu. Indeed, Kyushu could be said to be the heart of the Japanese ceramics world. Enthusiasts will want to get hold of a copy of the Japan National Tourist Organization's mini-guide entitled *Ceramic Arts and Crafts in Japan* (MG-087), probably in advance of their visit.

Back in Kyoto, you will quickly notice that the city is the center for **calligraphy**, Zen temple garden meditation, kimonos, *shakuhachi* (Japanese bamboo flutes), *shodo* (Japanese brush writing), woodblock printing, and much more. See the monthly magazine *Kyoto Visitors' Guide* for details, though it will be mostly of where to buy these things, rather than learn to make them. But the TIC will point you in the

right direction for the latter. All these kind of traditional items are for sale under one roof in the Kyoto Handicrafts Center, but it may not be to everyone's taste.

The important thing with specialty crafts is to make a contact early on in your trip. These are in many senses private, self-contained worlds, but a single Japanese individual who is a practitioner of, or an enthusiast for, one of these techniques will be of more use than all the general advice in the world. He or she will point you to one place, and the people there will point you on to others. Consequently, the importance of finding out just a minimum about the situation in Japan of the craft you are interested in before arriving, or immediately you arrive, is absolutely crucial.

YOUR CHOICE

You can also study Japanese full-time in Japan. Usually a student visa is required, but at Takushoku University's Language Center ((03) 3947-2261, you can follow a three-month course (beginning January, April, July and October) without this requirement. Their address is 3-4-14, Kohinata, Bunkyo-ku, Tokyo, two minutes walk from Myogadani Station on the Maronouchi subway line. The fee for the three-month course is ¥130,000. They also offer six-month courses, but for these you'll need a student visa.

Other universities offering **Japanese courses** are Waseda ((03) 3204-4141; Keio

A Kyoto artisan OPPOSITE fashions *noh* masks for a theater group and ABOVE the interesting showroom of Kei Tanimoto, a traditional potter working in Iga, near Kyoto.

((03) 2453-4511, extension 2323; and Aoyame Gakuin ((03) 3409-8111. All are in Tokyo, and all offer only six-month courses for which you will need to have a student visa.

Perhaps you are interested in **Japanese cuisine**? The problem here is getting instruction in English. One place that teaches how to make *sushi*, with English as the language of instruction, is the Sushi-making School ((03) 3797-5051 at 506 Miyamasuzaka Building, 2-19-15, Shibuya, Shibuya-ku, Tokyo. Lessons cost ¥5,000 for a two-hour introductory trial, ¥10,000 for a one-off six-hour session. You can observe free-of-charge by appointment.

Ice-carving take your fancy? You can learn this from English-speaking instructor as well at Tokyo's Shimizu Ice-Carving Academy ((03) 3320-981 in Nishi-Shinjuku. Telephone them between 10 AM and 8 PM.

Taking a Tour

We mention tours quite extensively in the body of the text. The adventurous will obviously prefer to travel on their own, but at least on a tour you can be sure of arriving at the right place, and being protected from mishap. The following is a sampling of a few (you'll find there are many more on offer when you check in to your hotel, enquire at the tourist bureau or visit a local travel agent) of the more interesting and convenient tours offered by **Sunrise Tours**, operated by the Japan Travel Bureau, Inc. Prices are correct at the time of writing but may have increased, we hope only slightly, by the time you step on board.

MOUNT FUJI AND HAKONE
One day tour; daily from mid-March till the end of the year. Travel by coach to the 'fifth station' — i.e. halfway up — on Mt. Fuji; lunch; to Hakone; cruise on the lake; cablecar up and down Mt. Komagatake (1,327 m or 4,300 ft); return to Tokyo by coach or (optionally) by *shinkansen*. Price: ¥14,000 with lunch;

¥12,000 without lunch; ¥17,500 with lunch, and home by *shinkansen*; ¥15,500 without lunch, and home by *shinkansen*.

KYOTO
One day tour; daily, except for a few days over New Year period. Tokyo to Kyoto and back by *shinkansen*. Lunch, then visit three historic locations. ¥49,000 (¥61,000 with Green Car, i.e. First Class, on the train).

RAPIDS SHOOTING
One day tour; from Kyoto; daily mid-March to mid-December. A 12-km (eight-mile) 90-minute downriver trip. Afternoons only. Price: ¥9,800 (children ¥8,500).

HIROSHIMA, MIYAJIMA, KURASHIKI, OKAYAMA
Two day tour; three times a week from mid-March to end of from November. Begins Kyoto or Osaka. *Shinkansen* to Hiroshima; see Miyajima shrine and Hiroshima Peace Park. Overnight in Hiroshima. Visit Kurashiki and Okayama second day, *shinkansen* back to Kyoto or Osaka. ¥84,000 (child ¥64,000).

MATSUMOTO, TAKAYAMA, KANAZAWA, KYOTO
Four day tour; various sites round Matsumoto; sites in Takayama; via Shirakawago (famous for its old farmhouses) to Kanazawa; sites in Kanazawa, and then to Kyoto. ¥159,000 (child ¥152,000), no meals included. Note: 15 days advance booking is required. Twice monthly between April and November if total numbers justify (four persons minimum to operate tour).

All these tours have special prices for children between six and eleven even if we don't mention them. They're usually around three-quarters of the adult fare, but occasionally more. And all tours offer vegetarian food if requested where a meal is included.

Rising majestically above the town, Shirasagi-jo Castle, in Himeji, is the finest castle in Japan. It dates back to the sixteenth century and was carefully restored in the late fifties and early sixties.

The Islands of Japan

SHRIMP OR DRAGON?

HOW BIG IS JAPAN? Economically, industrially, even militarily, Japan is one of the world's great powers. Routinely described as a Western country and included in Western counsels, she has climbed from the humiliation and poverty of the post war years to an impressive position where almost no one in the world is unaffected by what she does and makes.

Yet a glance at the map shows that this power and energy is concentrated in a country of puny dimensions, a slim string of islands arranged in an arc, more than 160 km (100 miles) of stormy sea from the nearest point on the Asian continent.

The Japanese themselves, with both pride and exasperation, have traditionally regarded their country as small and remote, contrasting it with the vastness and centrality of China. The modern novelist Yukio Mishima, looking at a map in which Japan was colored pink, was reminded of a shrimp hanging off the underbelly of Asia. But this isn't the whole story either.

Though its slimness would belie it, in area Japan is larger than most of the countries of Europe — roughly one-and-a-half times the size of the United Kingdom, for example. A large proportion of that area, perhaps 80 percent, is taken up by densely forested and precipitous mountains and is in consequence very sparsely inhabited. But within the remaining 20 percent, which consists of coastal plains, narrow river valleys and a few basins in the mountains, is crammed a huge population numbering more than 123 million people, making these zones among the most densely populated in the world.

As the perspective changes, the image alters once again, and again we are confronted with a giant: Japan's population is the seventh largest in the world.

These are some of the paradoxes that constitute Japan, a country where neither mountain nor sea is ever far away, where the primeval beauty of the alpine ranges, the forests and the many volcanoes contrast vividly with the meticulously cultivated paddy fields and the cheerful congestion of the great cities in the plains.

There are great variations of climate in Japan, both from season to season and from place to place. The narrow archipelago stretches from latitude 43° north to about latitude 28° north, with the result that while in March and April the people in the northwest of the country are still shivering in the tail-end of their bitter, snowy winter, the lucky inhabitants of the southern islands are dusting off their bathing suits. Congenially mild, sunny weather is to be found somewhere in the country at almost any time of the year. And although the famous cherry blossoms

are only at their best in any one place for a few brief days, by traveling gradually northward the dedicated *sakura* fiend could extend his pleasure to a full six weeks, from the end of March to the middle of May.

For those who prefer to stay in one place, there is the subtle and unending spectacle of Japan's changing seasons to be enjoyed. The way some Japanese talk you would think their country had a monopoly on the four seasons; yet there is a regularity to their rotation, and a distinctness to the changes they

Voluptuous roofs OPPOSITE in the grounds of Naiku, the inner shrine at Ise. ABOVE: A country full of paradoxes, Japan adheres to many of its traditions yet is able to embrace some totally different western values.

bring in their train, which is very special if not actually unique and which has etched itself deep into the Japanese psyche.

The mild spring, sunny and windy, is succeeded towards the end of June by a month-long rainy season. While it doesn't rain continuously, the downpour can go on for days at a time, and the humidity is high.

Summer is hot and close, uncomfortably so in the low-lying cities. Heavy work schedules prevent city-dwellers in Japan from fleeing in the manner of Parisians and New Yorkers, but they escape when they can and visitors are advised to do likewise. Both mountain and seaside resorts offer a great deal of relief from the heat.

Towards the end of summer, typhoons roar in from the southwest, but generally blow themselves out before reaching Tokyo. Then follow the cloudless skies and gorgeous colors of autumn. Winter, too, is a remarkably dry, bright season, and though snowfall is heavy on the Japan Sea side of the country, on the Pacific side there is little snow and the temperature rarely drops much below freezing.

For the visitor from more insipid climes it is the strongly defined character of the seasons which amazes. The rain, when it rains, is harder and more unrelenting than anything he has ever experienced, and the summer sun hotter; the periods of crystal-clear autumn weather are so perfect and prolonged he feels as if he has woken up in heaven.

Accommodating themselves to the dramatically different demands of these seasons, eking out a living from the narrow plains, gazing up at the beautiful, unyielding mountains are a people who, despite their huge numbers, are in many ways more like a tribe than the citizens of a nation-state — the Japanese.

THE JAPANESE TRIBE

Before the last ice age, Japan was attached to the Asian continent and, like their Korean and Chinese neighbors, the Japanese are a Mongoloid people. Korea is the nearest point to Japan on the continent and always provided the most convenient jumping-off point for migrants and travelers. Certain elements of the culture, such as the flimsiness of the early wooden architecture, suggest that there was an early influx of migrants from more southerly regions, but no archaeological evidence to support this has been discovered.

The picture is complicated by the *Ainu*, the hairy hunting and fishing tribes people who, until the eighth century, occupied the northern part of the main island of Honshu. They were pushed further and further northwards by the dominant Yamato Japanese and as a distinct people exist now only in small communities in the northernmost island of Hokkaido. However, large numbers of them have probably been absorbed over the subsequent centuries, as is attested by the bushy eyebrows and deep-set eyes of some of the Japanese today.

The salient fact is that large-scale immigration to Japan had come to a halt by the eighth or ninth century. Since that time — soon after the dawn of the nation's recorded history — the Japanese have been, and have regarded themselves as, a single, unified and homogeneous people. With the exception of the arrival of some half million Koreans earlier this century, as slave workers in the Japanese war effort, nothing has occurred during the intervening millennium to disrupt that state of affairs. When a Japanese describes himself as belonging to a single huge family, he has over 1,000 years of history to back him up.

The main reason for this is the country's geographical situation, in which it is arguable that the Japanese have been uniquely fortunate. They were never too far from the Asian mainland to get there when they really needed to, and generations of priests and scholars made the journey to China and Korea and back, bringing all those elements, practical and spiritual, of the culture of China which enabled Japan to attain a high level of civilization. But the journey was long and hazardous. Even the shortest route was more than four times the distance from Dover to Calais, while the distance to China was 520 km (323 miles).

This long and stormy stretch of water acted as a highly effective deterrent to both would-be migrants and invaders. The only

True to its name, Thunder Falls drops with a deafening roar into Matsukawa Gorge, part of the beautiful Japanese Alps.

general to challenge it was the Mongol conqueror Kublai Khan, who sent a great armada to invade Japan in the thirteenth century. A providential typhoon, dubbed *"kamikaze"* or "divine wind" by the Japanese, destroyed his fleet before he could inflict really serious damage.

Later, in the seventeenth century, when the intentions of the Western missionaries and merchants who had established a foothold in the country aroused the suspicions of the military ruler, the encircling seas enabled him to draw a curtain of isolation

around Japan almost without effort, and this state lasted for 250 years.

Blessed with the fruits of China's civilization but spared the bloody turmoil of her history, the Japanese have been, until this century, the most isolated and the most homogeneous of the world's great peoples. This has given them both the strengths and the weaknesses of a tribe. The strengths are a close identification of the individual with his people, the social harmony this brings and a great capacity for concerted effort. Weaknesses that one might point to would include the low priority given to the development and free expression of individual personality, the potential for nationalistic egotism which welled up during the years before the last war and a deep uncertainty about how to get along with the outside world.

Although Japan has been a member of the international community for more than 100 years now, these strengths and weaknesses continue to manifest themselves in both individual and national behavior. Alert visitors will be quick to notice them.

However, they will be even quicker to notice two other characteristics of the Japanese: their kindness and generosity. Lost, even in the middle of Tokyo, you can expect to be guided gently on your way; caught in a storm without an umbrella, you will frequently find one is hoisted above you. People who have tried hitchhiking report that drivers will go hours or even days out of their way to help them. And if you get a chance to spend time with a family or to visit a spot in the country where foreigners do not usually venture, you will be overwhelmed by the warm, thoughtful and solicitous welcome.

SUN GODDESS TO SHOGUN

It is probable that the Japanese arrived in their archipelago from Korea, but according to national myth they descended from heaven.

The grandson of the sun goddess, commanded to rule the country, arrived on Mt. Takachiho, a volcano which is still active in the southern island of Kyushu. It was the great-grandson of this god, the story goes, who became the first earthly emperor of Japan. He established the seat of his power in the plain of Yamato in the main island, Honshu, perhaps around the beginning of the Christian era, and his descendants have reigned (though rarely ruled) ever since.

Whatever the historical facts, this story has served the imperial family well. The emperor's supposedly divine origins meant that in the early centuries he was both the secular and spiritual ruler of his people. His secular power disappeared quite early on, but his holiness and the mythical link to the origins of his people ensured his survival. For long centuries the imperial family lived in powerless obscurity in Kyoto, but they were never threatened with extinction. And, as we shall see, they made an amazing comeback at the start of Japan's modern era. They are by a long way the oldest royal family in the world.

Yamato, the first emperor's base, is a plain in Kinki, the region which includes the modern cities of Kyoto, Osaka and Nara. Huge earth mounds dot this plain, marking the graves of Japan's prehistoric leaders. Pottery found with the mounds suggests that these earliest descendants of the sun goddess were horse-riding, sword-toting warriors, and forerunners of the samurai.

During the early centuries of the Christian era, contact between Japan and the continent was frequent, and Chinese influence continually seeped into the country. But during the sixth century, as China approached her glorious T'ang period, this influence became suddenly and dramatically stronger.

Buddhism, the Indian religion which the Chinese had made their own, was one of the early imports and brought much art, architecture and learning in its train. Also important was the model of centralized government, and the code of law and system of taxation which went with it. Some Chinese ways were unsuited to the Japanese situation and faded away once the initial enthusiasm gave out. Others, such as the system of selecting civil servants by examination, were too democratic to be acceptable to the clannish Japanese. But in many ways they did an amazingly good job of transforming their nation into a miniature version of the T'ang state.

And as Japan was spared the waves of invasion which rolled across China, flattening her early achievements, Japan is the best place to see the architectural and artistic styles of the T'ang today. The city of Nara, laid out in AD 710, was the country's first "permanent" capital (though it only lasted as a capital for 70-odd years). The temples and monasteries in the pleasant parkland at the city's old center reflect the purity of the Chinese influence at this time, and the fabulous achievement of the Japanese carpenters in mastering the foreign techniques.

Nara was abandoned for reasons unknown, and the reigning emperor decided to build a new capital called Heian-kyo (present-day Kyoto) a little further to the north. Like Nara, Heian was laid out like a chessboard in imitation of the Chinese capital Ch'ang-an, and this street-plan is still intact today. The city was to remain the nation's capital, at least in name, right up to 1868.

Heian-kyo was founded in 794. The T'ang dynasty was past its best by this time, and after three centuries of imitation the Japanese had gained enough confidence in their own abilities to go it alone. So from this time the Chinese influence began to dwindle, and in its place blossomed the culture of the Heian court.

Heian means "peace" and the Heian period was indeed a blessedly peaceful interlude. The imperial court, in accordance with Chinese practice, was supposed to be the center of government, but quite rapidly control devolved to local clan leader throughout the country. This left the court with plenty of wealth but very little to do except enact the empty ceremonies of power. The rest of the time they plotted, made love, dashed off countless poems, held elegant contests of aesthetic sensitivity and wrote diaries. The world's first novel, *The Tale of Genji*, written at that time

Early Japanese depiction ABOVE of an Englishman on horseback (ca 1861). LEFT: Outlandish-looking members of an early Japanese delegation, photographed in Honolulu. Photo courtesy of the *Mainichi Shimbun-Sha*.

by the woman courtier Murasaki Shikibu, paints an unforgettably vivid picture of this foppish age.

The Heian court was clearly too soft to last. The descendants of younger sons of the aristocracy, who had been sent into the countryside from the capital in earlier days, gradually acquired military as well as political power, and increasingly the most powerful of these tough, frugal warriors were called on by the court to protect them from gangs of armed Buddhist monks who had begun to terrorize the capital. Two principal fami-

lies, the Genji and the Heike, competed for this role of guardian, and before long they were fighting each other as well.

Two major explosions followed. The second and decisive one shattered what was left of the court's authority and left the country in the hands of the leader of the Genji clan, a fierce young warrior called Minamoto Yoritomo. He established his capital hundreds of miles from Kyoto in the obscure but easily defended fishing village of Kamakura, south of present-day Yokohama.

The culture of the Kamakura period which ensued, lasting for the next century and a

British soldiers march along The Bluff in Yokohama past the British Legation, preceded by a military band, in a late 18th-century print.

half, was a harsh and earthy contrast to that of the Heian court. But whereas the Heian period is utterly strange to modern Japanese, during the Kamakura period there came into being many of the ideas and values which have governed the people's minds ever since.

We could call it the age of the cultured warrior. Unlike his medieval European counterparts, the Kamakura samurai did not despise learning, and, when Zen Buddhism was introduced from China at the start of this era, he recognized in its simplicity of expression and its stress on self-discipline

and exertion as a way of attaining enlightenment the perfect complement to his Spartan military lifestyle. If the Heian period was like a hot, perfumed bath, the culture produced by this union of warrior and monk was as bracing as an icy shower.

This fruitful relationship between Zen and the Japanese ruling class continued for hundreds of years, far beyond the Kamakura period, and left its mark on many different aspects of the culture, from the tea ceremony and *tatami* mats to garden design and flower-arranging.

Meanwhile, Buddhism was enjoying a boom among the lower classes, too, as new Japanese sects sprang up, offering salvation through the endless repetition of devotional

The Islands of Japan

phrases. With their emphasis on personal salvation in a literal heaven, some of these sects bear a closer resemblance to Christianity than to Buddhism as practiced in other parts of Asia. They owed much of their success to the political and economic confusion at the start of the period.

The Kamakura shoguns survived the Mongolian menace at the end of the thirteenth century, but the structural weakness of their administration, based on the loyalty of a few chieftains spread throughout the country, gradually began to tell. When the

quixotic Emperor Godaigo (1288–1339) attempted to seize power by force of arms, the regime succumbed. Godaigo had no great success, but his attempt ushered in an era of war and confusion which lasted more than 200 years.

Central authority and the old estate divisions broke down during these turbulent years. As strong warrior chiefs, some still from old aristocratic families but many others of common descent, forced their way to power and then, as *daimyo* (feudal lords) staked out rational and readily defensible domains, Japan became a patchwork quilt of tiny fiefdoms. And as they consolidated their rule, candidates for top dog soon began to emerge.

This process was hastened by the arrival in Japan of the first Europeans. Approaching the country from the south, and dubbed for that reason "southern barbarians", the Portuguese arrived in Japan in 1543. They amazed the natives by their appearance and their manners, and delighted them with their tobacco, sponge cake, clocks and spectacles; but it was their harquebuses which left the deepest mark on Japanese history.

The military value of firepower was rapidly grasped, and within 20 years cannons and muskets were being widely and decisively used in battle. However, only the richest of the *daimyo* could afford to employ the new technology and to put up the monumental new castles which were the only effective type of defense against it. The struggle for power between the *daimyo* suddenly accelerated. Before the end of the sixteenth century, a resolution had been reached which was to last until the arrival of the next wave of destructive technology from the West 300 years later.

Clambering out of the smoke of battle into the center of the picture came three great generals, one after the other. Between them they crushed or won over all who opposed them, unified the country politically and ushered in a long age of authoritarian calm which is one of the wonders of world history.

The first, Oda Nobunaga, was a ferocious man, and one of the main objects of his ferocity was the Buddhist armies which had gained great power during the previous chaotic century. The enmity he had for them encouraged him to favor the Portuguese Jesuit missionaries, led by St. Francis Xavier, who had begun introducing Christianity into the country. For many years they enjoyed great success, converting as many as 300,000 Japanese to the faith until, losing favor with a later shogun, they and their works were stamped out and Christianity effectively disappeared from the country.

Hideyoshi, the second and most interesting of the three, was a small and famously ugly man who rose to supremacy from the rank of foot-soldier. He was a general of Alexandrian ambition: in an attempt to conquer China he had his troops overrun Korea, thereby poisoning forever the feelings of the Koreans to wards the Japanese.

But he was also an administrator of genius who balanced the forces of antagonistic and loyal *daimyo* throughout the nation to ensure the stability of his rule. In order to prevent other ambitious soldiers from treading in his footsteps he drew a strict and largely artificial line between samurai and commoners, and issued laws preventing members of different classes from changing their professions.

The third general, Tokugawa Ieyasu, who lived from 1542 to 1616, is remembered for his patience and his cunning, and also for his fantastically gaudy mausoleum at Nikko which illustrates how drastically the taste of the Japanese ruling class had changed since the Kamakura period. Tokugawa consolidated the work of his predecessors. He preempted opposition to his rule by insisting that *daimyo* spend alternate years at home and at his capital in Edo (modern Tokyo), thus wasting much time and money on the road, and by keeping their wives as permanent hostages in Edo. He also skillfully arranged for the succession to stay in his family, and the Tokugawas ruled Japan, at least in name, from 1603 to 1868. For all but the earliest years of that period the only contact Japan maintained with the Western world was through a tiny Dutch trading settlement on an entirely artificial island in Nagasaki Harbor.

There is a repressive quality about the long Tokugawa years which is deeply unattractive. Every aspect of the citizen's life, from his occupation and the size and design of his house to the style of his hair and clothes, was dictated by the government with the objective of freezing the social structure in place to ensure political stability.

So it is paradoxical that this period was in fact a time of great change and growth. The merchant class in particular, theoretically at the bottom of the social scale, grew enormously in wealth, and a whole new culture, flamboyant and frivolous, sprang up to entertain it. Most of those forms by which the rest of the world defines the word "Japanese" — *kabuki*, geisha, woodblock prints, for example — were part of that great surge of mercantile confidence.

And however unpleasant the means by which it was brought about, the long peace was a great blessing. While nothing resem-

bling an industrial revolution took place, craftsmanship in many different fields attained an extraordinarily high level. The standard of living of the common people rose, and education, provided by schools in temples, improved to the extent that about 35 percent of the population was literate by the nineteenth century.

Though deprived of the scientific advances enjoyed in the West, the Japanese were spared the humiliation and exploitation of colonialism. They survived, although blinkered and ill-informed, with pride and national integrity intact. When the shogunate — a very ripe fruit by the end — finally fell, the Japanese were, among all the Asian peoples, uniquely ready to take up the challenges of the modern world.

JAPAN'S AMAZING CENTURY

In 1854, under the threat of force from the American Navy, Japan grudgingly opened her doors to trade with the West. Six years later the first Japanese embassy was sent to Washington. A photograph survives from that mission: the ambassadors, posing with American naval officers and dressed in their samurai finery — split-toed socks, divided skirts, kimonos, shaved scalps and topknots, and two swords each — look wildly outlandish. Their befuddled, faraway expressions convey deep culture shock. They are obviously unaccustomed to sitting on chairs. No delegation of painted Papuan tribesmen could look more exotic or more distant from the modern world.

Yet less than 70 years later, the grandsons of these men, dressed in collars and ties, were to sit across the table from the world's great powers and participate with them on terms of perfect equality in the peace conference which ended World War I — the only non-Western power to do so.

The transformation was close to miraculous. How did it happen?

In a sense it was a reenactment, some 1,200 years later and under radically different conditions, of Japan's experience with China. In both cases, recognizing her back-

A glorious autumnal setting, fitting for such an architectural gem, complements Kinkaku-ji, the Temple of the Golden Pavilion, Kyoto.

wardness *vis-à-vis* the other country or countries, she set about learning with fierce determination what was necessary to even the score.

Japan's initial feeling towards the new intruders was quite simply revulsion, and anger with the weak shogunate for letting them in. People remembered the emperor again — "Honor the emperor and expel the barbarian!" was the popular slogan.

But once the shogun had been deposed and the emperor restored to his former glory (though as usual he had very little real power) in the new capital of Tokyo, things changed. The barbarian would not go away, and he was far too strong to be pushed out. Furthermore, some of his inventions — lightning conductors, steam engines and cannons, for example — were genuinely useful. A new slogan, "A rich country and a strong military", was adopted, and the new government, composed of young and highly enterprising samurai from the southwest, set about implementing it, and with fantastic dispatch.

The eagerness to learn which Japan demonstrated during the last third of the nineteenth century contrasts starkly with the pride in and stubborn adherence to tradition which characterized China during the period. Carefully choosing the most appropriate teacher for each subject, the Japanese learned avidly how to build a modern army and navy, a railway network, a textile industry, how to create an education system, a law code, a constitution. Cheerfully discarding their own "primitive" culture, they hurried to embrace the accessories of Western civilization — Western clothes, Western music, ballroom dancing and more.

No country in history had experienced such a rapid and drastic transformation. The period was crowned by two victories in war against gigantic opponents: China in 1895 and Russia in 1905. These amazed the world, not only because Japan won, but because of the civilized way in which the Japanese treated prisoners and civilians, a striking

contrast to their behavior in World War II. Japan became the first Asian nation to be admitted as an equal to the counsels of the rich industrial nations — and she remains the only one, even to this day.

Among the lessons Japan learned was parliamentary democracy. She applied this thoroughly alien concept with great care and caution, and the power of elected politicians was always checked in the early days by the strength of the military leaders and the "elder statesmen," founders of the new regime, who kept a keen, corrective eye on their juniors.

As the last of these elder statesmen died out in the early 1920s, and politicians who were neither soldiers nor aristocrats rose to high office for the first time, there was an interval of calm and moderation which suggested to the optimistic that a peaceful, democratic future awaited the country. A new modern literature blossomed. The prince regent — the late emperor — traveled to Europe, the first member of the imperial family to leave the country, and came back with a lasting love of oatmeal and golf.

Towards the end of the decade and with the onset of the Depression, however, people realized this pleasant prospect was a mirage. During the next ten years the system collapsed, undermined by corruption and weakness within and violent insubordination without. Angry and self-righteous young army officers, fiercely patriotic, repeatedly seized the initiative to deepen the nation's military involvement with China and to assassinate balky or pacific politicians.

By 1937 Japan was at war with Chiang Kai-shek in China, and in 1940 signed the Tripartite Axis Pact with Germany and Italy. In 1941, with no leader strong enough to halt the momentum built up during a decade of reckless and unplanned expansion, she crashed headlong into war with the United States and Great Britain. Despite early successes, the latter half of the war was a long nose-dive towards self-destruction. Perhaps only the sanity of the mild emperor, who took the decision to surrender, prevented the country from being laid to waste altogether.

Enduring national symbol of Japan, Mt. Fuji overlooks the docks at Yokohama. On the basis of its shipping movements, this port is consistently rated as one of the world's three busiest.

Even so, the damage was staggering. All the great cities, with the exception of Kyoto, were destroyed. In all, 40 percent of the built-up area of 60 towns and cities was burnt to the ground. Nearly 700,000 civilians were killed, including 100,000 on one night in Tokyo as a result of incendiary bombing. Even Japan's frequent earthquakes had never done damage on this appalling scale. The world's first use of nuclear bombs, dropped on Hiroshima and Nagasaki, completed the carnage.

remains in force today it has not prevented the country from rearming.

Gradually, during the 1950s and early 60s, as economic recovery got under way, the old strength and confidence returned. The Tokyo Olympic Games of 1964, the first ever to be held in Asia, signified that Japan was once again a full member of the community of nations, and the inauguration of the *shinkansen*, the fastest train in the world, in the same year gave a hint of the technological prowess with which she has been dazzling the world ever since. Her rapid

After the war, General MacArthur and the allied army of occupation took over and governed Japan until 1952. Under MacArthur's supervision the whole social and economic structure of the country was overhauled. A new constitution sheared the emperor of his divinity, while allowing him to remain a symbol of the nation. Farmers grew rich by means of land reform, and the educational system was remodeled along American lines. An attempt was made to dismantle the *zaibatsu*, the huge financial empires blamed for stoking the war effort. Then MacArthur's priority shifted to the creation of a staunchly anticommunist Japan. Article 9 of the new constitution renounced the use of force for aggressive purposes, and though the article

return to prosperity has been one of the wonders of the postwar age.

The new Japan has been described as a "fragile superpower," and in terms of her dangerous dependence on distant resources it is a fair description. Socially, however, despite the great changes of the past three decades, Japan remains in extraordinarily good shape. Crime and disaffection are still very low, and the industriousness and homogeneity of the people have been only marginally affected by the new material wealth.

Big problems remain, however. Internationally, the resentment of Japan's huge volume of exports increases every year; at home, political corruption is acknowledged to be widespread — the long-running "Recruit" shares-for-favors scandal being the most recent example, which resulted in the disgracing of many top politicians in the ruling Liberal Democratic Party — and many Japanese, even among the young, complain that spiritual qualities have been sacrificed in the postwar rush to catch up with the West.

We come back to our original question: how big is Japan? Sometimes the computers, the world-beating auto industry and the robots make her appear a great star in the center of the modern stage. At other times her self-obsession, and her apparent inability, in the field of foreign policy, to do anything but echo America, make her seem only a very curious bit-player right at the edge of things.

Attempts are now being made at a high level to tackle these limitations. Increasingly strident voices, especially on the right, urge Japan to stand up more robustly to America; the polemic by Dietman Shintaro Ishihara, *A Japan which Can Say No*, made waves right across the Pacific, and the end of the Cold War and greater flexibility in the Kremlin mean that a resolution of the old territorial dispute with the Soviet Union over the Kurile Islands off Hokkaido may now be in sight. *Kokusai-ka*, "internationalization", is one of the most frequently heard buzzwords today, whether applied to housing standards, consumer preferences or company hiring practices. Emboldened by the unprecedented, though sometimes volatile, strength of the yen, Japanese diplomats are for the first time in decades beginning cautiously to flex their muscles in the international arena. Increasingly the correct answer to the question seems to be: very big, and still growing.

Despite the disastrous results of World War II, Japan has bounced back to lead the world in technology. Familiarization with computers LEFT begins for tots in primary school and continues right through the educational spectrum. On the other end of the consumer scale, the motor industry RIGHT is healthy and expanding. Japan was the first country to announce commercial production of affordable, family-sized cars fueled by battery stored electricity.

The Culture of Japan

CUTTING THE CAKE

THE CULTURE OF JAPAN is rather like a layer cake. The top layer is the rich, gleaming, high-tech surface of the modern nation, borrowed with a meticulous eye for detail from the West but increasingly spiced with home-grown refinements. But below this, layer upon layer, are the fruits of nearly 2,000 years of civilization.

Elsewhere, in China or Europe, the new tends to replace what has gone before. Not so in Japan. In this country, which has never undergone a revolution and which until 1945 had never been invaded or occupied, habits, styles, religions or art forms which gain a foothold can cling on for centuries. Many of them are still there for our inspection. Some have been stagnant so long that only the form survives, ancient and leathery and requiring specialized knowledge to enjoy. Others though, while faithful to the original inspiration, retain an amazing vigor.

THE GEISHA AND THE ROBOT

The hostess-entertainers known as geishas ("art-persons") have excited so much curiosity abroad for so long that many foreigners probably know more about them than most Japanese. A few years ago there were estimated to be 60,000 of them in the country, but it is possible to live in Japan for years and still be very vague about whether they even exist any more. They impinge very little on the life of the ordinary person. The true geisha is a hostess for the big shots. Traditionally and still today, despite the great increase in the number of love marriages, most male entertaining and carousing goes on outside the home and marriage and in the context of work. In Japan, business is pleasure — and, conversely, pleasure is very big business. Some 500,000 women are reckoned to be employed in the bars, cabarets, theaters and massage parlors of the capital.

Geishas are at the top of the heap. The "tea houses" where they operate in the Akasaka, Shimbashi and Yanagibashi quarters of Tokyo are subdued and elegant in the traditional manner. The ladies wear thick white makeup and gorgeous kimonos and

have spent many years learning the arts required to soothe the big shots' worried brows: *shamisen* playing, singing, dancing. They are also adept at telling jokes, talking hilariously about nothing much and generally breaking the ice so that the customers, who may be setting up a political deal or negotiating the sale of 100 industrial robots, feel both important enough and comfortable enough to get down to doing business with one another. Many accomplished geishas are more like mothers to their guests than mistresses, but as many as one-third are believed to be

"sponsored" by one or more sugar-daddies. What they do offstage — beyond the tea house — may be as important economically as what they do on stage.

In the hot spring resorts and other pleasure zones, as well as in cheaper clubs in the large cities, the line between geisha and call-girl grows very fine.

THE WAY OF TEA

Tea was introduced into Japan, together with Zen Buddhism, in the twelfth century and was used by Zen monks as a way of warding off sleepiness during their long periods

---

OPPOSITE: The heavily made-up face of a Kyoto geisha. ABOVE: A *bona fide* tea master.

of meditation. They brewed and drank it in a formalized and starkly simple manner, and it was this ceremony which was adapted by laymen and became a popular pastime of the upper classes.

Ask an educated Japanese what is the heart of his country's traditional culture and he will probably say the tea ceremony. The tiny three-by-three meter (nine-by-nine foot), gloomy and rustic-looking cottage where the tea ceremony took place was the crucible in which Japanese taste was formed. And although the ceremony was mostly enjoyed

by the leisured class, its influence spread everywhere; it is still found even in the most garish high street, the humblest home.

If you enjoy the cool touch and green smell of *tatami*, you are appreciating the taste of the tea ceremony. If you find yourself admiring the simple elegance of the old architecture with its quaint and delicate woodwork and paper windows, or the roughness and spontaneity of the old pottery, you are on tea-ceremony wavelength. If you watch a shopkeeper wrap your purchase with deft and nimble fingers, you are witnessing at work the values the tea ceremony fostered.

Yet the tea ceremony was not really a ceremony at all — it was just a tea party. A small group of friends gathered in

surroundings they considered congenial, brewed and drank tea and talked. Great care and discernment went into the choice of everything used at the party: the tea-making utensils and bowls, the tea itself, frothy and bitter, the accompanying cakes, the arrangement of flowers, the scroll hanging on the wall. The conversation, too, was well considered and tasteful and revolved around the objects used or the beauties of the season. Silence was also permitted.

The object was to enjoy, in a brief space of time and in simple surroundings, a fragment

of eternity; to allow one's true nature, usually buried under noise, activity and desire, to come out and bask in tranquillity.

So there was a spiritual basis to the phenomenon, derived from Buddhism but without any overt religious observance, which is why it is sometimes called "Zen meditation for laymen."

The best way to get a feel for tea is simply to notice and relish those things —tatami, pottery and so on — which it has given to the society at large. Unfortunately, the ceremony itself has not only ceased to change, but has also turned slightly sour in its old age. Learning its thousand and one rules is now one of the main ways a young lady prepares herself for marriage. The naturalness and friendliness which must have played a part have been exorcized, and the ceremony, now truly ceremonious, is performed on stage and presented as if on a velvet cushion for the edification of visiting celebrities as "the heart of the culture." It's a pity.

There's a chance it may put down new roots overseas. An American who spent long years studying it in Japan is reported to have developed a new version in which a group of friends gather in congenial surroundings, brew and drink carefully selected coffee and listen to rock music.

history books say a match was first performed before the emperor in AD 100, and his modern descendant maintains the tradition, watching at least one match in Tokyo every year.

Sumo comes as a shock to those who imagine all Japanese to be small and slight. The typical sumo wrestler is an enormous man, tall and fat, who wobbles like jelly whenever he moves. Professionals live out their careers in *heya*, or stables, where a morning of hard training is followed by a hot bath and a huge lunch of meat, fish,

BLACK BELT BASEBALL

More than any other product of Japanese culture, it is the martial arts which have managed the difficult leap to the outside world.

Judo, "the way of gentleness" and the most famous, became part of the Olympic Games in 1964 when they were held in Tokyo. *Aikido* and **karate**, too, have soared in popularity in recent years. And **sumo**, the national sport and the only martial art practiced by professionals as well as amateurs, often inspires fanatical enthusiasm in the foreigners who get a chance to see it.

Sumo has been around the longest — 2,000 years according to some accounts. The

tofu, vegetables and large mountains of rice. The wrestler then snoozes away the afternoon while his meal converts itself happily into fat.

Modern sumo is a brilliant marriage of feudalistic ritual and highly telegenic drama. The elaborate Shinto ceremonies preceding and following the brief bouts have been simplified for the sake of modern audiences without sacrificing the sport's highly exotic flavor.

After several minutes of preparation, during which the combatants stamp, squat, gargle "power water" and scatter purifying

OPPOSITE and ABOVE RIGHT: Scenes from a sumo wrestler's life. ABOVE LEFT: Chiyononfuji, a past hero of this national sport, watches a contest.

salt on the clay ring, the bout begins — and is often over within seconds, with the loser either pushed out of the ring, sometimes somersaulting spectacularly into the arms of those in the front row, or forced to touch the ground with some part of his body other than the soles of his feet.

For the newcomer to the sport it may look like nothing more than fat men falling over; the aficionado is on the lookout for the skill with which the wrestlers use some of the 70-odd throws, heaves and pushes they are allowed to employ to bring the contest to an fairly swift end.

Sumo is very popular in Japan and champions are instant celebrities. The current top practitioners go under the names of Akebono and Takanohana.

Many of the other martial arts date back to the twelfth century when the samurai class first attained real power. Judo, or *jujutsu* as it used to be called, was the art of grappling and flooring an enemy on the battlefield. Like *aikido*, which was a different branch of the same art, it was modified in recent times and spread rapidly around the world. *Aikido*, the less aggressive of the two, depends on disabling an opponent by exerting painful holds on his vital points, then throwing him or pinning him down.

Kendo, "the way of the sword", is the samurai art *par excellence*. Combatants use bamboo staves in place of swords, wear protectors on the face and other parts of the body, and win by hitting the opponent's head, trunk or wrist or by jabbing him in the throat. It's possible to identify a *kendo dojo* (training hall) from some distance away, due to the feudalistic bellowing and screaming that issues from it.

Quite a number of other arts have survived from that early age. *Kyudo*, Japanese archery, was the subject of a famous book, *Zen in the Art of Archery*. *Yabusame* is archery on horseback, still exhibited regularly at Hachimangu Shrine in Kamakura, near Tokyo (see page 116 in FESTIVALS). **Ninjutsu** is the fiendish and multifaceted art of the *ninja*, the legendary spies and saboteurs of the feudal age. Though it was banned by the Tokugawa shogunate, its techniques have been passed on in secret down to the present day.

Karate is a special case. Originating more than 1,500 years ago in China, it was later introduced to the island of Okinawa, south of Kyushu, where it took on its modern characteristics. It arrived in Japan as recently as 1922 and has since become popular everywhere.

Among Western sports, baseball is undoubtedly the most popular, and golf, in a country drastically short of space and entirely lacking in rolling hills, the most incongruous. Those high-netted enclosures you see on your trips around Tokyo are for practicing golf driving.

Soccer, rugby and American football are among other sports with plenty of amateur followers. Indeed, thanks to the media's influence in popularizing western sports, Japan is hosting soccer's World Cup in the year 2002. On the other hand, however, cricket has failed to catch on. Japanese people often mistake it for croquet, the US version of which, gate ball, is much enjoyed by old-age pensioners.

SPORTS: WHERE TO SEE AND DO

Sumo. Professional tournaments are held in Tokyo for 15 consecutive days in January, May and September at the New Kokugikan Sumo Hall in Ryogoku, Tokyo. Similar events take place in Osaka in March, Nagoya in July, and Fukuoka in November. ((03) 3623-5111.
Judo. Full information is available from the All-Japan Judo Federation (*Zen-ju-ren*) ((03) 3818-4199.
Aikido. Information is available from Tokyo Aikikai ((03) 3203-9236.
Karate. Information from World Union of Karate-do Organizations ((03) 3503-6637/8.

For pro baseball, all fans and prospective fans should acquire a copy of the *Japan Pro Baseball Fan Handbook and Media Guide*. It contains team rosters and directories, league schedules, statistics from the previous season, profiles of foreign players, stadium diagrams and much other information (including statistics for all foreigners who have played since 1950). You can buy it in bookstalls, or direct from the author Wayne Graczyk at 1-12-18 Kichijoji Higashi-cho, Musashino-shi, Tokyo-to 180, enclosing ¥1,000, an envelope and return postage.

HOW DO THEY LIVE?

Meanwhile, 123 million human beings call Japan home. How do they make out? How do they live?

Take that youngish man in the blue suit sitting opposite you in the subway, his face hidden behind a newspaper. How does he support himself? What sort of place does he live in? And with whom does he share it? What does he believe? What are his dreams, his diversions?

In 30 years the *sarariman* (salaried worker) has replaced the farmer as Mr. Average.

LIVING TO WORK

Arriving at nine, he'll work through to five: that's the working day that gets into the statistics. However, he's likely to stay on for a couple of hours to finish up, then go off drinking with colleagues or clients. Japanese like to say they "live to work" (in the West they do the opposite) and if it's not as true as it used to be there is still something in it. (It's

FLOCKING OFF THE FARM

If we follow him off the train, he will lead us to his workplace: an office, the headquarters of a major company, 30 floors above Shinjuku in one of the skyscrapers there.

Fifty years ago, white-collar jobs like his were an impossible dream for the majority of the Japanese. More than 50 percent of the population were farmers or fishermen. By 1990 this proportion had dropped as low as 7.1 percent. Meanwhile, since the slump in oil prices, and with the proliferation of mass-production methods (robots are increasingly replacing men), the number of jobs in manufacturing has also begun to decline.

the reason, incidentally, why traveling around Japan off season, between national holidays, can be a blissful experience: even if the weather is good almost everybody is at work.)

The government, believe it or not, has been trying to persuade the workforce to take it a little easier — to stay home on Saturdays from time to time, for example. They are simply passing on the grumbles of other nations that the Japanese are too productive. The workforce does not like the idea — or so they say, and many of them are sincere.

Recreation in Japanese society takes many forms. ABOVE: A gay bar in Roppongi attracts its followers for after work fun and relaxation.

The Culture of Japan

Neither, it transpires, do many of their wives, some of whom are reportedly cracking up under the strain of having hubby around the house for two whole days.

Part of the reason for this is that the average Japanese home is not the best place in the world for relaxing. Let's follow our man home and have a look at him in his own environment.

REGULATION RABBIT HUTCH

Several years ago a European Union report

suggested that many Japanese houses resemble rabbit hutches. The remark stung, and stuck. They'll repeat it back to you, but it hurts. It's a bit too near the bone.

Our man is lucky enough to have his own house. It has two stories, and underneath the Mediterranean blue tiles and the fancy mortar finish it has a traditional wooden post-and-beam structure (it was constructed from the top down, starting with the roof). This structure means it sways in earthquakes (but does not collapse) and is cool in summer, but it's cold in winter and has a life expectancy of about 40 years.

It's a "4LDK" — four rooms plus living-room, dining-kitchen, tiny bathroom and separate toilet, and if he was trying to buy it today it would cost in the region of $1 million. Two of the rooms, one upstairs and one down, are traditional *tatami* rooms.

ABOVE: A young couple feeding the birds in Ueno Park. Compact in every facet of their lifestyle, these kindergarten children OPPOSITE LEFT are being taken for an outing. OPPOSITE RIGHT: Pedestrians wait for a green light before crossing this Tokyo street.

NATURE'S FRAGRANT CARPET

Tatami, rarely encountered outside Japan, is almost sufficient reason in itself for a visit to the country. The units are often called "*tatami* mats", which is confusing because "mat" suggests a thin carpet. However, *tatami*, about two meters long and one meter wide (six feet by three feet), is nearly seven centimeters (three inches) thick, so it's better described as a pad or flooring block.

Tatami, found in almost every home in the country (though in modern homes there may be only one small *tatami* room), is made by neighborhood craftsmen and consists of many layers of tightly braided rice straw. The sleek surface, green when the pads are new, is closely woven matting made of a reed called *igusa*. The mat has an edging of cotton or silk.

At the threshold of a Japanese home one removes shoes and puts on slippers, but at the threshold of a *tatami* room one removes the slippers. The pad is solid but gives slightly under one's weight. It is soft enough to sleep on directly (though this is rarely done) or for a baby to tumble around on. It is better than a carpet in summer as it remains cool, though in winter it can be downright chilly.

In wet weather or when the mat is new it gives off a sweet fragrance of straw. This sometimes makes foreigners feel nauseous but you find that you will quickly grow accustomed to it, and if you catch the smell again after an absence you may find it pulls at heart strings you never knew existed. Then you'll know how it feels to be a Japanese coming home from abroad.

Other Japanese smells which pull at the heart strings are:
- the first mosquito coil of summer,
- the smell of roasting tea (*hoji-cha* — cheap and delicious),
- mothballs (dramatic changes in temperature between seasons mean that half one's wardrobe is moth-balled for half the year), and, last of all,
- *yuzu*, a lime-like citron with a special fragrance, used in winter cooking.

All rooms in Japan are described according to the number of *tatami* mats which will fit snugly into them. It follows that rooms come in standard sizes: 3-mat, 4.5 mat, 6, 8,

10, 12 and so on. A 4.5-mat room is the classic size for a tea ceremony (also for romantic assignations); six or eight is normal for a living room. An eight-mat room is considered spacious, and when the only furnishings are a low table and a couple of flat cushions (*zabuton*), it feels spacious, too, at least until you stand up. When crammed with a sofa, armchairs, a coffee table, a 60 cm (24 in) TV plus LD and video equipment, a CD player, bookcases, a cabinet full of unopened bottles of scotch and a personal computer, it no longer feels spacious at all.

Futon are fluffy cotton mattresses, hung out in the sun every fine day (lazy bachelors don't hang out their *futon* and soon they become as hard as rice crackers, hence the phrase "*sembefuton*").

All the Saitos sleep in this room, the younger of the two children between Mr. and Mrs. This is one reason why love hotels are so popular in Japan, even with married couples. While Mr. Saito collapses into bed, we can poke around the house. It's soon clear why he doesn't like to spend too much time here: it really is small. The garden, as he

This may be one reason our man puts in such long hours at the office.

readily admits, is "no bigger than a cat's forehead."

WALL-TO-WALL PEOPLE

In our man's house — let's call him Saito — in Mr. Saito's home, however, it is the Western-style rooms which are full of furniture. The *tatami* room, the one upstairs, is full of people.

It's the bedroom, but only as long as the family is asleep. During the day it's a regular living room. At bedtime Mrs. Saito pulls from the deep built-in closet *futon*, sheets, blankets, quilts (in winter) and pillows and spreads them on the *tatami*, one sleeping space per pad.

LOVE AND MARRIAGE

In Japan, love and marriage increasingly go together like a horse and carriage. Mr. and Mrs. Saito met at work. He was a *sarariman* and she was an *o-eru* ("OL" = office lady). They dated in coffeeshops, went to movies, admired sunsets and views of Mt. Fuji and occasionally went to love hotels where at first they only kissed. More than 70 percent of modern marriages are actually "love marriages" like this, a dramatic increase over the number just 20 years ago. The other 25 to 30 percent are still arranged.

The arranged marriage is very alien to Western thinking, but the Japanese point out its advantages. The *nakodo*, or go-between, who brings the couple together is a friend of both families who can see the economic, social, even emotional ramifications of the union for both sides without misty-eyed sentiment confusing the issue. Traditionally, marriage is thought of not so much as a union of individuals as of families.

It's undeniable that this hardheaded system produces a lot of rock-solid marriages. Emotional expectations are realistically low

and burgeoning friendship between the partners is a pleasant bonus.

It's also a humane system, at least these days, as both partners are given ample chance to meet, weigh each other up and, if it smells wrong, call the whole thing off. This happens frequently. Living together for long periods without getting married is much, much rarer than in the West.

RITES OF PASSAGE

Like most Japanese couples, the Saitos solemnized their marriage with a Shinto ceremony at a wedding hall which has a shrine on the premises. (Shinto has shrines, *jinja*; Buddhism has temples, *o-tera*.) The groom

wore a *moningu* (a morning suit) and the bride a silk wedding kimono of fantastically rich design and an elaborate bonnet to hide her "horns of jealousy." After the ceremony she changed into a Western wedding dress and veil and they cut a huge wedding cake. The whole performance, including costume and feast, consumed about 33 percent of the year's income of the groom's family and about 50 percent of the bride's. Not surprisingly, divorce is frowned upon. Although on the rise, it is about half as common as in Western Europe.

A Shinto shrine is the normal place for a wedding, but when a member of the Saito family dies, a Buddhist priest will be called in. Hypocrisy? Confusion? The Japanese don't think so. Here's how it works.

HARMONY IN HEAVEN

Shinto is the native religion of Japan. Like many other primitive religions, it is animistic: worship is directed at the phenomena of nature.

The deities of Shinto are as varied and multitudinous as the natural world itself, and basically anything which struck awe and wonder into the hearts of the early Japanese was exalted as a *kami* or deity: mountains, trees, waterfalls, foxes, infectious diseases, military heroes, emperors. The intellectual content of the religion was minimal. The idea of purification was central. *Kami-sama* were invoked to bring prosperity and ward off misfortune.

When tolerant Buddhism entered the country from the continent, it soon reached an accommodation with Shinto. The deities of Shinto became identified with Buddhist *Bodhisattvas*. Shrines and temples were often built on the same sacred ground. In the case of at least one sect, the Shugendo, the two religions fused.

Both religions have suffered different vicissitudes over the years, but essentially their demarcation lines are clear. Shinto, bright, pragmatic, recoiling from "dirty" death, takes care of marriage; Buddhism,

LEFT: A banner at a Shinto shrine.
OPPOSITE: Elegant, elaborate, suffocatingly inhibited the traditional Shinto wedding ceremony is typical of the ceremonial side of Japan.

deeply philosophical, concerned with the essence of man's nature, takes care of death.

THOUSAND GODS AND NONE

It is often said that the Japanese are no longer a religious people, but it is hard to say whether or not this is true. Certainly they are not secular in the way the people of the Protestant countries of Europe have become secular during this century. Religious faith and ardor of the Christian type are rarities, but

In addition to these and many other observances, street festivals being the most visible, a huge panoply of new religions, usually focused on the teachings of a charismatic founder, has appeared in the last century.

Buddhism has been losing voltage for centuries. State-organized Shinto, associated with militarism, collapsed after the war. And less than one percent of the country's population is Christian. Yet among ordinary people religious belief and practice persist, like a quiet background melody you can hear only if you listen hard.

religious practices of all sorts are still extremely widespread.

When the people next door to the Saitos decided to rebuild their house, they went to stay with relatives nearby, but the grandmother of the house came to the site early each morning to pray to the *kami-sama* of the land to allow the operation to go through without harm. She put little cones of salt all round the site, with a lighted stick of incense in the center of each. When the old building had been demolished, a square of young bamboo trees in leaf was erected, connected by sacred rope, and a Shinto priest was called in to purify the ground. A similar groundbreaking ceremony took place at the site of a new TV factory nearby.

THE CATFISH STIRS

It's still the middle of the night but suddenly and simultaneously Mr. and Mrs. Saito are awake: earthquake! The floor is moving underneath them and the wooden posts and beams are squeaking and groaning. After a few seconds it stops. Neither of them has moved — they quickly judged it was only a small quake — but their pulses are racing all the same. There are three terrifying things, the Japanese used to say in the old days —earthquakes, thunder and a father's anger. The latter two don't bother anybody much these days, but nobody gets used to earthquakes.

Japan suffers hundreds of them every year, and the Tokyo area is one place where they are frequent. Most are too small to worry about, but every once in a while a big one strikes. Then, they say, the catfish which lives under Japan is thrashing its tail. The last really catastrophic one was the 1923 quake in which about 140,000 people died.

Fire is the worst hazard in an earthquake, so the first thing to do is to turn off the gas. Don't run outside; instead, take cover in an area which is structurally solid, either under a table, in a doorway or in a small room

for the top grade primary, junior high and high schools, and this in turn gives him a good chance of passing the entrance exam to one of the country's top universities — maybe even Tokyo University (*Todai*), which is *the* top. Once that hurdle is behind him, a career in government or one of the top companies is practically assured.

A hundred years ago there was no word for "competition" in Japanese. Now the education system is one of the most mercilessly competitive in the world. A high proportion of kids from age six up wards spend several

such as the toilet (leave the door ajar or you may later have to crawl out the window). Dangers outside include falling roof tiles and collapsing stone or brick walls.

Wooden houses make a terrible noise but are resilient to all but the strongest quakes. Modern highrise buildings in Tokyo are designed to ride out even those.

hours a day after school at cramming schools (*juku*), memorizing the facts they need to give them an edge in the exams. "Children without childhood", they were dubbed by one foreign observer.

At university they can relax and generally do. University students are renowned for doing as little as they can get away with. Who can blame them?

START RIGHT

After breakfast Mrs. Saito packs her six-year-old boy off to school. She has high hopes for him. When he was three he was selected for a prestigious kindergarten not far away, and this might prove to have been the single most decisive event in his life. It put him in line

OPPOSITE LEFT: Votive tablets and strings of folded paper cranes, two ways of petitioning for good luck. OPPOSITE RIGHT: The distinctive carp banners flying to celebrate Boy's Day Festival in early May. ABOVE: The band at a Shinto street festival in Osaka. OVERLEAF: Inauspicious *o-mikuji*, fortune-telling papers, tied to bushes at Heian Shrine in Kyoto.

One reason for the harshness of Japan's education system is that the country's class structure, one of the world's most rigid a century ago, has almost entirely collapsed in modern times.

Nearly 80 percent of the population believe themselves to be middle-class, while the level of literacy — one of the highest, not only in Asia, but in the world — is an amazing 99 percent. Japan is a true meritocracy — which means the scramble to get to the top of the heap must be replayed remorselessly every generation.

COMPULSORY CRAMP

When the teacher enters, little Saito and all the other children stand and bow to him and the teacher bows back. Mrs. Saito meets her *ikebana* (flower arrangement) teacher in the street and bows deeply, with her hands folded in front of her. Mr. Saito does the same when he meets his boss in the morning, but with his hands firmly at his side.

Japanese people start bowing when they are practically in the cradle. It's about as natural for them as yawning. A bow is simply acknowledgment that there is a difference in status between the two parties. The greater the gap, the deeper the bow, which is why students bow more deeply than their teachers. Getting the angle exactly right is important. A year or two ago a department store installed a machine to help train staff how to bow correctly to customers.

Westerners usually look — and feel — weirdly obsequious when they attempt a Japanese bow. It is not expected: a nod and a smile will see you through.

VALE OF TEARS

When Mr. Saito finally puts down his paper, give him a nod and a smile. He needs all the encouragement he can get. Every morning he has to struggle in to the center of the city on a transportation system which is one of the most crowded and one of the most efficient, in the world: Some 7,200,000 commuters, plus 4,800,000 other passengers, ride Tokyo's Japan National Railways trains daily.

This prospect stretches ahead of him five or six days a week, for the rest of his work-

ing life — or at least until the regular retiring age of 60. Mr. Saito's company, which is one of the larger and more prestigious, offers him and most other male employees lifetime employment. It's a great prospect when things are going well, but when he's wedged under someone's armpit in the morning crush he can't be blamed for his dreams of fleeing somewhere and opening a coffeeshop or *pension*-style guesthouse.

Mrs. Saito's life is not a bed of roses either. She is one of the 31 percent of Japanese women who graduated from a university —

just a two-year course, admittedly — but it landed her nothing better than a clerical job in the company and no prospects of advancement.

When she married she submitted to expectations and resigned. Like many educated women she's in a rut, with nothing to do with her wits but take care of an ultra-convenient home, perhaps take up another hobby, and prod her children on to ever-greater educational achievement. The *kyoiku mama* — education-obsessed mom — is a phenomenon of the new Japan.

So both Mr. and Mrs. Saito have their frustrations. The easiest way for them to forget these is to take a trip to the neighborhood *pachinko* parlor.

Pachinko is the vertical pinball game which began in Japan after the war and spread like fire. At the latest count, there were some 15,598 *pachinko* parlors nationwide. In a dense metallic cacophony of cascading silver balls, electronic slurrings and slushings and taped martial music, the troubled soul can fix his eyes on the machine and drift away. Continual refinements ensure that he doesn't get tired of it: some of the recent machines have tiny TV sets embedded in the center.

There are prizes to be won — they can be exchanged for cash illegally, at nearby shops

pulsion, the Japanese national myth revolves around a rude dance.

Affronted by another of the gods, the sun goddess (an ancestress, it was believed, of the imperial family) shut herself away in a cave, plunging the world into darkness. The other deities gathered round at the mouth of the cave and one of them performed a hilariously indecent dance, causing the others to fall about laughing. The sun goddess within the cave was overcome with curiosity. She emerged, and has been shining ever since.

— but except for the very keen or the very poor they are not the main incentive. Escape from reality is the name of the game.

THE PLEASURES OF JAPAN

Despite all the hard work, puritanism is a philosophy which has never taken root in Japan. The Japanese are a pleasure-loving people, and the good news is that a surprising number of their unique diversions are perfectly accessible to all visitors, and the enjoyment is, almost, unaffected by the language barrier.

Love of pleasure is engraved in the national character. While the Christian bible virtually opens with a story of sin and ex-

THEATER

Noh
The medieval *noh* theater, which nearly gave out at the start of the modern period, is strong and active again now and has had a big influence on the avant-garde theater of the West. This highly formalized and unrealistic type of drama was the favorite of one of the early shoguns, who had parts specially written for him and liked to rehearse before going into battle.

OPPOSITE: Housewives with time on their hands learn new skills, such as dance. A performance ABOVE of a *noh* play at the Meiji Shrine in Tokyo.

The beauty of *noh* is in the hypnotic and mysterious dancing, the masks — some blander than the Mona Lisa, some frighteningly demonic — and in the uncannily timeless atmosphere induced by these and by the music of drums and flute, punctuated by low wails and whoops. In this unworldly setting, where rules of time and space seem to be in suspension, old tales of loyalty, jealous passion and reincarnation unfold.

It is this atmosphere and the techniques used to bring it about which have excited the most interest in *noh* in modern times, but the stories too have an uncanny power. The great writer Yukio Mishima, notorious for his death by *seppuku* (*hara-kiri*) in 1970, reworked a selection of them into Western-style one-act plays, and reading these is perhaps the easiest way to get a feeling for the quality of *noh*. They have been published in English as *Five Modern Noh Plays*.

Noh is slow by the standards of modern theater and feels very ancient indeed — much more so than *kabuki*, for example — but once you are wrapped up in it you will forget about time. Try it, if only for the deep, meditative calm it can induce.

The **Kanze Noh-gakudo** (Shibuya ((03) 3469-5241) and the **Hosho Noh-gakudo** (Suidobashi ((03) 3811-4843) are two excellent places to see *noh*. Prices: ¥3,000 and ¥2,500 to ¥5,000 respectively. Performances start at 5:30 or 6 PM. Check *Tokyo Journal* (¥600 and monthly, in selected bookshops) for details.

Kabuki

Kabuki comes from the verb *kabuku*, which means to flirt, to frolic. It was first applied to another rude dance performed by a legendary lady called O-Kuni on a dry riverbed in Kyoto.

This remarkable thespian, said to have been rather plain but exceptionally clever, laid the foundations of the new art form at exactly the same time that Shakespeare was laying the foundations of his.

To add substance and interest to her dances she borrowed boldly from the *noh* theater and other contemporary forms, infusing her performances with the vigor and coarse spontaneity which had been deliberately drained from the aristocratic *noh*. Her performances finished with a "general dance" in which the spectators were welcome to take part — in any way they liked.

We can be sure that they did not restrain themselves, for the all-woman group was shortly closed down by the shogun on grounds of immorality.

It was replaced by an overtly homosexual all-male company from which *kabuki* as it exists today developed. During the long peace of the Tokugawa period, *kabuki* was the mouthpiece as well as the chief delight of the Edo towns man — merchant, shopkeeper, artisan. His materialism, his dash, his sentimentality and superstitiousness all found voice in the plays. As nothing much has changed in the productions of *kabuki* in a century or more, it offers the best insight into the tastes of that gaudy period — as well as being thoroughly enjoyable in its own right.

Everything in *kabuki* is on a huge scale. The revolving stage, wide and low, is equipped with traps and has every mechanical trick known to pantomime, carried off with a dozen times more panache and conviction. Costumes are gorgeous in the extreme — some weigh in at 18 kg (40 lb) — and the *hanamichi* or "flower walk" which runs from the stage to the back of the auditorium allows punters in the stalls to see them close up.

The plays go on all day, usually starting at 11:30 AM. The longueurs of the slow scenes are long indeed, but theaters like the **Kabuki-za** in Ginza are crammed with restaurants and kiosks to which the bored or hungry can retreat at any time.

Kabuki is a theater of spectacle and deserves to be seen close up. Then the full impact of the show — the dances, the transformations, the unearthly music of *shamisen*, flutes, clappers and drums coming from both sides of the stage, as well as the pathos of the separations and suicides and the glamour of the great battles — and all the vanity and charm of the Edo period pour over the happy spectator in a huge wave.

The Kabuki-za is perhaps the best place to see *kabuki*, although the **Shimbashi Embujo** and the **National Theater** are also fine. Tickets for *kabuki* and all other plays in

Moving away from tradition, street theater has become more popular in the urban centers of Japan.

Tokyo may be purchased from **Playguides** ticketing agencies, located in many department stores around town. Prices are lower than at the box office. Start queuing at 10 AM outside Kabuki-za to see that day's performance. Prices: Kabuki-za ((03) 3541-3131; between ¥2,000 and ¥11,000. National Theater ((03) 3265-7411, but 3230-3000 for reservations; between ¥2,500 and ¥9,000.

Bunraku

Bunraku, the puppet theater, started life at the same time as *kabuki*, shares many of its

characteristics, and was long in competition with it. It is certainly the most elaborate puppet drama in the world, and perhaps the only one which goes beyond the broadly comic to take on pathos and tragedy. Considering its age and strangeness, it is surprisingly easy to enjoy.

The largest of the puppets are two-thirds human size and require three operators, the master takes the head and right hand; his assistants the left hand and the feet. The repertoire, much of which it shares with *kabuki*, includes tales of revenge, sacrifice and suicide.

The love suicide plays are among the most engaging. As many of them were written about true episodes of thwarted love between humble shopkeepers and geisha which were

currently in the news, they abound with realistic detail and are some times really moving. Many a hard-bitten Westerner has found himself mopping the tears from his face at the climax of such a play.

Good seats are vital for the enjoyment of *bunraku*, even more so than for *kabuki*, due to the size of the puppets. Master puppet operators work with their faces uncovered, but when the play has you in its grip you will find you have forgotten about them. If you get tired of looking at the puppets, shift your attention slightly to the right and admire the art of the *joruri*, the narrators who, augmented by a *shamisen* player, recite the play's story and take on all the parts.

Bunraku is staged in May, September and December of each year at Tokyo's pleasant but aseptic **National Theater**. A trip to the **Asahiza Theater** in Osaka, where the company is based, would allow one to savor the *bunraku* atmosphere to the full. For more details see RELISH BUNRAKU, page 30.

Contemporary Theater

Modern theater flourishes in Tokyo, too. At theaters such as the **Nissay Gekijo** and the **Teikoku Gekijo** the *kabuki* tradition manifests itself in the elaborate staging and the tendency to glittering fantasy in modern works, some of which feature stars borrowed from the *kabuki* companies. Internationally known companies such as the Waseda Shogekijo and Tenjo Sajiki, playwrights like Hisashi Inoue and Juro Kara, theaters like the **Honda Gekijo** in Shimo-kitazawa — all these demonstrate the liveliness of Japanese contemporary theater. See the monthly *Tokyo Journal* for details of these and more.

Another theater experience for the curious is **Takarazuka**, a modern all-female company which stages lavish and sticky-sweet fantasies in Tokyo every six or eight weeks.

Butoh

And then there's **Butoh**. Shaved, all but naked, totally whitened male figures writhing in shafts of light, *butoh* is an apparently absurdist spectacle that suddenly blossoms into the most extraordinarily beautiful, if somewhat bizarre, effects. It originated in the nihilistic atmosphere of Japan in the 1950s, and has been seen as an attempt to recapture the shamanistic origin of Japanese dance and give it a new life as modern art.

If you've never seen it and are reasonably adventurous in your theatrical tastes, you should go along. Two companies currently riding high in esteem in *butoh* circles are Sankai-juku ("Mountain/Ocean School") and Byakkosha ("White Tiger Regiment"). For enthusiasts they're a reason for going to Japan in themselves.

Details of *butoh* performances can be found among the entertainment listings in *Tokyo Journal*.

FESTIVALS

We go over festivals in Japan at greater length starting on page 58 in YOUR CHOICE. So here we detail some of the most famous and splendid.

TOKYO

Dezome-shiki or New Year Ceremony (January 6th). Firemen's parade, featuring a display of traditional acrobatics by fire men on top of tall bamboo ladders. Location: Chuodori, Harumi (Tsukiji subway station).

Zojoji Matsuri. Large and colorful procession in memory of St. Honen, founder of the Jodo sect of Buddhism; continues for three days. Location: Zojoji Temple, Shiba

Park (Shibakoen station, Toei Mita municipal subway).

Kanda Myojin Matsuri (Mid-May). One of the capital's two greatest *matsuri* (the other one is at Hie Shrine) and one of the "big three" nationwide, this festival involves many magnificent *o-mikoshi* and ancient dances. Location: Kanda Myojin Shrine, Tokyo (Kanda station, JR). Held on even-numbered years — 1998... 2000... 2002.

Sanja Matsuri (3rd Friday, Saturday and Sunday in May). A famous and splendid festival, featuring more than 50 huge

o-mikoshi and troops of Shinto priests. Location: Asakusa Shrine (Asakusa subway station).

Sanno Matsuri (10 to 16 June). Tokyo's other great *matsuri* with dancers, wood-wheeled carts, *o-mikoshi* and gilded lions' heads. Location: Hie Shrine, Tokyo. Held on odd-numbered years — 1999, 2001, 2003....

Hanabi Taikai or **Grand Fireworks Display** (last Saturday in July). Fireworks are a spectacular feature of Japan's sticky summer, and this recently revived display is one

---

OPPOSITE: The decorated prow of a boat at the *Mifuni Matsuri*, the annual Boat Festival in Kyoto. ABOVE: Launching a kite, and tattooed kite-flyer, at the Hamamatsu festival. OVERLEAF: A giant kite at the Hamamatsu festival.

of the best in the country. Time: 7:15 to 8:15 PM. Arrive early. Location: Sumida River at Asakusa (in the Asakusa subway station).

NIKKO
Grand Festival of Toshogu Shrine (May 17 and 18). A grand procession recreates the days of the Tokugawa shogunate against the background of Japan's most gorgeous shrine. Location: Toshogu Shrine, Nikko, Tochigi Prefecture.

KAMAKURA
Tsurugaoka Hachimangu Spring Festival 2nd to 3rd Sunday in April). Many parades and other events under the cherry blossoms in Japan's medieval capital, just one hour from central Tokyo. Location: Tsurugaoka Hachiman Shrine, Kamakura, Kanagawa Prefecture.

Hachiman Matsuri (mid-September). A festival featuring *yabusame*, the martial art of archery on horseback, in the grounds of Kamakura's biggest shrine. Location, as above.

HAKONE
Hakone *Daimyo* Gyoretsu or **Hakone Feudal Lord Procession** (November 3). About 200 local people in feudal costumes parade through the streets of the handsome old spa town of Hakone-Yumoto. Location: Sounji Temple, Hakone-Yumoto, Kanagawa Prefecture.

SHIMODA
Kurofune Matsuri or **Black Ships Festival** (May 16 to 18). The arrival of the American Commodore Perry in his "black ships" was the most crucial single event in the opening of Japan to the outside world. The event is recreated and commemorated at this port in the Izu Peninsula, two and a half hours by rail from Tokyo. Location: Gyokunsenji Temple, Shimoda, Shizuoka Prefecture.

HAMAMATSU
Hamamatsu Odakoage or **Big Kite Flying** (May 3 to 5). One of Japan's most famous kite festivals which kites of all sizes engage in battles. The expert contestants try to cut the strings of opposing kites by means of glass or other sharp objects fastened to their own

strings. Hamamatsu is a town famous for musical instruments and motorcycles and is nearly two hours by *shinkansen* ("bullet" train) from Tokyo. Location: sand dunes some three miles from town. Shuttle buses leave from outside the station on festival days.

KYOTO
Aoi Matsuri or **Hollyhock Festival** (May 15). Japan's oldest festival, dating from the sixth century, and one of the most elegant. The procession features an imperial messenger and his retinue in costumes from the Heian period and a cart with huge wooden wheels decorated with wisteria flowers and drawn by a garlanded ox led by ropes of orange silk. Location: Kamigamo and Shimogamo Shrines, Kyoto.

Mifune Matsuri (3rd Sunday in May). Prettily decorated boats with figure heads in the shape of dragons and phoenixes sail down the River Oi bearing musicians, and commemorate the river-borne excursions of the Heian court. Location: River Oi at Arashiyama, near Kyoto.

Gion Matsuri (July 17 to 24). Perhaps the single most famous festival in Japan and another of the "big three." The procession features towering, teetering carts which are dragged through the streets, all of ancient origin and each with a story to tell. Many other events connected with the festival occur throughout July. Location: Yasaka Shrine, Higashiyama-ku, and Shijo-Kawaramachi amusement quarter, Kyoto.

Daimonji Okuribi or **Great Bonfire Event** (August 15 and 16). A great bonfire on a Kyoto hillside burns in the shape of the character *Dai*, meaning "Great", and is visible for miles. Location: Mt. Nyoigadake, Kyoto.

Jidai Matsuri or **Festival of the Ages** (October 22). For a vivid rundown on how the costumes of Japan's ruling class have changed over the last millennium this festival is unbeatable. The long procession begins with soldiers of the Meiji period (1868–1912) and works backwards to the nobles and archers of the eighth century. The attention to authenticity of details is meticulous. Location : Heian Shrine, Kyoto.

Ukai or **Cormorant Fishing** (May 11 to October 15). A lighted stick draws *ayu*, a type of trout, to the surface of the river where cormorants on leashes are waiting to snap them up and deliver them whole to the waiting boatmen. A highly popular occasion for a summer party on the water. Location: Nagara River, Gifu Prefecture, and Uji River, Kyoto Prefecture.

NARA
Mando-e or **Lantern-Lighting Ceremony** (February 3 or 4). All 3,000 lanterns of Kasuga Shrine are lit, welcoming the coming of spring. The ceremony is repeated on Au-

O-mizutori Matsuri or **Water-Drawing** Festival (March 1 to 14; main event on night of March 12). A solemn evening festival, the greatest event of the year, at the temple which houses Nara's Great Buddha. Huge torches illuminate the temple, the eerie wailing of conchs echoes through the air and at midnight the festival culminates in the drawing of holy water from the Wakasa well. Location: Todaiji Temple, Nara.

OSAKA
Tenjin Matsuri (July 24 or 25). A richly

gust 15, in the O-bon season (Festival of the Dead) to light the way for visits from departed spirits. Location: Kasuga Shrine, Nara.

Onio-shiki or **Demon-Driving Ceremony** (February 4, but variable). February 1 marks the end of winter and the beginning of spring and is the season of *setsubun* when the chant of "Demons out! Luck in!" is heard, and roasted beans are chucked around the house and elsewhere as a means of ritual purification. This rite is taken to a picturesquely literal extreme at the Kofukuji Temple, where men dressed as demons invade the temple grounds and are then chased out by disguised priests. Location: Kofukuji Temple, Nara (also at Horyuji Temple, Nara, and Nagata Shrine, Kobe).

picturesque festival with processions on both land and river, this is the third of the "big three". A Chinese-style lion dance and a huge drum played by six men in immensely tall hats are among the attractions. Location: Temmangu Shrine, Osaka.

HIMEJI
Kenka Matsuri or **Fighting Festival** (October 14 and 15). One of the few festivals Japan with an element of danger. Participating *o-mikoshi*-bearing teams jostle and barge one another in an effort to come first. Location: Matsubara Hachiman Shrine, Himeji City, Hyogo Prefecture.

Late afternoon visitors to an Osaka shrine, dressed in some gloriously gaudy kimonos.

HIROSHIMA
Heiwa Matsuri or **Peace Festival** (August 6). Hiroshima's most important annual event, commemorating those who died as a result of the atom bomb which fell on the city at 8:15 PM on August 6, 1945. It is a solemn occasion with songs of peace, prayers and lighted paper lanterns which float down the river. Location: Heiwa Koen (Peace Park), Hiroshima.

MIYAJIMA
Kangen-sai Matsuri or **Music Festival** (mid-

July). A fleet of brightly decorated boats makes a sea parade in the vicinity of the holy island of Miyajima, accompanied by *gagaku*, the ancient music of the imperial court. Location: Itsukushima Shrine, Miyajima, Hiroshima Prefecture.

SHIKOKU
Awa Odori or **Awa Dance** (August 12 to 15). This is the season of *O-bon*, the Festival of the Dead, much more cheerful than it sounds as it is the occasion for the spirits of dead loved ones to return home for a season, and they are given a properly uproarious welcome. Dancing and festivities take place nation wide, but Tokushima in Shikoku is famous for making a really big thing of it; in

fact, this may be Japan's most truly festive festival. Parading, dancing and drinking continue day and night throughout the three-day period. Location: Tokushima City, Tokushima Prefecture, Shikoku.

NAGASAKI
Peiron or **Boat Race** (Sundays and holidays from late May to August). Thirty-five men crowd into each of a number of long and bulky boats and paddle to the rhythm of gongs and drums as they strive to win this grueling, race derived from the Chinese.

Location: Nagasaki City, Nagasaki Prefecture, Kyushu.

Okunchi Matsuri (October 7 to 9). Nagasaki is one of the closest spots in Japan to China, and the fabulously gaudy carts and dragons in this brilliant festival show strong Chinese influence. Location: Suwa Shrine, Nagasaki.

TAKAYAMA
Sanno Matsuri (April 14 and 15) and **Takayama Matsuri** (October 9 and 10). Takayama has 23 enormous, and enormously ornate *yatai* or festival wagons, covered in carvings and tapestries, some with mechanical figures which perform tricks. Twelve of these are dragged through the streets in the spring

Sanno Festival, the other 11 in the autumn Yahata festival; both are among the nation's most magnificent. The 23 beautiful old floats in these processions testify to the strength of tradition in this well-preserved town, located on the old "back way" from Edo (Tokyo) to Kyoto. Location: Hie Shrine, Takayama, Gifu Prefecture.

KANAZAWA
Hyakuman-goku-sai or **The Lord's Million-Measures-of-Rice Event** (June 13 to 15). A large and fascinatingly varied parade, inc-

now often, and regrettably, of polyethylene. Location: Sendai, Miyyagi Prefecture.

MATSUSHIMA
Matsushima Toronagashi or **Lantern Event** (August 16). In the island-spotted waters of this famous bay, thousands of little boat lanterns are set sailing. Location: Matsushima, Miyagi Prefecture.

AOMORI
Nebuta Matsuri or **Dummy Festival** (August 1 to 7). Two million people pour into

luding geisha, old-fashioned firemen, and demonstrations of the tea ceremony. Location: The Oyama Shrine, Kanazawa, Ishikawa Prefecture.

SENDAI
Tanabata Matsuri or Seventh of July Festival (old calendar) (August 6 to 8). Two stars, Kengyu and Shokujo, are separated by the Milky Way, but once a year around this time they meet. The annual rendezvous of the heavenly lovers, as a Chinese fairy tale describes them, is celebrated with a gaudy but processionless festival in many parts of the country. Sendai's is the most famous. The streets are hung with extremely elaborate decorations, originally made out of paper,

this otherwise undistinguished city in the far north of Honshu for one of the most dramatic of summer festivals. The special feature is the procession of huge, beautifully painted and illuminated papier mâché floats which are hauled drunkenly through the city during the festival's two-day climax. Location: Aomori City.

AKITA
Kanto Matsuri or **Balancing Festival** (August 5 to 7). Reputedly the most enjoyable of Tohoku's "Big Three" summer festivals

OPPOSITE: Dressed up for a visit to the shrine and the finishing touches on festival day. ABOVE: Scene from Hamamatsu's Kite Festival.

(the other two are in Sendai and Aomori), this festival features the boys and men of the city who balance huge bamboo frameworks covered with lanterns and weighing some 60 kg (132 lb) on their foreheads, shoulders, hips, hands and even mouths while they slink down the street to the accompaniment of traditional music. Location: Akita City.

SAPPORO

Yuki Matsuri or **Snow Festival** (First or second week of February). The capital of the northernmost large island, Hokkaido, takes advantage of its freezing winter with a famously kitschy festival of snow sculpture, plus a costumed parade and skating. Shrewd publicity has induced foreigners to visit the festival in large numbers, but some have complained that it is basically a PR stunt for the Self-Defense Forces who construct many of the larger sculptures, and that it lacks the spontaneity and fun of more traditional festivals. Location: Sapporo, Hokkaido.

The festivals listed above are not only fascinating and charming in their own right; most of them occur in towns and cities which offer other compelling reasons for a visit. These places crop up again in the two chapters that follow, JAPAN: THE BROAD HIGHWAY and OFF THE BEATEN TRACK, where their particular attractions are described in more detail. By careful planning it is possible for the visitor to enjoy both a famous festival and the more serene pleasures of sightseeing in one and the same trip.

Besides these regular annual events, there are many once-only festivals around the country every year, and innumerable tiny but delightful neighborhood festivals of the type described at the beginning of this section. Details of the former can be obtained from the Tourist Information Centers (TICs) in Tokyo, Narita International Airport and Kyoto; stumbling across the latter is a matter of luck.

Checking with the TIC is a must anyway, whatever the festival: dates vary from year to year, old festivals give up the ghost, even older ones are suddenly revived. Information is regularly monitored by the TIC, and they will supply you with confirmed dates and useful details. If you can't get to one of their offices, use the Japan Travel Phone service, toll-free outside Tokyo and Kyoto, to get information. For details of this service see TRAVELERS' TIPS.

RYOKAN

The single most pleasant way to immerse yourself in things Japanese is to spend a few days at a *ryokan* or Japanese inn. They are described in STAY IN A *RYOKAN*, page 24 in TOP SPOTS.

Hotels all over the world are much the same and, like airports, have the effect of homogenizing the experience of travel. In a *ryokan*, on the other hand, the Japanese experience is at its most piquant. Furthermore, if you are prepared to put up with some inconveniences, you will probably end up agreeing that a good *ryokan* is at least the equal of a good hotel for comfort.

But make sure it is a real *ryokan*. The building will usually be no higher than two stories and constructed of wood, and there should be a garden, however small. In contrast to much else in Japan's modern cities, its appearance, with pine trees, paper windows and a step up from the *genkan* (entrance) to the body of the house, should declare plainly that you are now in Japan.

Most visitors fall in love with the *ryokan* experience, but there are undeniable drawbacks. Sitting on the floor becomes painful before long. Toilets are often of the crouching variety. There are no Western-sized desks to write or read at.

The ideal answer would be a hybrid, combining the best of the traditional elements — the wooden structure, the *tatami*, the *futon*, the bath — with Western conveniences. Unfortunately, no *ryokan* fitting this description exists as yet — or so we believe. Any reader who discovers one would do us a favor by letting us know.

Tax and service charges, as well as two meals, are usually included in the price quoted. This may be as low as ¥7,000 (or even ¥5,000) per person, or may be much higher. For instance, Kyoto's famous **Sumiya Ryokan** costs between ¥30,000 and ¥80,000 per night, which makes it nearly twice as expensive as the swankiest hotel in Tokyo. Reservations at a *ryokan* can be made through a travel agent.

JAPANESE BATHS

In your *ryokan* you will have experienced a traditional bath. But they are also available in their own right all over the country. Water is the one natural resource which Japan has in abundance. And due to the countrywide volcanic activity, hot water, rich in health-giving salts and minerals, bubbles out of the earth at innumerable places and has long provided the Japanese with one of their cheapest, yet richest, delights: hot spring bathing.

Several renowned bathing areas are described in the chapters that follow. Among the most famous and/or accessible are:

Hakone-Yumoto
Ninety minutes by Odakyu line's Romance Car, a truly luxurious train, from Shinjuku in Tokyo, this is a charming old spa town on the old Tokaido road to Kyoto.

Atami
"Shinjuku-on-sea", 55 minutes by *shinkansen* (bullet train) from Tokyo, Atami is one of the

Soak away the day's strains in the startlingly hot water of the large bath in your *ryokan* and you are already tasting that pleasure. But to get the full effect you should travel to one of the many resort towns which have grown up around particularly generous or salubrious hot springs. The water may be murky and reek of sulfur but once you are immersed in it you will feel the difference.

Fantastic medicinal properties are claimed for many baths and almost all are said to be good for "ladies' sicknesses" and skin diseases. The beautiful skin of some of the old ladies in these spa areas suggests that the latter is true. But for most visitors, Japanese and foreign, the real reason for bathing is it is one of the idlest and easiest of pleasures.

biggest spa resorts in Japan and the best place to see metropolitan Japanese at play. Too much concrete for some nature lovers. Be sure to take the Shinkansen's Kodama train: the Hikari flashes straight through Atami.

Beppu and Ibusuki
These are two of the most famous spas in Kyushu, the southernmost of Japan's main islands. Both feature hot sand baths, in which the lucky guest is buried to the waist or beyond in naturally steaming hot sand, and jungle baths, huge tropical greenhouses

ABOVE: The architecture of Ryokan Jippoan is all that one imagines a Japanese inn should be — clean lines and a tranquil interior fashioned out of wood and paper.

dotted with pools of different colors and temperatures.

Noboribetsu Spa
One of the baths in this town in the northern-most island of Hokkaido is one of the few attested mixed baths still remaining in Japan.

BATH ETIQUETTE

It will assure anxious natives that you know what you are about if you follow the same procedure as you do when bathing in your

ryokan. Before entering the bath, wash your-self with soap and hot water and rinse off thoroughly, sitting on one of the small stools provided and using hot and cold water from the taps. Rinse the small towel or flannel you have brought with you and take it with you into the bath to preserve your modesty. You may like to follow Japanese custom and place it on your head while you are in the water. Don't let your hair get in the water. If the bath is mixed, refrain from obvious staring or drooling. Rinse again on leaving the bath, in cold water if you like, but avoid pouring a bucketful over your neighbor.

Up to her neck in sand ABOVE this visitor is taking a therapeutic sand bath in Ibusuki. RIGHT: The Jungle Baths, Beppu are also extremely popular.

The average cost of staying overnight at a spa (*onsen* in Japanese) is ¥13,000 includ-ing dinner and breakfast. Reservations, particularly at weekends and holiday sea-sons, are essential. Solicit help from the TIC.

Warning!
The Japanese bath is *hot* — temperatures range from 35° to 60°C (95° to 140°F) plus. The hardest part is getting in. Once in, if you then sit still, your troubles are over (until you have to get out). However, for older people and especially those suffering from high blood pressure, the temperatures can be dangerous. If you want to risk it anyway, turn on the cold tap before entering and stay in that cooler region.

For people who have no time or inclin-ation to make a special trip to a resort, and who are staying in, say, a Western-style busi-ness hotel, a way to sample the pleasures of the bath is provided by the *sento* or neigh-borhood public bath. In the old days every-one went to the *sento*. Now most Japanese have baths in their own homes but a few bathhouses survive in most urban areas, serving the needs of students, the poor, the nostalgic and people on the move.

You can identify the *sento* by its high chim-ney, often belching black smoke. For some visitors these chimneys confirm their worst fears about Japan's lack of zoning laws, but their function is to keep the water hot.

As soon as you're through the *noren* (cur-tain) at the entrance, you split up according to sex, men going into one changing room, women another. You pay a standard charge of ¥310, plus a surcharge if you wash your hair. Children get in cheaper. Undress, leav-ing your clothes in a basket or locker, and go through glass doors to the bathing area, also segregated by sex. Then simply follow the etiquette described above. You will have to put up with some staring, particularly if you are hairy, but you may get into some inter-esting conversations. Enjoy the naive paint-ing of Mt. Fuji or another countrified scene on the back wall.

Some *sento*, notably in the working class areas of big cities, are still flourishing. In the Jujo section of Tokyo, one stays open to 1 AM, and is enlivened near 12 PM by the arrival of the local *kabuki* troupe, still in their makeup.

Sauna baths have caught on in Japan in a big way, and Tokyo has a number of all-night saunas. The city's many Turkish baths have recently been persuaded to change their name to "Soapland." Numbering around 2,000 nationwide, they sprang up in the wake of the 1956 anti-prostitution law — and it wasn't a coincidence. See TOKYO AT NIGHT, page 148, for more on that subject.

FOOD

Japanese food is discussed in more detail in

GALLOPING GOURMETS, page 62. Listed below are representative restaurants (and phone numbers) in 25 towns and cities throughout the country, in cases where it was possible to determine it, a figure suggesting roughly what a meal for one will cost.

While traveling around Japan there is no need to put up with inferior food. A variety of options exist. Restaurants of a decent standard are to be found in almost every town of any size. Many towns and cities have their *meibutsu*, the product or dish for which that particular area is renowned, and discovering and sampling these can lend an extra dimension of adventure to your journey.

Beautifully presented dishes ABOVE and a local eatery OPPOSITE in Tokyo.

"Course" (Japanese *kosu*) means a full set meal. Ordering à la carte, it is usually possible to eat more cheaply than the course price suggests.

Unless you speak Japanese the easiest way to use the list below is to get a Japanese person to call the restaurant in question (maybe your hotel clerk) to make a reservation (if this is necessary or possible) and obtain directions.

A Few Recommendations

Note: Restaurants can be a problem in Japan. Menus are frequently in Japanese only and the food, healthy though it undoubtedly is, is often challenging to the palate on initial acquaintance. In addition, establishments can be hard to identify on the ground. Trying to find a restaurant can be difficult indeed for often the name, like the menus, is only written in Japanese script, and not only are buildings unnumbered, but streets can be unnamed.

Consequently in this book, we have adopted a policy of indicating a few hotels and other types of accommodation for most major cities and areas, and restricted restaurant recommendations to the Tokyo region (see page 145, under TOKYO, WHERE TO EAT), and a few other establishments in the country that are personally recommended by the authors.

We feel most visitors will be in better hands eating in either their own, or other, hotels. Here menus are much more likely to be in English, or an English (or other European language)-speaking member of staff available to guide you through the intricacies of the cuisine.

This is not to say that you can't stumble on wonderful places more or less by chance. It looks enticing from the outside, there are other Westerners eating within, and you decide to chance your arm and check it out, possibly with the help of those other foreign diners.

There are also chain restaurants to look out for, some of them offering what are by Japanese standards, exceptional value.

One of the best of these is the **Yoshinoya** company's array of fast-food outlets. Unexpectedly, the food is freshly cooked and not pre-frozen; the prices are very low, and the choice illustrated on printed placemats laid out on the trays. US$3 could see you supplied with a bowl of rice and meat, miso soup and a dish of pickled cabbage.

Also, the ubiquitous plastic replicas of the dishes on offer in many of the cheaper places are a godsend to foreign travelers in the country.

Lastly, bento boxes are available to travelers and supermarkets have good selections of *sashimi* and *sushi* ready to take away.

KAGOSHIMA
Nagura ((09937) 62-5026. *Katsuo* (bonito *sashimi*) and other dishes. ¥1,500 and up.
Satsuma-ji ((0992) 26-0525. Traditional local *satsuma ryori* cuisine. ¥3,500 and up.

KANAZAWA
Kanazawa ((0762) 23-4439. *Robata-yaki*.

KAMAKURA
Monzen ((0467) 25-1121. In this town of Zen temples, *shojin ryori*, the elaborate vegetarian temple cuisine, is the special (though expen-

BEPPU
Marukiyo ((0979) 22-4055. Fish, including *fugu* (blowfish).

HIROSHIMA
Chez Yamarai ((0822) 94-1200. French-style food, including oysters. ¥5,000 and up.
Kakifune-Kanawa ((0822) 41-7416. Japanese-style. Special course ¥5,000 and up.

ISE (ISE-SHI)
Tekonejaya ((0596) 22-3384. *Sushi, sashimi*.

ISE (KASHIKOJIMA)
Shima Kanko Hotel ((05994) 3-1211. Famous for French cuisine and lobster dishes. ¥20,000 and up.

sive) treat. *Monzen* means "outside the gate" and it is indeed just outside the gate of En-kakuji in Kita-Kamakura, one of the town's most august monasteries. *Shojin ryori*, starts ¥4,000; and the elaborate *kaiseki ryori*, ¥5,000.

KUMAMOTO
Tagosaku ((0963) 53-4171. Country-style Japanese food, including horsemeat *sashimi*, a local specialty. Lunch: ¥4,500 up; dinner: ¥10,000.

KYOTO
Daimonjiya ((075) 221-0605. The specialty is elaborate and beautiful *bento* boxes which can be eaten on, or off, the premises. ¥7,000 and up.

Daitokuji Ikkyu, meaning "in front of the gate of Daitokuji Temple" ((075) 493-0019. *Shojin ryori*. Lunch: from ¥3,500; dinner: ¥7,000 and up.

Tagoto ((075) 221-3030. 100 years of serving *soba*. Lunch: from ¥3,000.

MATSUMOTO

Furusato ((0263) 33-3717. *Soba* (buckwheat noodles) shop. ¥515 and up.

MIYAZAKI

Sato (Miyazaki Kanko Hotel) ((0985) 27-

1212. *Sashimi*, including very rare mushroom *sashimi*.

NAGASAKI

Fukudaya ((0957) 22-0101. *Unagi* (broiled eel). ¥870 and up.

Shikairo ((0958) 22-1296. Nagasaki *chanpon* local Chinese-style noodles. ¥820 and up.

NAGOYA

Gomitori ((052) 241-0041. Loaches, frogs, spare ribs. ¥1,500 and up.

Kishimen Tei ((052) 951-3481. *Kishi men* or flat white noodles, are a specialty of Nagoya: A good place to sample them. ¥400 to ¥1600.

Torikyu ((052) 542-1889, 522-6331. High-class *yakitoriya*. Course ¥6,500 and up.

NAHA

Ryotei Naha ((098) 868-5577. Features traditional Ryukyu (Okinawa) cuisine to the accompaniment of Ryukyu dance.

NARA

Tonochaya ((0742) 22-4348. *Chame shi* (dishes with rice cooked in tea) specialist inside Kofukuji Temple. Also *somen* (a Nara *meibutsu*). *Chameshi* set ¥2,570 and up.

NIKKO

Nikko Kanaya Hotel ((0288) 54-0001. Elegant old hotel specializing in trout dishes (*nijimasu*). ¥2,800 and up.

OSAKA

Imai ((06) 211-0319. *Udon* house in famous Dotonbori area. ¥380 and up.

Itoy ((06) 341-2891. *Okonomiyaki*, delicious — and cheap — do-it-yourself omelette-cum-pancake. ¥500 and up.

SAPPORO

Sapporo biruen ((011) 742-1531. Steak and lamb dishes ("Genghis Khan") in converted nineteenth-century brewery. ¥3,090 and up.

Kanikko ((011) 231-4080. *Kani* (crab) dishes. ¥4,000 and up.

SENDAI

Kakitoku ((0222) 22-0785. Oyster dishes. Course ¥4,000 and up.

TAKAMATSU

Hamasaku ((0878) 21-6044. Fish *tempura*-style. ¥800 and up.

TAKAYAMA

Suzuya ((0577) 32-2484. *Sansai* (wild mushroom vegetables), beef, *hoba* (special local *miso* cooked on a leaf). ¥2000 and up.

TOKYO

See the listings in WHERE TO EAT, page 145 under TOKYO in JAPAN: THE GREAT HIGHWAY.

TOKUSHIMA

Saijo ((0886) 95-2775. *Udon* (fat white noodles) are the specialty of **Shikoku**. Also served here is the *tarai udon*, which mean literally "bathtub *udon*" in wooden bathtub-shaped dishes. ¥300 and up.

YUMOTO

Hatsuhana ((0460) 5-8287. *Soba* (buckwheat noodles) specialist. ¥850 and up.

LEFT: *Soba* noodles and *tempura*. RIGHT: Look out for the cheery, red lanterns indicating less expensive places to eat and above all, to drink.

Japan:
The
Broad
Highway

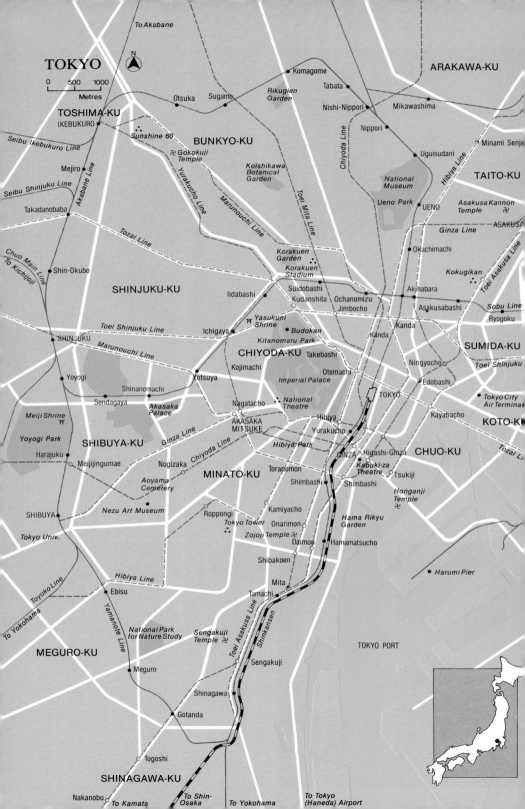

HONSHU

FOR MANY VISITORS TO THE COUNTRY, Japan is the island of Honshu: they never travel beyond its shores or venture into the neighboring islands. The reason is simple: Tokyo, Kyoto, Osaka, Hiroshima and Nagoya are all on Honshu, and although the archipelago comprises over 4,000 islands, it is on Honshu, the largest island in the whole group, that the majority of the Japanese people live and play. It is also the usual point of entry to visitors coming to Japan.

TOKYO: THE CITY AND BEYOND

If you've just arrived in Japan, you are probably in Tokyo. You know all the bad things already — the smog, the crowds, the "rabbit hutches" people live in. Now for the good news: it's safe, it's friendly and it's one of the most energetic — and energizing — cities in the world. It's much less smoggy than it was, and fish are returning to the rivers. There are not enough parks, but a couple of hours from the center there are volcanoes, lakes and primeval forests. Now read on.

BACKGROUND

Coming in from Narita airport, Tokyo seems to go on for ever. Sombre, gray and brooding, the megalopolis appears a place of immense power, much less futuristic than you expected for the capital of a nation that has conquered the world with its high-tech products, but nevertheless stubbornly forging its way inexorably into the future.

With its vastness and monochrome sophistication, Tokyo is a city that on first sight seems strangely familiar. Haven't we been here before, first-time visitors tend to ask themselves. And indeed, to people familiar with the great cities of Europe and America, Tokyo appears far less "different" than they might have expected.

Yet, unimposing though it is to look at, Tokyo is endlessly fascinating to experience. Who would have thought that august department store was home to a surrealist theater company, or that faceless block was in reality a love hotel?

With a population of nearly 12 million, Tokyo vies with Shanghai as the largest city in the world. For population density it has few competitors, for chaotic lack of planning none. One glimpse can be enough to send new arrivals scuttling back into the hotel lobby.

It's important to remember that this monster doesn't bite. It's both harmless and wholesome. You can, and probably will, lose your way within moments — the idea of using street names was introduced by the Americans after the war but never caught

on — but no harm will befall you. You can't read the signs, you can't ask the way, you feel as helpless as a toddler — but, despite the frenzied activity, there are thousands of people out there ready to guide you gently on your way. As capital cities go, Tokyo is remarkably friendly.

This friendliness seems to be bound up with its lack of any rational plan. The city has been almost entirely razed to the ground twice this century, once in the 1923 earthquake, once in the bombing of 1945. Both times it was rebuilt at top speed without any semblance of overall planning. Both times

For the finest choice in state-of-the-art technology, Akihabara ABOVE offers virtually wall-to-wall electrical goods stores.

this was deplored by architects and many other enlightened people as a shocking waste of opportunity. Both times it probably saved the city's soul.

Why? Because the human fabric of the city has managed to survive these waves of destruction, almost intact. Tokyo, today, consists of the dozens of villages which once dotted the Kanto Plain. Despite the destruction, despite the immigrants who still flood in from all over the country, the village feeling persists, sometimes almost as far as the city center.

The Past

The Kanto Plain, which Tokyo dominates, is the largest area of fairly flat land in Japan, but it was developed much later in the nation's history than the smaller plains around Kyoto and Nara. As in most Japanese towns, the nucleus was a castle, and the first one was built here in the fifteenth century.

The first Tokugawa shogun made Edo, the city's old name, his capital in the sixteenth century, and it began to expand rapidly, gobbling up without quite destroying many surrounding villages in the process.

Edo was the *de facto* capital throughout the 250 years of the Tokugawa period. The capital in name, however, was still Kyoto. In 1867 the shogun was deposed and the emperor restored to his former position of prestige. He moved with his court to Edo Castle and the city was renamed Tokyo — "Eastern Capital." Expansion continued apace.

A British envoy who visited the city at that time praised it as one of the most beautiful in the Orient. This century's earthquakes and bombs have ensured that this compliment is unlikely to be repeated, unfortunately, and the city has few buildings of great antiquity or historical interest.

But it is very much the hub of the nation — more so than many capitals — and it is the best and biggest showcase for the new Japan: for the electronics, the motorbikes, the cars, the fashion, the architecture. It has the most museums and galleries, the best stores, the best theaters and cinemas, many of the best restaurants and the most exciting and varied night life in the country.

Finding Your Way Around

Whether it's the green-uniformed, white-gloved guards who gesture you invitingly onto the trains, and only push you when they feel they must, the hooters that sound when the doors are about to close (at exactly the same pitch as those in the Paris Metro), or the astonishingly comfortable, upholstered seats (should you be lucky enough to get one), the subway trains of Tokyo are a delight. A major earthquake? Well, no one can deny it's a possibility, albeit a remote one. If you're really worried, you'll have to confine yourself to the overground JR Yamanote Line.

And indeed Tokyo's subway system is one of the most elaborate in the world. The JR Pass — see page 253 in TRAVELERS' TIPS — is not valid on the subway, however. Instead, tickets are bought from automatic vending machines; if in doubt of the fare to your destination, buy the cheapest ticket and pay the excess at the other end.

The system virtually constitutes an underground city. At the larger stations there are kiosks, small restaurants, and even quite elaborate shops. Shinjuku Station, which serves both subway and overground rail systems, is the most heavily used train station on earth. Once you begin to understand your way around there, you can consider yourself an honorary citizen of the Japanese capital.

Finding your way around any of the Tokyo subway stations is made easier thanks to the color-coding system. Once you know the color for the line you are looking for, you will be unerringly led to the platforms by

---

Hi-no-maru ("round sun") flags ABOVE wave to the Emperor on his birthday. Pachinko parlors RIGHT provide amusement for the bored and lonely.

following that color on direction-pointing signs. Then all you have to do is decide which of the two platforms you need, a decision easily executed by looking at the list of stations served. Stations ahead are printed in black, those behind are in grey.

So — where shall we start?

THE HUB OF THE HUB

Imperial Palace in the center of the city is one of the few historical musts for the tourist, but you can't see much of it because the

emperor still lives there. Reliable sources say it is considerably harder to penetrate than Buckingham Palace. You can admire the moat which surrounds it and the massive stones of the outer walls. Admire, too, the white walls of the palace itself, though temper your admiration with the knowledge that they were recently rebuilt in ferroconcrete.

The **East Garden**, across one of two bridges from the Plaza, is open to the public daily between 9 AM and 3 PM except on Mondays and Fridays. If you want a closer look, the palace itself throws open its gates just on two days a year, December 23 (the emperor's birthday) and January 2, 9 AM to 3:30 PM. The Hibiya-station is the best subway stop for the palace.

Important museums and halls are located near the palace. Near Takebashi (Takebashi subway) are the **National Museums of Modern Art, Science and Craft. The National Theater** is diametrically opposite Takebashi on the other side of the Imperial palace (Nagata-cho subway), while near Kudanshita subway is the massive **Nippon Budokan** hall, the main Tokyo venue for visiting big-name rock bands when it is not hosting tournaments of judo and *kendo*.

The large area between the palace and Nihombashi is the business heart of the city and is as smart and sterile as one would expect. Linger not, except to sample the delicious pumpkin pies at **Steinmetz's** near the north exit of Tokyo station (Yaesu-guchi side) and the **English-language bookshop** on the third floor of **Maruzen** (Nihombashi subway).

In the area of Nihombashi, by the way, lived William Adams, the first (the only?) English samurai and model for the hero of James Clavell's novel *Shogun*.

The Silver Mint

The **Ginza** ("Silver Mint") area southeast of the palace (Ginza subway) is the swishest, sleekest part of town and has been in the forefront of things for a century or more. Tokyo's first trams and subways ran here, and this was where the smart set came to drink coffee and show off their Western-style umbrellas and watches.

Now it's where the elite "salaryman" comes to put his entertainment account to proper use in some of the world's most expensive hostess clubs. Those using their own money are advised to be careful in this area and to check prices before ordering, or they could wind up paying several thousand yen for a single drink.

Emerge from the subway at **4-chome** crossing: the **Wako** jewelry establishment and the **Mitsukoshi** department store are typical of Ginza's huge and sophisticated attractions. It's often hard to get your bearings in this area. Best is to ask a passing friendly face, *"Sony Biru doko?"* ("Where is the Sony building?") and move in the direction indicated.

In the sidestreets you pass on your left are smart little boutiques, coffeeshops, clubs and restaurants and occasionally, if you look hard enough, a stubborn old traditional shop selling authentic craftware. The **Sony Building** itself has demonstration models of all the famous electronic company's current equipment.

Back on the main drag **(Harumi Dori)**, and going in the same direction, you run into a warren of little shops near the Yamanote line, known collectively as **Sukiyabashi Shopping Center**, and offering all manner of tax-free electronic goods, and so on. In the past few years this section has had a major

commercial boost with the opening of glitzy new *Seibu* and *Hankyu* stores. The people who work there are used to foreign customers and are helpful. **Akihabara**, however, is probably cheaper (see below).

Down at the other end of Chuo Dori, beyond Higashi-Ginza station, is the ornately Oriental ferroconcrete of the **Kabuki-za**, while further still is the **Tsukiji Fish Market**. The *sushi* shops around here are, reasonably enough, among the best in Tokyo.

Stiffer and Looser

Edge round to the south of our original hub, the palace, and you enter another pleasure zone. **Akasaka** is both stiffer and looser than Ginza: stiffer in the north where the **Diet**

(Parliament) convenes; looser in the west, behind Akasaka-Mitsuke station, where the young and beautiful dance the night away at discos. It's a handy area to boogie in, being only a short stumble to several of the city's top hotels (New Otani, Hilton, Tokyu) and bed. But be careful you don't get run over by a rickshaw: a few geishas still practice their soothing arts close by.

Two Outsiders

An outsider, craning and jostling for position — that's how **Roppongi** ("Six trees")

looks on the map in relation to the areas described above. And it's true: Roppongi is younger, crazier, later, noisier — and a little cheaper than elsewhere.

Practically surrounded by embassies, Roppongi has been a favorite hangout of Tokyo's foreign community for many years, but its transformation into one of the centers of the city's youth culture is a more recent event. The *gaijin* (foreigner) presence remains strong, however, and with models, whiz kids and embassy people thronging cheerfully together on the streets, it's almost like being back in the West.

OPPOSITE: The Imperial Palace, central Tokyo. Asakusa ABOVE LEFT and Akihabara ABOVE RIGHT known for its electronic goods stores.

Start your tour from the **Almond** coffee-shop near Roppongi station and walk towards **Tokyo Tower**. Most of what matters around here is on, or behind, this main street, and it includes discos, English- and American-style bars, live jazz spots and international (truly international) restaurants. Some of Tokyo's most startling and inspiring modern pop architecture is to be found here and in Kamiyacho, next door.

Roppongi may have got as big as it's ever going to. Now that everyone knows about it and the clubs are filling up with 9-to-5ers,

sale from many foreign capitals, and several provincial cities in the United States as well.

From the JR and subway station, go out to where there's a famous statue of a dog on the station forecourt. This is a well established meeting-point for locals, and opposite (i.e. looking away from the station) is where much of Shibuya's action is. To the Shibuya enthusiast, Roppongi can look a trifle shabby by comparison.

High and Low

A short way to the north of Shibuya via JR's

the beautiful people are fleeing to Hiroo, the next subway stop west. Curious visitors may care to poke around there and see what's happening.

Much of the action, anyway, has these days shifted over to another satellite town, Shibuya. For cinemas (21 screens at the time of writing), restaurants, and shops specializing in the latest trends, this is where many of the fashionable young now head. Shibuya's **Tower Records**, for instance, has one of the finest English-language bookshops in the city, with in addition newspapers on

Yamamote Line is **Shinjuku**, a Tokyo parvenu on the grand scale. Shinjuku station is the biggest in the country, and one of the most bewildering, although people will tell you, if you complain, that it is quite straight forward, really.

The station is the dividing line between Shinjuku's two utterly different sections. On the west is a cluster of brand-new sky-scrapers, the background for innumerable commercials and the symbol of the hopes of (some) Tokyoites for their city's future.

Attractions for visitors include some good, and sky-high, restaurants, staggering panoramic views and, down in the basement of the Sumitomo Building, the **Do Sports Plaza**, one of the few places in Japan where

PREVIOUS PAGES: Tokyo Cathedral. An interesting mix of architectural styles ABOVE in the center of Tokyo while modern buildings OPPOSITE sprout skyward in whatever space that is available.

you can play squash (among many other things).

East of the station, on the other hand, is one of Tokyo's most lushly low-life quarters. Dozens and dozens of tiny bars and restaurants skirt the station; beyond spread whole tracts of porno cinemas, strip clubs, gay bars and more. There's a strong gangster (*yakuza*) presence here, and it is one of the few parts of town that can on occasion turn nasty, but compared with similar sections of most other cities in the world it is still extremely innocuous. In Kabuki-cho, unlike almost everywhere else in Tokyo, the action goes on all night, and is as crowded at 4 AM as at 9 PM.

On the more sober-sided main street, still on the east side, are several department stores as well as the excellent **Kinokuniya** bookstore — foreign books are on the fifth floor. Try visiting on a Sunday: like the Ginza area, the main street is closed to traffic on that day and it's a good chance to observe Japanese youth at play without risking a carbon monoxide swoon.

Rocking Round the Shrine

An even better chance is provided on Sundays at **Harajuku**, a couple of stops down the Yamanote line, where hordes of trendy teenagers, known as *Takeno kozoku* — the Bamboo-shoot Gang — jive away the afternoon to tapes of antiquated rock 'n' roll.

If you get a headache trying to work out the sociological implications of this one, soothe it in the lovely grounds of **Meiji Shrine**. This and neighboring **Yoyogi Park** form Tokyo's most spacious areas of green, and the shrine, though less than a century old, is classically simple and elegant. The shrine's association with the growth of State Shinto, the ideology behind the Japanese militarism of the 1930s, is the only thing that might cast a shadow over one's enjoyment of the place. The completion recently of a grandiose new entrance to the shrine fuels suspicion that rightist forces are pushing hard for a revival of the dangerous cult.

The area east of the shrine was remodeled in the early 1960s for the benefit of the athletes who came to the 1964 Tokyo Olympics and it is green and spacious. Walk down boulevard-like Omote-Sando towards the subway station of the same name. Two-

thirds of the way down on the right is the **Oriental Bazaar**, one of Tokyo's best shops for traditional goods of every description, stocked with foreign preferences in mind. Buy all your souvenirs here and you will be able to persuade your friends that the Japanese still wear two swords and a topknot.

Old Town

Another nice park, and a mecca of museums, is to be found at Ueno, a few stops north of Tokyo on the Yamanote line. The museums include the **Tokyo National Museum**, the **National Science Museum**, and the **Tokyo Metropolitan Fine Art Museum**. The park in which they are set has many cherry trees and is a favorite spot for cherry blossom viewing (*hanami*). Thousands of people gather under the trees during early April and — write poems? meditate? think great thoughts? No: they drink, dance and roar with laughter. It's a great sight, and if you play your cards right you will be invited to join in. (See LAND A 747 AIRCRAFT, page 14 in TOP SPOTS for more on Ueno's museums).

Get back on the Yamanote line and go two stops south towards Tokyo station: here is **Akihabara**, famous the world over for cut-price electronic goods. The prices are low — some say the lowest in the world — and the quality is high. The only danger is of buying an appliance which will not work back home without adjustment — or at all. Many salesmen speak some English, but why not have someone at the front desk of your hotel write out this anxiety in Japanese, just in case?

Not far from here, at the end of the Ginza subway line, is one of the few places in Tokyo with some of the charm and atmosphere that much of the city must have possessed before modernization. **Asakusa** it's called; to the foreign tongue it is readily confused with Akasaka, but they are worlds apart.

The main attraction is the **Asakusa Kannon Temple**, with its huge red lantern and the tiny image of the goddess of mercy enshrined in it, and the long avenue of shops and stalls, many selling beautifully made traditional goods, which leads to it. It's worth setting aside a few hours to browse through

火傷しそうなクリスマス。

"Life is a party" declares this shop window. The traditional granny, however, has yet to be convinced.

this area at leisure, and to marvel at the changes that have come over the capital in a century.

This is the first temple we have had cause to mention in Tokyo. Temples — tranquil, removed from the city bustle, often set at the foot of steep green hills — seem at odds with Tokyo's raucous, cheery character. It's somehow appropriate that the Asakusa Temple should be the focus of a huge market, and that the temple's most famous emblem, the red lantern, should also be the customary sign for a bar.

Stranded on the far side of the Yamanote loop line, Asakusa bustles less madly than elsewhere in Tokyo, but has more than its fair share of excellent traditional restaurants.

Tokyo Disneyland

California is now only a 25-minute subway ride from the center of Tokyo. In April 1983, what was then Walt Disney Productions' third theme park, and the first outside the United States, opened its gates to the public. The huge amusement park, built on reclaimed land in Chiba, east of the city, is one-and-a-half times the size of the original in

Anaheim, but its attractions are basically the same. The park's 58-hectare (143-acre) area is divided into six "themed lands": Critter Country, Adventureland, Westernland, Toontown, Fantasyland and Tomorrowland. Within each of these environments are a number of rides, including a jungle cruise, a trip through Snow White's adventures and the much-praised space trip. The park is also crammed with performance areas, shops, cafés and restaurants, each carefully harmonized with the setting in which it is located.

The bad news for homesick Americans is that Tokyo Disneyland's *lingua franca* is Japanese. The good news, perhaps, is that the food available will at least be roughly similar to that at the original. The surprise for anybody unfamiliar with Disneyland in America is the attention given to detail in making this a seamless and self-contained four-dimensional theater and the extravagantly high quality of the finish.

Fear of overcrowding led Tokyo Disneyland's management to stipulate, before the park opened, that all visitors must book in advance, but this policy has been abandoned as unnecessary. Now you are almost guaranteed entrance on any day in the year, though if it's really packed you may be asked to wait awhile. The management point out that mornings and evenings are relatively slack, and they also suggest that visitors consider eating before or after the regular lunch hour (noon to 1 PM in Japan): the lines outside the restaurants can be horrendous, and picnic lunches are not allowed inside the grounds. Admission costs ¥3,670 (adults), ¥3,260 (12 to 18 year-olds), ¥2,550 (4 to 11 year-olds), while a "Passport", including admission and access to all rides and attractions except the Shootin' Gallery, costs ¥5,200 for adults, ¥4,590 for 12 to 18 year-olds, and ¥3,570 for 4 to 11 year-olds.

To get to Tokyo Disneyland take the JR Keiyo Line or Musashino Line from Tokyo Station to Maihama Station. The trip takes around 15 minutes.

More museums

In addition to the museums mentioned above there are others worth seeing. The **Kite Museum**, for example, is on the fifth floor of the Taimeiken Building, 1-12-10, Nihom-

Disneyland ABOVE pulls in the crowds. OPPOSITE: Solitary in his work, this window cleaner hangs high above the city.

bashi, Chuo-ku ((03) 3271-2465, a two-minute walk from Nihombashi subway station. 11 AM to 5 PM, closed Sundays and public holidays. Entrance ¥200.

Then how about the **Japanese Sword Museum**. It's at 4-25-10, Yoyogi, Shibuya-ku ((03) 3379-1386, a 10-minute walk from Sangubashi station on the Odakyu Line. Open 9 AM to 4 PM, closed Mondays. Admission fee is ¥515.

Not far away from the Sword Museum is the **Meiji Jingu Treasure Museum**. It contains objects used by the Meiji Emperor (1852–1912), and it's at 1-1 Kamizonocho, Yoyogi, Shibuya-ku. It's open 9 AM to 4 PM (4:30 PM March through October), closed the third Friday of the month.

Tourist Information

Yurakucho (pronounced Yaruk'cho) station is one stop south of Tokyo on the Yamanote line and here is the visitor's single most useful address: the **Tourist Information Center**. It's just five minutes from Yurakucho JR station, in Basement One of the Tokyo International Forum building. This is the place to go for maps and tour brochures. Also, although not on display, the TIC people have a large number of very reliable mini-guides, giving detailed information on a large number of tourist hot-spots. These are also available bound together in one volume. See TRAVELER'S TIPS, page 242 for more details.

Touring Tokyo

Getting to know Tokyo's interesting ins and outs takes time. If you're in a hurry, why not join a tour? The Japan Travel Bureau (JTB) offers several, advertised as Sunrise Tours, with the foreign visitor in mind, and though the buses tend to get clogged in the capital's frightful traffic they will take you to places you would have trouble finding on your own. The following are a few of the regular ones:

Tokyo Disneyland. A full-day tour of the hugely popular theme park closely modeled on the versions in Anaheim and Florida. Fare adults ¥8,800; juniors aged 12 to 17 years old, ¥8,000; and children four to 11 years old, ¥5,700. Saturdays, Sundays and public holidays (with certain exceptions, including Disneyland holidays) year-round.

Panoramic Tokyo. A full-day city tour, including **Meiji Shrine, Imperial East Garden** (or **Imperial Palace Plaza**), **Asakusa, Tokyo Bay cruise,** drive through **Ginza.** Daily, March through November. Adults ¥9,350, children ¥7,150, lunch included.

Tokyo Morning Cityrama. The above minus lunch and the Tokyo Bay cruise. Daily (except New Year). Adults ¥3,500, children ¥2,700.

Kabuki Night. Dinner, night ride through the city, *kabuki* theater show. Adultd ¥10,950, children ¥8,800. Daily, except where no *kabuki* show is scheduled.

Tokyo Wondernight. Monorail ride, highrise view of the city, dinner, topless dance show in Roppongi. ¥11,400 (over 18 only). Daily except New Year period.

WHERE TO STAY

Room rate indications—Budget: ¥5,000 or under. Moderate: ¥ 5,000 to ¥11,000. Average: ¥11,000 to ¥22,000. Expensive: ¥22,000 and up. A (*) denotes hotels offering Western and Japanese-style rooms. A (ß) denotes business hotels with mostly single rooms.

Akasaka Prince Hotel ((03) 3234-1111 FAX (03) 3262-5163, 1-2, Kioi-cho, Chiyoda-ku. 806* rooms. Rates: expensive.

Asia Center of Japan ((03) 3402-6111 FAX (03) 3402-6111, 8-10-32, Akasaka, Minato-ku. 172 rooms. Rates: moderate.

Hotel Ginza Daiei (ß) ((03) 3545-1111 FAX 3545-1177, 3-12-2, Ginza, Chuo-ku. 106* rooms. Rates: moderate.

Hotel Okura ((03) 3582-0111 FAX (03) 3582-3707, 2-10-4, Toranomon, Minato-ku. 825* rooms. Rates: expensive.

Hotel Sun Route Shibuya (ß) ((03) 3464-6411 FAX (03) 3464-1678, 1-11, Nampeidai, Shibuya-ku. 181 rooms. Rates: moderate.

Takanawa Prince Hotel ((03) 3447-1111 FAX (03) 3446-0849, 3-13-1, Takanawa, Minato-ku. 414* rooms. Rates: average and upward.

The New Otani ((03) 3265-1111 FAX (03) 3221-2619, 4-1, Kioi-cho, Chiyoda-ku. 1,612 rooms. Rates: average and upward.

Toko Hotel (ß) ((03) 3494-1050 FAX (03) 3490-4569, 2-6-8, Nishi-Gotanda, Shinagawa-ku. 337* rooms. Rates: moderate.

Tokyo Yoyogi Youth Hostel ((03) 3467-9163 FAX (03) 3467-4417, 3-1, Yoyogikamizono-cho, Shibuya-ku. 150 beds. Rates: inexpensive.

Tokyo International Youth Hostel ((03) 3235-1107, 18th floor, Central Plaza, 21-1, Kaguragashi, Shinjuku-ku. 138 beds. Rates: inexpensive.

Imperial Hotel ((03) 3504-1111 FAX (03) 3581-9146, 1-1-1, Uchisaiwai-cho, Chiyoda-ku. 1,059 rooms. Rates: expensive.

Okubo House (Hostel) ((03) 3361-2348, 1-11-32, Hya kunin-cho, Shinjuku-ku. 18* rooms plus 10 (bunk beds). Rates: inexpensive.

Taisho Central Hotel (ß) ((03) 3232-0101 FAX (03) 3209-2349, 1-27-7, Taka danobaba, Shinjuku-ku. 200 rooms. Rates: moderate.

Ours Inn Hankyu ((03) 3775-6121 FAX (03) 3778-3861, 50-5, Ooi 1-chome, Shinagawa-ku (opposite Ooimachi station). 800 rooms (single rooms only). Rates: moderate.

English House ((03) 3988-1743, 2-23-8, Nishi-Ikebukuro, Toshima-ku. 15 rooms. Rates: inexpensive.

Hotel Okura ((03) 3582-0111 FAX (03) 3582-3707, 2-10-4, Toranomon, Minato-ku. 10* rooms. Rates: expensive.

Mickey House ((03) 3936-8889, 2-15-1, Nakadai, Itabashi-ku. 15 rooms. Rates: inexpensive.

Okubo House ((03) 3361-2348, 1-11-32, Hyakunin-cho, Shinjuku-ku. 18* rooms. Rates: inexpensive.

Ryokan Chomeikan ((03) 3811-7205, 4-4-8, Hongo, Bunkyo-ku. 36 rooms. Rates: moderate.

A peaceful spot in the ultra-luxurious Imperial Hotel, Tokyo.

Ryokan Mikawaya Bekkan ((03) 3843-2345 FAX (03) 3843-2348, 1-31-11, Asakusa, Taito-ku. 12 rooms. Rates: moderate.

Sansuiso Ryokan ((03) 3441-7475 FAX (03) 3449-1944, 2-9-5, Higashi-Gotanda, Shina-gawa-ku. Nine rooms. Rates: inexpensive.

Lastly, for those who are changing flights and need to spend a night at the airport or connecting very early in the morning, accommodation can be found there.

Holiday Inn Narita ((0476) 32-1234 FAX (0476) 32-0617, 320-1, Tokko, Narita. 500* rooms. Rates: average and upward.

WHERE TO EAT

There are a number of garden restaurants for alfresco dining.

Among them are **Chinzan-so (** (03) 3943-111, in Bunkyo, at 2-10-8, Sekiguei. Specialties are *shabu-shabu* and Japanese barbecue. ¥ 6,000 to 25,000. Open from noon to 10 PM; **Hazawa Garden (** (03) 3400-2013, in Shibuya, at 3-12-15, Hiroo. *Kaiseki* cuisine and *shabu-shabu* (¥16,000 and up). Barbecue ¥5,000 to 6,000. Beer garden (reservations recommended). Open 11 AM to 10 PM; and **Jisaku (** (03) 3541-2391, in Chuo, at 14-19, Akashicho. Kaiseki food; lunch ¥8,000, dinner ¥15,000. Other prominent hotel restaurants, this time

with extensive views over the city are the Keio Plaza Continental's **Restaurant Ambrosia (** (03) 3344-0222, in Shinjuku, at 2-2-1 Nishi-Shinjuku, open 11:30 AM to 3 PM, 5 to 10 PM; the New Otani's **Top of the Tower, Virgo,** and **Tower Grill** restaurants **(** (03) 3238-0023, 3238-0020 and 3238-0021, respectively in the Akasaka district; open for breakfast, lunch and dinner (Tower Grill only); and the Sunshine City Prince Hotel **(** (03) 3988-1111, in Ikebukero, with its **Le Trianon** restaurant, open for lunch and dinner. These restaurants offer all types of food.

For natural food **Tenmi (** (03) 3496-9703, in Shibuya, at 1-10-6, Jinnan, Shibuya-ku, offers vegetable dishes plus a few fish dishes at dinner. Also in Shibuya is **Mominoki House (** (03) 3405-9133, 1st floor, You Building, 2-18-5 Jingumae, closed on Sundays. Open for lunch and dinner, they serve meat, fish and vegetable dishes.

The **Blue Gardenia** restaurant in the Akasaka Prince Hotel **(** (03) 3234-1111 is open for breakfast, lunch and dinner, and in keeping with this famous hotel, offers fine cuisine.

In the Word Trade Center Building is the **Rainbow Restaurant (** (03) 3435-2600, in the Hamatsu district. It's open from 11:30 AM to 5 PM only, serving lunch and tea on the 39th floor. One minute's walk from Yurakucho (pronounced "Yurak'cho") JR station, in Yurakucho district is the **Tokyo Kotsu Kaitan (** (03) 3212-2775, where the **Ginza Sky Lounge** is open from 11 AM till 10 PM, 9:30 PM Friday and Saturday). Again, a wide variety of food is on offer.

Seryna ((03) 3403-6211 in Roppongi, is renowned for its *shabu-shabu*.

Ten-Ichi Honten ((03) 3571-1949 in Ginza is known for its *tempura*. A much cheaper place, also recommended, is **Tsuruoka (** (03) 3408-4061 in Shibuya-ku.

Ashibé ((03) 3543-3540 in Tsukiji, near Tokyo's fish market is known for *fuga*; they also serve turtle cuisine (*suppon*). As the *fugu* here is fresh it is only served between the end of October and March.

Nodaiwa ((03) 3583-7852 in Higashi-Azabu, is for the best in eel cuisine.

There are also chain restaurants to look out for in Tokyo, some of them offering prices which are, by Japanese standards, exceptionally good value.

One of the best of these is the **Yoshinoya**
company's array of fast-food outlets. Unexpectedly, the food is freshly cooked and not
pre-frozen; the prices are very low, and the
choice illustrated on printed sheets laid out
on the trays. US$3 could see you supplied
with a bowl of rice and meat, miso soup and
a dish of pickled cabbage.

CULINARY HOMESICKNESS

What if you are struck with homesickness?
What if you're in Tokyo and you crave a spot
of home cooking, nothing too pretentious,
but something that is perhaps familiar from
home or traveling elsewhere in Asia?

Foreign-style restaurants abound in Tokyo, but in the vast majority Japanese cooks
prepare Western and other food for Japanese
taste buds. It may be good, but it may not be
what you had in mind.

There are an increasing number of exceptions to this rule, offering the discerning (and
the homesick) something approaching the
real thing. Some examples follow.

Tokyo, today, has become an eclectic city which
addresses the tastes, culinary and otherwise, of a
large range of people. Here, various locals show
another influence of the West — fashion directly out
of the fifties and sixties.

GERMAN
Ketel's ((03) 3571-5056, Hideyoshi Building,
5-5-14 Ginza, Chuo-ku. Famous restaurant
dating from the 1930s. You have a choice of
a beer-hall or a more formal restaurant. Dinner only (5 to 9:45 PM; 8:45 PM on Sundays
and holidays).

FRENCH
Le Maestro Paul Bocuse ((03) 3505-0121, Ark

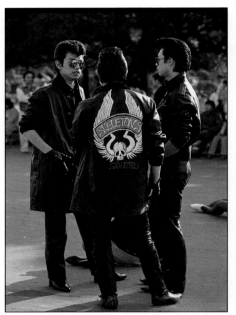

Mori Building, 2 F, 1-12-32 Akasaka, Minato-
ku. Expensive: huge cellar and *cordon bleu*
food. Dinner from ¥12,000 to 18,000. Lunch:
11:30 AM to 2 PM; dinner 5:30 PM to 9:30 PM.

Citrus ((03) 3464-8647, 1-18-7 Jinnan,
Shibuya-ku. Californian-French, an offshoot
of one of the most famous restaurants in Los
Angeles. ¥5,000 to 10,000. Open noon to
10:30 PM (10 PM Sundays and public holidays).

For another taste of Europe, there is the
Brasserie Lecomte ((03) 3479-2838, the **Loire
Coffeeshop (** (03) 3475-1756, the **Restaurant
Din Don (** (03) 3475-1795, and more. All
moderately priced (¥1,000 to 2,000), such
places contribute yet more of the Paris ambiance to what is becoming, in its general feel,
an increasingly Parisian city.

INDIAN
Moti ((03) 3479-1939, Roppongi. Delicious

tandoori dishes, *sag*, piping hot *nan*. A Tokyo institution. Call for details of three other branches. ¥2,500 to 4,000. Take-away available. Open 11:30 AM to 10 PM daily.

ITALIAN

Domani ((03) 3412-4011, 4-37-7 Ikejiri, Setagaya-ku. Long-established mid-priced restaurant, much-loved. Open evenings only, from 5:30 PM.

DJ's Pizzeria ((03) 3479-5711, 6-4-5 Roppongi, Minato-ku. Excellent low-price Italian food — more than just pizzas, in other words. Open daily 11 AM to 11 PM.

Sabatini ((03) 3573-0013, Sony Building, 7F, 5-3-1 Ginza, Chuo-ku. Classy traditional Italian dishes cooked over traditional Japanese charcoal. Homemade pasta. Lunch: ¥3,800 to 7,500. Dinner: ¥10,000 to 15,000. Lunch noon to 2:30 PM; dinner 5:30 to 10 PM.

SPANISH

Puerto de Palos ((03) 3574-7387, Kikumura Building, 7-2-11 Ginza, Chuo-ku. Exceptionally reasonable in price and good. Set lunch ¥1,000 and up.

CHINESE

Oh-Ho Nittaku Building, B1, 3-8-15 Roppongi, Minato-ku. Opens 5 PM; closes 5 AM Mondays to Saturdays, 11 PM Sundays.

'Course' ¥5,000 to 12,000, but individual items are more reasonable. A fair choice of dishes.

ENGLISH

Wedgewood Tea Room ((03) 5458-8024, 11-6 Sarugakucho, Shibuya-ku. You're tired? Fancy collapsing and enjoying teatime, English-style? Then this is the place for you. Pots of tea, cucumber and other types of sandwiches, scones and cream. All for ¥2,000. Open 11 AM to 8 PM, so it doesn't even need to be teatime.

AMERICAN

Victoria Station ((03) 3479-4601, 4-9-2 Roppongi, Minato-ku. American salads and roast beef at down to earth prices. There are many other branches; in Shibuya ((03) 3463-5288; Ogikubo ((03) 3399-1129; and Waseda ((03) 3205-0844, and elsewhere. This is a place a beleaguered Westerner can be sure of getting a decent, well-priced meal. Open daily from 11 AM to midnight (11 PM Sundays and holidays).

Chicken's ((03) 3586-5554, 3-1-6 Azabu-dai, Minato-ku. Chicken, salad, potatoes, pizza, beer and wine, all at extremely low prices. No decor at all — like eating on a building site, only indoors. Open for lunch and dinner (closed 3 to 5:30 PM).

Specializing in healthy food is **Home** ((03) 3406-6409, situated on floor B2 in Crayon House, 3-8-15 Kita Aoyama, Minato-ku.

THAI

Siam ((03) 3770-0550, 1-15-8 Jinnan, Shibuya-ku. Thai buffet for ¥1,000. Many branches, for instance at 5-8-17 Ginza ((03) 3572-4101, and 3-9-4 Akasaka ((03) 3505-0550. Open for lunch and dinner (i.e. closed from 3 to 5:30 PM).

SUBWAY FARE

And then there's the subway. Subway sta-

tions are awash with small, and these days frequently European-style, restaurants. For an example, take a look at **Aoyama-ichome station** on the Ginza Line. The station precinct (in the Ayoma Twin building) is home to half a dozen small restaurants specializing in French cuisine; this is becoming rather common in Tokyo, but the concentration here is still unusual. You will have to leave the platform area, and therefore surrender your ticket, but these bistros are right in the underground passages adjacent to the station exit. Understandably for what is largely a

ABOVE: Chinese restaurants can be found in most of the cities throughout Japan. A glitzy topless show OPPOSITE in a Tokyo music hall is always guaranteed to pull in the crowds.

business and government-office area, they specialize in the lunchtime trade.

TOKYO AT NIGHT

Tokyo after dark is a bizarre world that fascinates, repels and bewilders all at once. The main streets are bright with some of the world's most extravagant neon, but it's down the winding, scruffy alleys near the big stations that the action seems to be happening. These streets were made with the night in mind. By day they may be mean, cheap, tawdry; at night they glow and buzz with life. They are dotted with fortune-tellers, erect and solemn before their little tables with lantern and charts. A smell of hot *sake*, soy sauce and barbecuing chicken blows out of that *yakitori-ya* on the corner where shirt-sleeved businessmen huddle on beer crates. Disco sounds bombard the street from one doorway where a man dressed up as a monkey is selling lottery tickets, while from an open window just around the corner come the staccato notes of a *shamisen*, like drops of hard rain hitting an iron roof one at a time. Gangs of boys and pretty girls spill out of a restaurant, pour into a club, laughing and kidding. A door slides open behind a little curtain, granting the shortest glimpse of a tiny "snack" with a huge white grand piano.

It's all very strange and convivial. How can you join in?

The main clubbing areas are Roppongi, Nishi Azabu (west of Roppongi), Shinjuku and Shibuya (with neighboring Aoyama).

Roppongi, not so long ago the new place in town, is nowadays long-established, though somewhat rundown, with drug dealers seemingly on every street corner. Nevertheless a number of clubs remain extremely popular.

Club 99 Gaspanic ((03) 3470-7180, offers a classic evening out, and you can down a few beers at **Deja Vu** ((03) 3403-8777, next door before going in. The long-established **Lexington Queen** ((03) 3401-1661, is American-glamorous, while next door **Desperado Tokyo** ((03) 3475-6969, plays live rock-n-roll and boasts a drinking space that has no cover charge. **DX3000** ((03) 3470-8556, offers different special attractions night by night, but nevertheless has a distinctive style all of its own that remains the same. **Java Jive** ((03) 3478-0087, offers house and reggae music from early evening.

For simple drinking, **Salsa Sudada** ((03) 5474-8806, has, as you'd expect, a Latin ambiance, **Pint's** ((03) 3408-1134, has a big TV for those big sporting fixtures, while the very popular **Gaspanic Bar** ((03) 3405-0633, is another outlet for these night-life specialists.

Nearby in Nishi Azabu, the fashionable **Vitamin-Q** ((03) 3405-6204, has an always interesting lineup of live bands, while at

music till 10 AM, **Pylon** ((03) 3478-1870, open weekends only, and **Milk** ((03) 5458-2826, a venue for local underground bands.

And for bars, try **Bar Aoyama** ((03) 3498-4415, for good music or **What the Dickens** ((03) 3780-2099, for a London pub atmosphere with draught Guinness.

Take your chance. Many of the above places are designed for the younger set, but if you ask to take a peep inside before paying at the door you'll usually be allowed to (get someone from your hotel to write the request down in Japanese before you set out).

Yellow ((03) 3479-0690, they specialize in the latest sounds for the youngest crowd.

As for bars, you can eat and drink well in **Acaraje Tropicana** ((03) 3478-4142, and eat according to the latest Marin County fashion in the Beach Loft Café ((03) 3478-6855.

Shinjuku is home to the **Liquid Room** ((03) 3200-6831, a major Tokyo live venue, and its associated Club Venus. Meanwhile, **Automix** ((03) 3358-2256, is a place for techno dancing on two floors.

Some way away is the elegant **Mission** ((03) 3583-6332, while **Volga** ((03) 3433-1766, offers Russian food and an old-world aristocratic ambiance.

Shibuya/Aoyama has **Maniac Love** ((03) 3406-1166, which plays house and techno

Many more such places, plus details of programs for the week in question, are available in *Tokyo Journal* (¥600), the best magazine guide to what's happening in the city. It also carries good instructions for how to find these clubs and bars — almost always a problem in Tokyo's frequently baffling night regions.

Phone all the clubs in advance, or check carefully in *Tokyo Journal*, before turning up, especially early in the week, as several are closed one or more nights.

Then there are the things that go on after dark in Tokyo that you wouldn't believe. There is, for example, the notorious club in Shibuya where the staple entertainment is live sex. The semi-nude female performer

tours the low circular stage offering the punters, mostly of student age, a dildo with which to do their worst to her, then later coaxes the more drunk, or more daring, up on stage to have sex. The only thing more astonishing than the frankness of the performance — which has the eyes of old Bangkok hands popping — is the atmosphere of innocence which prevails. Checking tickets at the entrance is a benign-looking old granny who lends this grim dive the air of a public bathhouse.

Tokyo's steamiest greeting awaits those who learn enough Japanese to read the word "Soapland", plastered over scores of establishments as Shinjuku, Ikebukuro in the west and Senzoku in the east, the latter being the location of the famous "nightless city", Yoshiwara, that flourished during the Edo period. Known as *toruko* until recently, these bath houses began to spring up in 1956 when the police closed down all the conventional cat houses. The 20,000-odd masseuses who work in them nationwide have unique techniques for helping you to relax. They are hard to get into without Japanese company, and not cheap even then. The average fee for a bath and "additional services" is from ¥45,000 to ¥80,000!

Taken together with love hotels, Turkish baths are now a 13-billion-dollar industry. If you and your girlfriend (or boyfriend) are fed up with paper-thin walls and lockless doors, a love hotel is the most discreet place you could retreat to. They tend to be crowded together near the amusement areas of major sub-centers such as Tokyo's Shinjuku, or else out on the freeways. Many are masterpieces of pop architecture. There are no lobbies, no dining rooms, no registers. You rent a room for an hour or two — it's possible to stay the night, but most people don't — and pay about ¥7,500 for a couple of hours. But it's not just any old room; it may be equipped with wraparound mirrors, video, S/M equipment. There are reckoned to be an incredible 35,000 love hotels through out the country, soaking up a greater proportion of the GNP than is spent on defense. Access for foreign visitors is no problem.

After your love hotel you may like to cool off with a movie. A few little-known cinemas in the capital show movies all night, with a mixture of Japanese, American and European films. Some of the programs are excellent. Try Theater Shinjuku ((03) 3352-1846, or Theater Ikebukuro ((03) 3987-4311. Programs at both start around 10 PM. *Tokyo Journal* may be the only English-language journal which carries useful listings of such movies.

Tokyo is great in small doses, but after a while you will have the urge to escape. Where to go? The following are the most attractive and popular destinations within half a day's striking distance of the capital.

NIKKO

After spending some time in Tokyo's lowlands it is a source of joy and amazement to find that Japan is full of splendid mountains. One of the best places for enjoying them, and indeed for seeing some of Japan's richest (and most uncharacteristic) architecture, is Nikko, about 140 km (87 miles) north of the capital.

The chief attraction at Nikko is **Toshogu Shrine**, the gorgeous mausoleum of the mighty shogun Tokugawa Ieyasu, who died

Large neon signs and publicity OPPOSITE define the Ginza skyline. Fall foliage in mountainous Nikko ABOVE heralds the onset of winter.

in 1616, and his grandson. But Nikko's history as a religious center goes back much further than that.

It is one of the centers of a curious cult called Mountain Buddhism. When Buddhism first arrived in the country, about 1,500 years ago, it mingled with certain native ascetic practices to produce a new cult whose devotees scaled mountains, lived as hermits and immersed themselves in icy water, all as a means of attaining spiritual enlightenment. Clad in white, these men and women still congregate at **Nantai-san**, the

conical mountain at the heart of the Nikko region, in early August each year. So Nikko was already famous when it was chosen over 370 years ago as the appropriate site for Ieyasu's mausoleum.

Ieyasu was the first shogun of the Tokugawa line. It was he who, having united the country, fettered it so successfully that his heirs ruled for the next 250 years without serious challenge. The mausoleum was built to glorify his achievement, and all the apparatus and imagery of religion was harnessed to that cause.

It can be a confusing place for the visitor. For a start, it is totally unlike any other shrine or temple in the country. Most Japanese Buddhist temples are somber, even gloomy

places, with structures of unpainted wood and little decoration. Shrines are often painted — typically an orange-red color — but usually in a simple manner. The gorgeous colors and overwhelming richness of decoration and carving at Nikko are unique in the country, and much more reminiscent of Chinese and Korean temples than of others in Japan. In fact, many of the craftsmen who worked on the shrine were of Korean stock.

The other respect in which Nikko is confusing is the carefree way it mixes elements of Buddhism and Shinto. The two religions are radically different (see THE CULTURE OF JAPAN, page 102), although early on they learned to live with each other. At Nikko, however, the most picturesque and impressive features of the architecture of the two religions are intermingled, not for religious reasons but to create an image of magnificence. The *torii* (gate) at the shrine's entrance, a Shinto feature, stands next to a Buddhist-style pagoda. Inside, but before the main gateway, stands a trough of water with wooden ladles where visitors wash — purify — their hands and mouths, another Shinto feature. But the indescribably rich gateway itself is based on Buddhist models. And so on.

See how freely we control these gods and Buddhas, the shogunate seems to be saying. How much more freely, then, do we control you, the people! This secular orientation of the shrine is one of the reasons — another being the large number of visitors — for the lack of any strong religious atmosphere. Here are the roots of the secularism and materialism of modern Japan.

To put Nikko into perspective it is a good idea to visit one or two "purer" temples and shrines elsewhere. Almost any of the temples in Kyoto or Kamakura will do, while the best shrine to visit is the most important one in the country, the bone-bare **Ise Jingu** (for more details see the ISE section, page 186).

For an instant contrast, **Chuzenji Temple**, above Chuzenji Lake not far from the shrine, is recommended. The eighth-century statue of Kannon, goddess of mercy, enshrined there was carved from a living tree and practically glows with spirituality.

The lake is reached by one of the two hairpin Irohazaka Driveways; the second is used for the descent. The scenery here is lovely, particularly in autumn. **Kegon Waterfall** near Chuzenji spa is also worth visiting. If you have time take the lift down to the observatory at the bottom. The waterfall used to be a favorite spot for love suicides — something that the guides don't tell you.

If you're in Nikko and you're interested in pottery, why not make a side trip to the pottery town of **Mashiko** on the way back? This was for many years the home of Shoji Hamada, a great potter whose vigorous and simple work, decorated with a rapid tech-

some of the foreign potters based in the town do very fine work.

HOW TO GET THERE

You can get to Nikko either by Japan Rail (JR) or the private Tobu Line (for which, however, your Japan Rail Pass will not be valid). If you go on a Tobu train the route's direct; if you go by JR you'll have to change trains at Utsunomiya.

For the Tobu Line, leave Tokyo from Asakusa Station, and arrive in Nikko one

nique that became his trademark, helped spread the fame of Japanese folk ceramics through out the West. Hamada died a few years back, but his old farmhouse home is still there, as is his "climbing kiln" (*noborigama*) — a wood-fired clay kiln with several chambers built on a slope with the chimney at the top — and a small museum of folk-art objects he collected on his travels.

Mashiko has been a pottery town for 150 years. Hamada moved there because of his admiration for the rough, folksy forms the town's potters produced, but he became so famous that, ironically enough, most of them are now producing rather uninspired imitations of *his* work. How ever, there are a few interesting potters among them, and

hour, 45 minutes later; there are seven trains that leave Asakusa between 7:20 and 12:30 AM and the fare is currently ¥2,530.

For the JR trains, leave from Tokyo or Ueno stations; it's 90 minutes, plus the time you have to wait when changing at Utunomiya; the fare if you don't have a JR Rail Pass is ¥5,430.

All the tour companies offer trips to Nikko, usually including Lake Chuzenji, or sometimes Mashiko as an alternative. The problem with these, and indeed all tours, is that if you hold a Japan Rail Pass you are

OPPOSITE: Not far out of Kyoto is the impressive Kegon Waterfall, once an infamous suicide spot! ABOVE: Evening light picks out Nikko nestling between the hills.

paying for a longish train trip you could have had for free. In addition, the Mashiko visits don't usually last long enough for you to try making a pot yourself — something that's possible there if your time's your own. On the Sunrise Tours' trips, for instance, only three people are 'chosen' to try their hand at pot-making, and the company advises that 'participants may not have enough time to complete the process of shaping a pot'. If nevertheless you would like a tour — and taking one does have the advantage of making sure you do get to the various places of interest — then contact any of the many companies that operate trips to Nikko via your hotel reception desk.

For more on Nikko refer to SEE NIKKO, page 18 in TOP SPOTS.

WHERE TO STAY

Room rate indications—Budget:¥5,000 or under. Moderate: ¥ 5,000 to ¥11,000. Average: ¥11,000 to¥22,000. Expensive:¥22,000 and up. A (*) denotes hotels offering Western and Japanese-style rooms. A (ß) denotes business hotels with mostly single rooms.

Nikko Kanaya Hotel ((0288) 54-0001 FAX (0288) 53-2487, 1300, Kam i-Hatsui shi-machi. 80 rooms. Rates: average and upward.
Nikko Youth Hostel ((0288) 54-1013, 2854, Tokorono. 48 beds. Rates: inexpensive.
Pension Turtle ((0288) 53-3168, Takumi-cho, 2-16. 10* rooms. Rates: in expensive.
Chuzenji Hotel ((0288) 55-0333 FAX (0288) 55-0415, 2478, Chugushi, Nikko. 100 rooms. Rates: average and upward.
Hokino Yado Konishi ((0288) 54-1105 FAX (0288) 53-2246, 1115, Kami-Hatsuishi-machi. 22 rooms. Rates: moderate.
Nikko Green Hotel ((0288) 54-1756 FAX (0288) 54-1144, 9-19, Honcho. 43 rooms. Rates: average and upward.

MOUNT FUJI

Every mountain in Japan is sacred according to the Shinto view of things. And Mt. Fuji (*Fuji-san*), the highest at 3,776 m (12,388 ft) and the most beautiful, is the most sacred of all.

After weeks of cloud and rain, the skies over the capital clear and suddenly the

mountain appears to the south west, astonishingly high and sharply defined. Sometimes only the peak is visible, hanging in the air like the Cheshire Cat's smile. Towards dusk it is often the mountain's silhouette which dominates the skyline, black against the deepening blue of evening. No matter how many pictures one has seen, the volcano never loses its ability to startle and impress.

Before modern times it was frequently visible from Tokyo, as the various place-names including the prefix Fujimi ("Fuji visible") attest. During the notoriously smoggy years of the 1960s and early '70s, it disappeared almost entirely except for a few magical days in autumn and winter, and although things have improved since, and in really fine weather you can see it all the way from Narita Airport, it is best to get a little closer.

A trip round the **Fuji-go-ko** (Fuji-Five-Lakes) area in the national park at the mountain's base provides pleasant scenery and diversions such as boating and fishing, should the mountain decline to put in an appearance. For those determined to sit it out there are plenty of hotels and *ryokan*, but be warned that really clear days are rare except in autumn and winter.

Kawaguchiko is the name both of one of the five lakes and of the resort on its shore. See TRAIN TO KAWAGUCHIKO, page 34 in TOP SPOTS for more on this destination.

Or you can climb the great mountain itself. About 300,000 people do this every year, most of them during the open months of July and August. See OFF THE BEATEN TRACK, page 212 for details of how to set about it.

WHERE TO STAY

Room rate indications—Budget:¥5,000 or less. Moderate: ¥ 5,000 to ¥11,000. Average: ¥11,000 to¥22,000. Expensive:¥22,000 and up.

FUJI-GO-KO (Fuji Five Lakes District), Yamanashi Prefecture
Hotel Bugaku-so ((0555) 62-1100, 508, Hirano, Yamana-kako-mura, Minami-Tsuru-gun. 24 rooms. Rates: moderate.

Spectacular views of Mt. Fuji from the "Ropeway", the Japanese term for a cable car.

Kawaguchiko Club ((05557) 2-0554
FAX (05557) 2-0939, 51-1, Azagawa, Kawagu-chiko-machi, Minami-Tsuru-gun. 16 rooms.
Rates: moderate.

HAKONE

Mt. Fuji is the focus of an area, including the Fuji Five Lakes, the Izu Peninsula and Hakone, which might be called Tokyo's playground. The mighty, forested flanks of the mountains and the pure waters of the various lakes in this area have been spared most

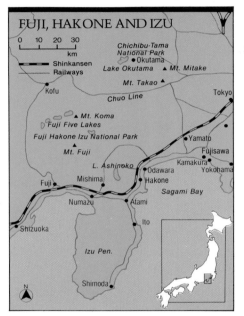

of the nastier intrusions of the modern world. Healing, sulfurous waters boil and bubble underground, spectacularly breaking the surface here and there and supplying the many inns and hotels with smelly but salubrious hot water.

Hakone, bordered by mountains and lying within the crater of an extinct volcano roughly 40 km (25 miles) across, is the most accessible and perhaps the most rewarding area for the visitor. Tokyo lacks gardens and green space in which to relax: Hakone is the compensation, paid in one splendid lump sum. Only ninety minutes from the capital by express, half that by *shinkansen*, it is the perfect place to relax and replenish your oxygen supply.

Gateway to the area is **Odawara**. Here you can leave your gleaming "bullet" and board a smart little train from another era on the Hakone Tozan line which will haul you up with many a switchback into the heart of the mountains.

You will pass through several intriguing villages full of hot spa hotels, but the first imperative stop is **Chokoku-no-Mori**. This means "Woods of Sculpture" and is the name of the magnificent open-air sculpture museum which borders the railway line. Admission is expensive, but includes the impressive Picasso Hall and as such is worth it. The works of art, including several very famous pieces by Moore, Hepworth and others, are imaginatively displayed against the lush backdrop of the mountains. With diversions for children and plenty to eat and drink, boredom is impossible.

Getting back on the train and going to the end of the line you change to a cablecar which carries you even higher to aptly named **Owakudani**, the "Valley of Greater Boiling", A foul stench of hydrogen sulfide fills the air. Vivid yellow gashes mark the places where the steam belches from the earth. And in one or two small pools strange gray material is indeed boiling away with great frenzy. It's all very impressive and is said to be the only place of its type in Japan. Hot water from Owakudani is piped to hot spas for miles around.

One of the finest views of Mt. Fuji — should it be visible at all, of course — is from the ropeway which swings you down the steep mountainside from Owakudani to **Lake Ashinoko**. Having arrived there you can continue this carnival of transportation by crossing the lake on what is claimed to be a replica of a seventeenth-century English man-of-war, "modeled after the baroque manner as percise (sic) as possible."

The Tokaido, the old road which led from Edo (Tokyo) to Kyoto and Osaka, passed through Hakone. Near where the ferry docks at Hakone-machi is the old **Barrier Guardhouse** where travelers in pre-modern days were searched and their documents rigorously checked. The guardhouse has been reconstructed in the original style and contains life-size models of travelers and guards. In a nearby museum, mystifyingly described as **Hakone Materials Hall**, are many old relics from those days.

And if you want a taste of what transportation was like way back then, the course of the old road has been preserved for several miles east of the Barrier Guardhouse. Winding and precipitous, though paved with large stones for much of the distance, it inspires respect for the messengers of those days who, clad in loin cloths and straw sandals, dashed across the country along roads like this.

Ashinoko is 723 m (3,400 ft) above sea level. On July 31 every year there's a Lake Festival

HOW TO GET THERE

There are two options. Either take the Tokaido Shinkansen from Tokyo station to Odawara, a 42-minute trip. Alternatively, the Odakyu (private) line's luxurious Romance Car train runs between Shinjuku in Tokyo and Yumoto in Hakone, via Odawara, in 75 minutes.

WHERE TO STAY

Room rate indications—Budget: ¥5,000 or less.

there, with floating lanterns, and fireworks positioned so that they reflect on the lake's surface.

Formal parks are everywhere in Hakone. There's a **Wetlands Botanical Garden** and in spring the magnificent display of azaleas close to the Hakone Hotel and the Barrier Guardhouse is justly famous. The Hakone Detached Palace Garden is situated on a promontory on the lake shore.

These are some of the delights Hakone offers. Others include camping, skating, at the peak of **Mt. Koma**, the area's central peak, and golf. For more ideas and information see the TIC's mini-guide (MG-035-2), *Mt. Fuji and Fuji Five Lakes*, which provides comprehensive coverage of this district.

Moderate: ¥ 5,000 to ¥11,000. Average: ¥11,000 to ¥22,000. Expensive: ¥22,000 and up. A (*) denotes hotels offering Western and Japanese-style rooms.

Hakone Prince Hotel ((0460) 3-1111 FAX (0460) 3-7616, 144, Moto-Hakone, Hakone-machi. 218* rooms. Rates: expensive.
Hakone-Sounzan Youth Hostel ((0460) 2-3827, 1320, Gora, Hakone-machi, Ashigarashimo-gun. It has 27 beds. Rates: inexpensive.
Hotel Yamadaya ((0460) 2-2641 FAX (0460) 2-2641, 1320, Gora, Hakone-machi, Ashi-

ABOVE: Pleasure boats on the shores of Lake Ashinoko, one of the five lakes found in the Hakone region.

gara-Shimo-gun. 15 rooms. Rates: average plus.

Matsuzaka-ya ((0460) 3-6315 FAX (0460) 3-6530, 64, Moto-Hakone, Hakone-machi, Ashigara-Shimo-gun. 20 rooms. Rates: average and upward.

Naraya Ryokan ((0460) 2-2411 FAX (0460) 2-6231, 162, Miyanoshita, Hakone-machi, Ashigara-shimo-gun. 20 rooms. Rates: expensive.

Suizanso ((0460) 5-5757 FAX (0460) 5-5750, 694, Yumoto, Hakone-machi, Ashigara-shimo-gun. 25 rooms. Rates: average and up.

KAMAKURA

Tourists usually stop in Kamakura, a seaside town about one hour south of Tokyo, to see the **Dai-butsu** (Great Buddha). This is a good reason, for the 11.4 m (37 ft) high bronze figure is strikingly beautiful, but there are many reasons for prolonging the visit beyond the customary half hour.

For one thing, Kamakura is the nearest really attractive town to Tokyo. Enclosed on three sides by small but steep and densely wooded hills, and on the fourth by the sea,

its atmosphere is much older than Tokyo's, while its air is much fresher.

The hills and the sea made it marvelously easy to defend in the Middle Ages and this is why the first shogun, Minamoto Yoritomo, chose to raise it from a humble fishing village to capital of the country when he seized control in 1192. The Great Buddha was one of the greatest products of the Kamakura period (1192 to 1333) which ensued, but there are many others.

In the middle of the town, 10 minutes from the station at the far end of an avenue of cherry trees, is the magnificent **Hachiman Shrine**, devoted to the god of war and built by Yoritomo in gratitude for his victory. Among the votary creatures kept in the shrine's grounds is a flock of doves.

Not long after Yoritomo's rule began, Zen Buddhism was introduced from China, and several fine old temples of the Rinzai Zen sect are tucked away in the hills around the town. Best for atmosphere, perhaps, are **Engakuji**, opposite Kita-Kamakura station, and **Kenochoji**, just 10 minutes from Engakuji on the road to the city center. In particular, Engakuji's tall trees, shady paths and soulful old buildings reverberate with the somber spirituality of the Kamakura period.

Kamakura's Hachiman Shrine LEFT and its wooden tablets RIGHT bearing the names of the shrine's benefactors. OPPOSITE: Visiting the shrine.

Among the many other temples is the **Hase-dera Temple** which contains a statue of the 11-headed Kannon that is over a thousand years old.

Several well-marked and well-tramped hiking courses follow the ridges of the town's hills. The **Dai-butsu** course, for example, goes from near Kita-Kamakura station to a spot near the Great Buddha. It's about an hour's pleasant stroll from end to end. On the way, you can drop in at **Zeni-Arai Benten**, a very popular shrine, to wash your money. It should double in value — sometime.

And finally, what about the Great Buddha? It is a remarkable piece of work. Cast in bronze in 1252, it has survived the storms, typhoons and earthquakes which destroyed the temple building that used to enclose it. The rock-solid posture and the sublime calm of the face successfully embody the ideals of Buddhism.

Kamakura has a lighter side, too — the seaside, where Tokyoites flock in their thousands every summer weekend to swim, sail, windsurf and sunbathe. The lack of alternatives helps them to ignore the quantities of garbage that are continually washed up on the beach. Foreign visitors do not always find it so easy.

Along the scenic coast between Kamakura and the nearby city of Fujisawa runs the single-track Enoden railway line. Some 15 minutes from Kamakura it stops at Enoshima, and 10 minutes' walk away is the holy island of that name, reached by a bridge. It's small, steep and notably overdeveloped, but the shrines and tower at the top of the island are popular. If your legs ache by the time you reach the shrine precincts you can, for a small sum, take an escalator to the top.

The Kamakura City Tourist Association runs a telephone information service from 9 AM to 6 PM at ((0467) 72-3350.

HOW TO GET THERE

Japan Railways' Yokosuka (pronounced "Yokos'ka") line covers the distance from Tokyo to Kamakura in just over an hour.

The platform at Tokyo is underground, on the Marunouchi side of the station.

If you wind up your visit in Enoshima, there are two other ways of getting back to Tokyo.

The private Odakyu line runs between Odakyu Enoshima station and Shinjuku, in the heart of Tokyo. The fastest trains (*Tokkyu*, special express), which run roughly once an hour, cover the distance in 70 minutes. Like most private lines,

the Odakyu line is much cheaper, and consequently more crowded, than JR.

Alternatively, you can take an exhilarating 13-minute ride on the monorail that swoops and climbs through the hills between Enoshima and Ofuna, and catch JR's Tokaido line to Yokohama and Tokyo from there.

Touring Hakone and Kamakura

JTB's Sunrise Tours has a Discover Kamakura One Day By Local Train and Walking tour. It seems expensive at ¥12,000 for adults and ¥11,000 for children. But at least you get a guide to see you right. Wednesdays and Saturdays, spring and autumn only (!). Check with JTB for details.

WHERE TO STAY

Room rate indications—Budget:¥5,000 or less. Moderate: ¥ 5,000 to ¥11,000. Average: ¥11,000 to ¥22,000. Expensive:¥22,000 and up. A (*) denotes hotels offering Western, and Japanese-style, rooms.

ENOSHIMA, Kanagawa Prefecture
Ryokan Iwamotoro Bekkan (also known as Enoshima Grand Hotel) ((0466) 26-4111 FAX (0466) 26-4115, 2-16-6, Katasekaigan,

Fujisawa. 51* rooms. Rates: average and upward.

KAMAKURA, Kanagawa Prefecture
Kamakura Kagetsuen Youth Hostel ((0476) 25-1238, 27-9, Sakanoshita, Kamakura. 49 beds. Rates: inexpensive.

NAGOYA

The fastest Tokaido Shinkansen train, the Hikari, stops only once between Tokyo and Kyoto: at Nagoya. The two million-plus people who live and work in this city's remarkably wide, clean and carefully planned streets constitute Japan's fifth-largest urban population. It is not known as a center for tourism, and even native Nagoyans are hard put to name their city's charms. But it is a major business and conference center, and if you have cause to visit you will find a variety of ways to while away the time.

Nagoya is also the gateway to two of Japan's most worthwhile sightseeing areas: Ise and Toba to the south, and the Hida area, including the city of Takayama, to the north.

NAGOYA'S HISTORY

In the seventeenth century, the great shogun Tokugawa Ieyasu built a major castle where Nagoya Castle now stands, and as so often happened in Japan, a city grew up around its skirts. Crafts which had been practiced in the area since ancient times — especially pottery — flourished, and the city became a major cultural center.

Unfortunately, nearly all vestiges of this culture were destroyed in the war, but the people of Nagoya took advantage of the disaster to rebuild the city on a grid plan. In 1959 they also rebuilt the castle, prudently in ferroconcrete. The old trades — porcelain, cloison and textiles — flourished again, but were overtaken in importance by modern heavy and chemical industries: iron and steel, automobiles, shipbuilding, plastics, fertilizers, drugs. Ideally located on the Pacific and in the center of the great Tokaido industrial belt, well-watered Nagoya is one of the modern world's most massive and smoothly turning dynamos.

WHAT TO SEE

The **Kanko Annaisho** ((052) 541-4301 — the Tourist Information Office (not to be confused with the TIC) — is on the east side of Nagoya station. The people there are helpful and have useful English-language leaflets. City sightseeing bus tours are conducted in Japanese but are a good way of getting acquainted with the city quickly. There are several every day, the earliest leaving at 9:30 AM.

Nagoya Castle is the high-point of most tours. Although the main building is less than 25 years old, it is a faithful copy of the original (unlike Osaka Castle, for example, which

Winter time in Nagoya. ABOVE: Part of the castle walls and OPPOSITE a temple in the city.

is smaller than its model) and some of the gates and turrets around it have survived from the seventeenth century. It's a bit obvious that it is made of concrete, but the lift which whisks visitors to the fifth floor will be appreciated by anybody who has trudged up the hundreds of steps in a genuine Japanese castle. On the way down, in the well-lit exhibition spaces, there are weapons, armor, painted screens and, on the fourth floor, cases of beautiful paper dolls representing the city's October parade of feudal lords. The nearest subway station is Shiyakusho on the Meijo Line. Entrance costs ¥300, for which you also get an informative and well-written leaflet.

Atsuta Shrine, the most important in the city, is one of the oldest in the country and draws streams of pilgrims. Its buildings are reminiscent of those at Ise (see page 186). The nearest subway station is Jingu Nishi on the Meijo Line.

Nagoya's city center, Sakai, is dominated by the 180 m (590 ft) TV tower, and the garden-cum-boulevard in which the tower stands, Hisaya-odori Park, is remarkably spacious. Close to the Tower is the **Aichi Arts Center** (theater and museum). Nearest subway station: Sakae, on the Higashima and Meijo Lines.

The **Nagoya City Art Museum** and the **Nagoya City Science Museum** stand side by side in Shirakawa Park (10 minutes on foot from the subway stop Yaba-cho, on the Meijo Line; also accessible from Fushima Station, on the Higashiyama/Tsurumai Lines).

In the port area there are the **Antarctic Museum,** "Fuji", housed in the former icebreaker vessel of the same name and, across the bridge, the Port of Nagoya Public Aquarium (opened 1992). Access: Nagoyako subway station on the Meijo Line.

Through no fault of its own, Nagoya is miserably short of old buildings, but a 60-minute bus ride away from the city center is a treasure house of Japanese architectural history. Called **Meiji Mura**, it is the highlight of one of the regular daily bus tours.

Unique in Japan, the large hillside park is home for more than 50 of the most significant buildings of the Meiji period (1868–1912). Like all such parks, it rates nil for atmosphere, but as a series of vivid demonstrations of the way the Japanese variously

imitated, adapted and resisted Western architectural styles, it is unbeatable. Among the attractions are a prison, a bathhouse, a small *kabuki* theater and the house occupied in turn by the novelists Mori Ogai and Natsume Soseki. The park fronts onto a lake, Iruka Pond (rowboats for rent).

To get there on your own, take the overground Meitetsu Komaki Line train from Nagoya Station to Inuyama, and then the Meitetsu Bus to Meiji Mura. Don't attempt to get all the way there by rail — it's a two-hour hike from the nearest station (Gakuden). Save your energy for the amble up the nearby hill known as Owari Fuji Mountain.

Inuyama is also a place to see cormorant fishing; for details see GIFU (below).

Back in the city, but not included in any of the regular tours, is the model factory of **Noritake**, Nagoya's famous porcelain firm. *Kanko Annaisho*, the Tourist Information Office, will help arrange your visit.

Due to the city's grid plan, finding your way around is straightforward, and the subway system is easy to use (it may also be the only one in the world with curtains). The subway will take you as far as **Nagoyako**, Japan's third-largest port, where some of the vast number of Japanese cars which are for sale overseas will probably be lined up for your inspection.

NAGOYA AT NIGHT

Sakae, two subway stops from Nagoya station, is the place to go for evening entertainment. Due to its wide streets and four-square architecture, Sakae has neither the style of Tokyo's Roppongi nor the cheerful garishness of Dottonbori in Osaka. There is, however, plenty going on.

An invaluable guide to straight entertainment (theater, movies, concerts) as well as daytime events is the monthly English-language *Nagoya Calendar*, published by Kokusai Center. If you can't get a copy at the Tourist Information Center, call Kokusai (which means International) Center and ask about it. Their number is ((052) 581-5678.

The only guide to the less formal nightlife, however, is your own nose. There are many restaurants, bars, "snacks" and cabarets. Nagoya's only culinary specialty is *kishi-*

men, wide, flat wheat noodles in broth, but excellent food of all sorts is available.

One particular shop deserves special mention. **Gomitori**, a *nomi-ya* (bar) in the heart of town, serves an amazing selection of exotic delicacies at reasonable prices in rooms charmingly decked out with Japanese antiques. Specialties include horsemeat *sashimi*, loaches, frogs (in season), spare ribs, *natto* (fermented soybeans), turtle soup and *kushiyaki* (barbecued kebabs of chicken). There are two branches, one close by Nagoya Kanko Hotel. For directions (in Japanese) ((052) 241-0041.

HOW TO GET THERE

It's not difficult. Nagoya is 105 minutes from Tokyo, 50 minutes from Kyoto (and one hour from Shin-Osaka) by the Hikari *shinkanzen*, the fastest train available on a Japan Rail Pass. The super-express Nozomi takes 96 minutes. All *shinkanzen* trains running west from Tokyo stop at Nagoya.

TOURING NAGOYA

The Japanese-language city bus tours were mentioned above. There are no scheduled tours of the city conducted in English.

Nagoya is one of the best places to begin (or end) trips to the holy shrines of Ise and the seaside area of Toba (to the southwest) and to the well-preserved villages of Tsumago, Magome and Narai and the elegant city of Takayama to the northeast.

WHERE TO STAY

Room rate indications — Budget: ¥5,000 or under. Moderate: ¥ 5,000 to ¥11,000. Average: ¥11,000 to ¥22,000. Expensive: ¥22,000 and up. A (ß) denotes business hotels with mostly single rooms.

Nagoya Kanko Hotel ((052) 231-7711 FAX (052) 231-7719, 1-19-30, Nishiki, Naka-ku. 505 rooms. Rates: average and upward.
Nagoya Green Hotel (ß) ((052) 203-0211 FAX (052) 211-4434, 1-8-22, Nishiki, Naka-ku. 103 rooms. Rates: moderate.
Nagoya Youth Hostel ((052) 781-9845, 1-50, Kameiri, Tashiro-cho, Chikusa-ku. 92 beds. Rates: inexpensive.

Park Hotel Tsuchiya ((052) 451-0028 FAX (052) 451-9361, 2-16-2, Noritake, Naka-mura-ku. 22 rooms. Rates: average.

Nagoya is also close (40 minutes by train) to the old city of **Gifu**. No longer very picturesque (blame the bombs), Gifu is nonetheless a center of picturesque trades — parasol and lantern making. It is also, more significantly, the center of the ancient sport of *ukai*, or cormorant fishing.

Every summer night (except when there is a full moon) fishing boats prowl up the Nagaragawa River at Gifu. Suspended from

the prow of each is a fiery torch; and each boat also contains a number of cormorants on leads. Lured by the light, *ayu* (delicious sweetfish) rise to the surface, where the cormorants snap them up and bear them to the boats. This very ancient ritual takes place under the eyes of hundreds of spectators, almost all of them river-borne too, and most of them enjoying snacks or fullblown picnics washed down with quantities of *sake*. It costs ¥2,700 to ¥2,900 exclusive of food and drink. Reservations can be made at JTB offices, or in Gifu on the day. Cormorant fishing also takes place at Inuyama (see under MEIJI MURA, page 162).

ABOVE: A Nagoya mother and child. OVERLEAF: The Pavilion at Kinkakuji Temple, Kyoto.

KYOTO

Kyoto is only 30 minutes from Osaka by the fastest train, but the dialect, *Kyoto-ben*, is quite different — and it's one of many profound differences between the two cities. People elsewhere in Japan say that when a woman speaks *Kyoto-ben* it sounds like poetry, but when a man speaks it makes you squirm, and this is indicative, too. Kyoto is one of the most feminine of places and contrasts starkly with the rough practicality of Osaka down the track.

Kyoto is also the one place in Japan you should visit, even if you go nowhere else. Capital of the country for more than a thousand years, it is the cradle of almost everything that is uniquely Japanese, and though designed along Chinese lines it is the place where the medieval Japanese first shook off that tradition and started to go their own way.

As the only Japanese city of substance to escape wartime bombing — at the plea, it is said, of a highly placed American Japanophile — a great deal of this ancient beauty survives: in temples, shrines, palaces, castles and aristocratic villas. There are also theaters, craft workshops and museums, geisha houses — and beautiful women. The young women of Kyoto do full justice to their surroundings.

You can "do" Kyoto in a day or less, but you should stay longer if you can. It is an elusive city, and with its modern steel and ferroconcrete and snarled-up traffic it doesn't at first seem anything out of the ordinary. Much of the charm is on a delicate scale: give yourself time to drop in to that little temple or small shrine that you would otherwise march right past, to get lost in the geisha district, to follow the winding course of a city stream.

There are no grand European-style prospects in the city, and the view from the 131-m (430-ft) Kyoto Tower outside the railway station (the proprietors claim it harmonizes well with classical Kyoto) is banal in the extreme. You have to get close to the city, absorb what it has to offer, and become a part of the picture before you can start to relish it.

KYOTO'S HISTORY

Kyoto was founded in 794 as the capital of Japan. Like nearby Nara, the capital for the preceding 70-odd years, it was designed according to Chinese concepts, with nine broad streets running from east to west, intersected by a number of wide avenues running from south to north. This gridlike street plan persists to the present day and makes the city a blessedly easy place to get about in.

Heian-kyo — "Capital of Peace" — was one of its early names, and its golden age was the Heian period, from its foundation to the twelfth century. During these years the imperial court lived in great splendor and the city's artisans developed the skills necessary to satisfy the courtiers' luxurious tastes. These were the centuries when Kyoto was the country's true capital.

In the twelfth century, power was wrested from the court by military leaders based near present-day Tokyo, and the city began a long and gentle decline. The transfer of emperor and court to Tokyo in 1869 might have been a final disaster but the city survived, its old

A Kyoto parade of geishas is a great sight for the visiting tourist.

trades shored up by modern industries. The atmosphere of the city remains as refined and aristocratic — and snobbish, many Japanese say — as ever. The enthronement ceremonies for new emperors still take place there.

WHAT TO SEE AND DO

First stop for all visitors who wish to explore Kyoto is the TIC on the ground floor of the Kyoto Tower Building, two minutes' walk from the main station (north exit). The busy but friendly and very helpful staff will give you a map, an explanatory pamphlet and any other help or advice you require. Brochures describing city tours are freely available and there are notices advertizing upcoming concerts, plays and festivals.

The center is open from 9 AM to 5 AM on weekdays and 9 AM to noon on Saturdays. It's closed on Sundays and national holidays.

Armed with your map, you are ready to set out. Here are some of the places you should see.

Temples

Kyoto has an amazing number of temples — some 1,500 in all. Many of the most charming are located around the city's edges where they enjoy the serenity of the encircling mountains. Note that most temples these days charge an entrance fee of between ¥300 and ¥600.

The first one you will encounter when you start walking, however, is slap bang in the middle of town — **Higashi Honganji**, the city's largest wooden building. The victim of many fires, it was most recently rebuilt in 1895. Most of the temple's buildings are closed to the public, so content yourself with an "ooh" and an "aah" and pass on.

The famous pagoda of **Kiyomizu Temple** is one of the city's most splendid. Its verandah projects over a cliff and is supported by 139 m (456 ft) high wooden columns: vertigo is assured. The temple is on the east of the city, a stiff 10-minute walk from Kiyomizu-michi bus stop up through the narrow streets where much of Kyoto's characteristic pottery is produced and sold. The temple was founded in 798 but re-erected in 1633. The veranda is a miracle of wooden engineering and offers great views of the city.

Keeping close to the hills and moving north a little, we reach **Nanzenji Temple**. The easiest access is from Keage station on the Keishin line. This enormous temple, which contains 12 subordinate temples, is noted for its *fusuma* (sliding door) paintings and its exquisite gardens. It is a Zen temple, headquarters of the Nanzenji school of the Rinzai sect.

In the grounds there is a curious red-brick Victorian aqueduct. Following this to the end we find that its only function is to feed the little waterfall which is the main feature of one of the gardens. From the place where the garden is designed to be admired, the aqueduct is, of course, invisible.

The road leading to Nanzenji is lined with restaurants which specialize in *yudofu*, literally *"tofu* with hot water", though the reality is a bit more interesting than that. Still, prices are high for what is basically a simple dish, fancily presented.

Daitokuji Temple in the north of the city (Daitokuji-mae station) is another enormous Rinzai Zen establishment with numerous subsidiary temples. Pretty gardens and artworks of great age and beauty abound. Some of the sub-temples are open to the public, but an entrance fee must be paid for each one. It is generally worth it: they are full of charming surprises.

In the grounds of the temple there is also a restaurant which specializes in Kyoto's vegetarian cuisine. It does not look like a restaurant so much as another temple, and the atmosphere is appropriately hushed and meditative. The food is, needless to say, very pretty. Go with a friend — ideally a Japanese one.

West of Daitokuji is the famous **Kinkakuji**, the "Temple of the Golden Pavilion" in Yukio Mishima's novel of the same name (Kinkakuji-mae station, one stop west of Daitokuji-mae). The pavilion of this temple, situated on a small lake, has two claims to fame aside from its extraordinary beauty: its walls are entirely covered in gold leaf, and it was burnt to the ground by a deranged priest (the hero of Mishima's novel) in 1950. It was rebuilt exactly as before — and not, for once, in ferroconcrete — in 1955.

A couple of kilometers from Kinkakuji to the southwest is **Ryoanji Temple** (no convenient railway station). This temple's austere and simple stone garden, composed of a few mossy rocks arranged in a sea of gravel which is carefully raked into place daily, is the most famous of its kind in Japan. Yet "garden" seems the wrong word for it: apart from the moss, nothing grows here at all.

Ryoanji's fame, which has gone round the world, has perhaps been counter productive. People who have read ecstatic descriptions of the garden and its metaphysical meaning arrive burdened with grand ideas and ex-

tion, is a remarkable temple known as **Sanjusangendo**, which glitters with the reflected light of a thousand and one small images of Kannon, the goddess of mercy. The tall "thousand-handed" image of Kannon around which they cluster was carved in 1254. The temple is a great favorite with all visitors.

Shrines

Kyoto is dotted with shrines, though they are not nearly as numerous as temples. As elsewhere in Japan, they are distinguishable

pectations and often go away disappointed, because the garden is very simple. Happy is the visitor who, knowing nothing about it beforehand, arrives and dangles his legs over the veranda — and, looking at his watch, finds that an hour has slipped by since he started gazing at it. Words maul a place like this.

Unfortunately, this type of experience is almost impossible due to the loudspeaker which babbles on all day about the garden's tranquillity. Arrive early in the morning — before 9 AM — to avoid this. The temple will not be officially open but a monk should let you in.

Back in the center of town, about a kilometer (around a half mile) east of Kyoto sta-

from temples by the *torii* (gate) which invariably marks the entrance to the sacred ground. This is often painted red, as are the shrine's buildings.

Suspended outside the shrines' main hall is a bell which makes a dry rattling noise when shaken by means of a rope which hangs below it. This is one way of arousing the attention of the enshrined deity before praying — another is clapping your hands.

Kyoto's most impressive shrine, though not the oldest, is **Heian Jingu**. This monumental piece of work was built in 1895 to commemorate the 1,100th anniversary of the city's foundation, and every year it is the

ABOVE: Part of the Ryoanji Temple in Kyoto where the art of a Japanese garden is brought to the fore.

locus for the city's **Jidai Matsuri** (Festival of the Ages), a historical costume parade on a grand scale (see FESTIVALS, page 116).

Despite its enormous proportions, Heian Jingu is in fact a smaller replica of a much older shrine, built in 794. It's within walking distance of Nanzenji Temple.

An older and more restrained and soulful shrine is **Kitano**, a short distance east of Ryoanji Temple. Others are scattered around the city, charming but not worthy of special mention. Note how local children use the precincts of shrines as playgrounds: this is

At the same time you can apply for permission to visit one of Kyoto's architectural musts, the **Katsura Rikyu mansion**. Say you hope to see it a day or two later (longer in the blossom and autumn leaves seasons) and the imperial bureaucrats will usually consent.

If you take a Japanese friend with you to the palace he will have to wait outside: only foreigners are allowed such easy access. Japanese have to wait months for permission and many are turned down flat.

Nijo Castle, 20 minutes' ride from the TIC on a Nº 9 or 50 bus, was the home of the

one of Shinto's public functions. The public park is a modern idea imported from the West.

Palaces

Kyoto's **Old Imperial Palace** (*Kyoto Gosho*), which covers a large area in the centre of the city, was the emperor's home before he packed his bags and moved to Tokyo. Getting to see it is something of a hassle: you must visit the offices of the Imperial Household Agency located there, fill in an application form, show your passport and wait for a short while. You are, after all, in the presence of the ghosts of many emperors and the descendants of the sun goddess! There are tours beginning at 10 AM and 2 PM.

great shogun Ieyasu whenever he was in Kyoto and is the best place to get a glimpse of his luxurious (and his highly security-conscious) lifestyle. The castle, designed as a lavish habitat rather than a fortress, is crammed with invaluable works of art and craft, including carvings, paintings, metal work and furniture.

The single most famous feature of the castle is the *uguisubari*, the "bush warbler floor" of the corridor in the first building, which warbles under the lightest tread. This was to warn guards that an intruder — perhaps a would-be assassin — was on the premises.

The castle is surrounded by a pleasant garden but the trees in it are new: in the old days there were none. The sight of falling leaves was said to be too depressing for the resident samurai.

If you go to the trouble of getting permission to visit **Katsura Rikyu**, you won't regret it. According to many it is the crowning glory of Japanese domestic architecture.

In Japanese the adopted word *man shon* means a block of flats. Katsura Rikyu, however, is a mansion in the old English sense — a country pile. But it has none of the grandiloquence or pomposity of Western equivalents. With its clean lines and masterly proportions, it is almost a modern building, except that the quality of the craftsmanship which greets the eye at every turn is beyond the dreams of any modern architect.

In the spring of 1982 the building was reopened to the public after six years of work, during which it was entirely reconstructed from scratch. The fact that it was possible to reproduce the seventeenth-century craftsmanship of the original to the same high standards speaks volumes for the strength of Japanese craft traditions.

And what of those traditions? How are they faring elsewhere?

Arts and Crafts

Many cities, towns and villages in Japan boast of one particular craft which has been practiced in that place for generations and cannot be found in exactly the same form anywhere else. Kyoto, however, has not one craft but a whole spectrum, including dyeing, silk weaving, cloisonné, embroidery, lacquerware, woodblock prints, bambooware and others.

Some of these, such as silk weaving, date back to the foundation of the city in the eighth century. Some, again with weaving and dyeing as examples, have developed into modern industrialized concerns with an annual output worth hundreds of millions of dollars. But even in these cases the traditional craft techniques are maintained as a relatively small but vital part of the industry.

Other crafts such as lacquer and bambooware are quite resistant to radical modernization, but their fame within Japan allows the craftsmen to ask high enough prices to keep going. Craft is a fascinating as well as a vital aspect of the city's life, and there are a number of opportunities for visitors to

learn more about them. Here are some of the most interesting:

For the **Kyoto Handicrafts Center** board the N° 206 bus from Tokyo Station (it takes 20 minutes). Dropping in here is the single most convenient way to see crafts men at work, weavers, potters and wood block makers among them. A good selection of their products is on sale as well.

The area of steep, narrow streets leading up to **Kiyomizu Temple** is Kyoto's well-known pottery-producing area, and potters can be seen at work in several of the shops

here. One of the greatest of them lived in this neighborhood. His name was Kanjiro Kawai and his house is open to the public. Here you can inspect his work and the traditional "climbing kiln" in which he fired it.

The house is closed Mondays, like so many of Japan's museums, (or the following day if the Monday falls on a national holiday), August 10 to 20, and December 24 to January 7. Otherwise it's open from 10 AM to 5 PM. The address is Gojo-zaka, Kyoto. TIC have a leaflet that contains instructions in Japanese for taxi-drivers. Some 200 m (660 ft) east of Nishi-Kyogoku station is

Rich in color, the Heian Jingu Shrine OPPOSITE is on the top of the list for most visitors to Kyoto. ABOVE: A craftsman fashioning *geta*, wooden clogs.

Kyoto Yuzen Cultural Hall, and here you can observe the traditional method of silk-dyeing in progress — although painting give a closer idea of how the craft looks in action. This is how they make the material for those gorgeous kimonos you see around town. Enjoy the serenity of the atmosphere in the workshop: pure Kyoto.

As well as these live attractions there are a number of museums which specialize in crafts of various sorts:

The **Kyoto Center of Traditional Crafts** (Fureaikan). Completely rebuilt in 1996, this

Kyoto at Night

Kyoto may not boogie like Tokyo but it has some suave steps of its own. It's one of the few Japanese cities where in the early evening the citizens do the Mediterranean thing and stroll along the streets, at least during the warmer months. Join them: it's a pleasant way to get to know the city at night.

Drift around the **Gion** section on the east bank of the Kamo River, admire the quiet elegance of the old town houses there. In a number of these geisha still live and work. Cross the bridge at the **Minamiza Theater**,

museum is in the Myako Messe Building. It has a great collection of traditional craft products as well as a reproduction of a traditional Kyoto house. It's to the right of the **National Museum of Modern Art** near Higashiyama Sanjo station.

Costume Museum. Located near Nishi-Honganji station, this museum charts the various ways in which Japanese costume has changed over the past 2,000 years.

Other interesting cultural sites include the **Nishijin Textile Center and the Kodai Yuzen-en and Gallery**. For details contact the TIC.

home of Kyoto's *kabuki* theater, back to the west bank, then turn right up the narrow street closest to the river and parallel to it running north.

This is **Ponto-cho** and it's the heart of the city's amusement quarter. Many bars and restaurants line the street, some forbiddingly traditional or expensive (remember to check before ordering), others welcoming and relatively cheap. The ones on the right look out over the river: there you can feel cool, even in summer.

There are plenty of other ways to pass the time: first-rate cinemas, *kabuki* and *noh* plays, coffeeshops specializing in Beatles records or jazz (some people call Kyoto the jazz capital of the world).

ABOVE: The imposing lines of *torii*, gateways, at the Fushimi Inari Shrine, Kyoto. The bright, inviting clutter OPPOSITE of a Kyoto side street.

Back on the east bank of the river is **Gion Corner** (also known as **Gion Kaburenjo Theater**) where you can catch one of the twice-nightly presentations of traditional arts and drama. The tea ceremony, flower-arrangement and *bunraku* puppet plays are among the arts demonstrated, and a handier way to sample traditional Japanese culture has not been devised.

Shopping

Kyoto is the best place to buy locally made craft products. A map available at the TIC, the *Shopping Guide Map of Kyoto*, shows where. For general shopping, Kyoto has a number of excellent department stores.

Miscellaneous

The **Toei Movieland** (*Toei Uzumasa Eigamura*) is a working outdoor film studio specializing in historical movies (see page 13 for details). You turn up and watch as the cameras roll.

Eigamura, the name it's usually referred to by, is open daily from 9 AM (except from December 21 to January 1, when it's shut). The gates close at 4:30 PM (3:30 PM between December 1 and the end of February). To get there take the № 71, 72 or 73 Tokyo bus from Kyoto Station to Uzumasa Koryuji. If in doubt, the TIC office opposite the station will love to point you in the right direction; they consider it one of Kyoto's prime sites. Admission: ¥2,100 (adults), ¥1,100 (secondary school students), ¥900 (primary school students, aged four upwards).

A well-known figure in Kyoto is the **English-speaking guide** Hajime Hirooka, better known to visitors as Johnnie Hillwalker (more on page 14). Tours begin at 10:15 AM every Monday, Tuesday, Wednesday and Thursday from the beginning of March to the end of November (i.e. no walks in the winter). The total distance is an easy three kilometers, and the total time taken is three hours. The cost? ¥2,000 per person, with couples charged ¥3,000, and children taken along for free. Give him a try.

And the **Women's Association of Kyoto (WAK)** will take you to places in Kyoto of special interest to women (kimono-dressing, flower arrangement, Japanese cooking, and many more) as well as advise on good buys

in these areas of interest. Contact Michi Ogawa on ((075) 752-9090 FAX (075) 762-2201.

Lastly, there's a finely-produced magazine called the *Kyoto Journal* which uses the historic city as a base from which to contemplate world issues of environmental degradation and the quality of life on the planet, as well as matters more specific to Kyoto. Nature and meditation could be said to be its key points of reference. It contains poetry, sophisticated photographs and artwork, and is generally a very useful source of information on the best Kyoto has to offer.

Even the advertisements that it carries are as good as valuable recommendations in themselves. It is published by the Heian Bunka Center ((075) 761-1433 FAX (075) 751-1196 E-MAIL kyo794jo@beehive.twics.com.

HOW TO GET THERE

The quickest way is by Hikara *shinkansen* from Tokyo station, which stops at only one station on the way (Nagoya) and covers the 513 km (319 miles) in two hours and 37 minutes. (Japan's fastest trains, the all-reserved Nozomi *shinkansen*, take two hours and 15 minutes but they are not available on a Japan Rail Pass). The stopping Kodama train takes over four hours.

For those on a tight budget, JR runs convenient night buses, leaving the Yaesu side of Tokyo station at 10 PM and 11 PM and getting to Kyoto station at 6:00 AM and 6:50 AM. When the bus is not crowded it's possible to sleep fairly soundly in the reclining seats. The fare is ¥8,180.

Alternatively, you can fly to Kyoto, either from within the country or from overseas, landing at Osaka's domestic airport (Itami) or the newer Kansai International Airport. Frequent buses ply between both airports and Kyoto's major hotels. The JR rail service

from Kansai International to Kyoto takes an hour and 15 minutes — change at Tennoji and Shin-Osaka stations.

TOURING KYOTO

Once you've arrived, several lightning tours are available to give you a taste of the city.

JTB's **Kyoto Morning Tour** visits Nijo Castle, the Imperial Palace (Nishijin Textile Centre on Sundays and holidays), Kinkakuji and the Kyoto Handicrafts Center. Departing from major city hotels between 8:20 and 9 AM, it returns at noon. The adult fare is ¥5,200.

Japan Travel Bureau offers an **Afternoon Tour** calling at Heian Jingu, Sanjusangendo and Kiyomizu Temple. The adult fare is ¥5,200. In the case of Fujita you can stitch morning and afternoon tours together to make a full-day tour. See Kyoto TIC for leaflets giving details of all these tours.

Other tours with trips to Nara, including those originating in Tokyo, are described at the end of the NARA section below.

WHERE TO STAY

Room rate indications — Budget: ¥5,000 or under. Moderate: ¥5,000 to ¥11,000. Average: ¥11,000 to ¥22,000. Expensive: ¥22,000 upwards. A (*) denotes hotels offering Western and Japanese-style rooms. A (ß) denotes business hotels with mostly single rooms.

Higashiyama Youth Hostel ((075) 761-8135, 112, Shira kawabashi-goken-cho, Sanjo-dori, Higashiyama-ku. 126 beds. Rates: inexpensive.

Holiday Inn Kyoto ((075) 721-3131 FAX (075) 781-6178, 36, Nishihirakicho, Takano, Sakyo-ku. 270 rooms. Rates: average and upward.

Kyoto Central Inn (ß) ((075) 211-1666 FAX (075) 241-2765, Shijo-Kawaramachi-nishi-iru, Shimogyo-ku. 150* rooms. Rates: moderate.

Miyako Hotel ((075) 771-7111 FAX (075) 751-2490, Sanjo Keage, Higashiyama-ku. 480* rooms. Rates: average and upward.

Chigiriya Ryokan ((075) 221-1281 FAX (075) 255-4949, Takoyakushi-dori-Tominokoji-nishi-iru, Nakagyo-ku. 45 rooms. Rates: expensive.

Izumiya Ryokan ((075) 371-2769, Nishi-Nakasuji Shomen-sagaru, Shimogyo-ku. 18 rooms. Rates: moderate.

Kaneiwaro Bekkan ((075) 351- 5010, Kiya-machi-dori-Matsubara-sagaru, Shimogyo-ku. 23 rooms. Rates: average and upward.

Matsubaya Ryokan ((075) 351-3727 FAX (075) 351-3505, Higashinotoin-nishi-iru, Kamijuzuya-machi-dori, Shimogyo-ku. 11 rooms. Rates: inexpensive.

Miyako Hotel ((075) 771-7111 FAX (075) 751-2490, Sanjo Keage, Higashiyama-ku. 527* rooms. Rates: expensive.

Ryokan Hiraiwa ((075) 351-6748 FAX (075) 351-6969, Ninomiya-machi-dori, Kamino-kuchi-agaru, Shimogyo-ku. 20 rooms. Rates: inexpensive.

Sumiya Ryokan ((075) 221-2188 FAX (075) 221-2267, Fuyacho-dori, Sanjo-sagaru, Nakagyo-ku. 23 rooms. Rates: expensive.

Tani House ((075) 492-5489, 8, Daitokuji-cho, Murasakino, Kita-ku. 10 rooms (dormitory style). Rates: inexpensive.

Tawaraya Ryokan ((075) 211-5566 FAX (075) 211-2204, Fuyacho-Aneyakoji-agaru, Nakagyo-ku. 19 rooms. Rates: expensive.

Kyoto is the perfect base for making excursions to other places of interest in the Kansai district. Foremost of these should be a visit to Nara.

NARA

Kyoto was not the first city the Japanese built under the inspiration of China. That honor goes to Nara.

Before Chinese influence began to surge into the country, and while administration was still a simple matter, it was the custom

iers and common people, the servants and warriors and worshipers have all vanished. Only tame deer and tourists remain.

It's a great place to visit, if only for a day. Setting off from Kyoto in the morning — a very pleasant 50-minute ride on the luxurious privately-run Kinki Nippon line train — you can see most of what should be seen before returning, sated but happy, in the evening. Alternatively, you can put yourself in the hands of the JTB or Fujita Travel Service, both of which run afternoon Nara tours (a full day tour is also run by the JTB) from

for each new emperor to choose a new capital. In 710, however, the empress *regnant* decided to pitch camp for good: a city was laid out — though never more than partially constructed — along rectangular Chinese lines, and although it only lasted 74 years those years encompassed the reigns of seven successive emperors.

In 784 the capital was transferred to the southwest of present-day Kyoto and Nara's tide began to recede. The process has been going on ever since. Of Japan's old capitals, Kyoto is still thriving in its own quiet way, while the population of Kamakura is almost exactly the same as it was in the thirteenth century. Nara alone has slipped, and is now a grassy ghost town. Many of the temples and shrines are still standing, but the court-

Kyoto hotels. See the end of this section for details.

(As a passenger on the Kinki Nippon train you are by definition a Kinki Nippon Tourist. If you want to explain the joke to a Japanese friend, have a good dictionary handy and be prepared for a long haul. He or she will then explain patiently that "Kinki" means the Kyoto/Nara/Osaka area.)

Several, though not all, of Nara's attractions are located in **Nara Park** which is close to the station. Really nice parks are unusual in Japan so enjoy this excellent specimen to the full. If you plan a picnic, however, bring

OPPOSITE: This old wooden building bears witness to Kyoto's ancient lineage. ABOVE: Some of the 3,000 lanterns at Nara's Kasuga Shrine. They are lit twice a year, once in February, once in August.

plenty for the deer, which are harmless but always hungry.

As Nara was the first city to be established under Chinese influence, it is not surprising that it was also the first place in Japan where Buddhism flourished. This was very much a state-sponsored affair with imperial magnificence clearly in view. The temples are large, dignified and purely Chinese in style — in fact, they are the best surviving examples anywhere of architecture of China's T'ang dynasty. The ones on the continent were destroyed during the Mongol invasions.

Typical of the Chinese style — although the present building is a later reconstruction — is Nara's biggest attraction, **Todaiji**, the world's largest wooden building, containing the world's largest bronze figure, the Great Buddha.

This Buddha is 16.2 m or 53.1 ft high, and is taller than the 11.4-m (37.4-ft) Great Buddha in Kamakura. It is certainly impressive, and somehow the temple's gloom makes it seem even huger than it is. It has had an unhappy history, however; decapitated in earthquakes, partially melted in fires

and patched together numerous times — and these accidents have left the statue with a slightly offputting Frankenstein monster quality.

The JTB's official guide tells us that the image is "Worshipped with the utmost reverence." This may be so but it is also true that the sect which focused on the image disappeared centuries ago. The sea of popular devotion has long since retreated, leaving monuments like this sticking up like rocks out of the sand.

Kofukuji Temple is another of Nara's great landmarks, famous for its two pagodas, one five-story and the other three-story. It was founded by a member of the most powerful court family. After a period of decline during which it moved twice, its name was shrewdly changed to Kofukuji which means "Happiness-Producing Temple". Result: instant popularity.

Kasuga Shrine is hidden away deep in the woods in the east of Nara Park and is a place to experience the tranquility of Shinto: you can almost smell the sanctity. **Ise Jingu**, Shinto's most important shrine (see below), has this quality to an even stronger degree. Like Ise, Kasuga used to be reconstructed regularly every 20 years. The custom continues at Ise but has apparently lapsed here.

There are 3,000 lanterns at Kasuga and they are lighted twice a year. See under NARA in the FESTIVALS section starting on page 113 for further details.

AROUND NARA

Byodoin Temple is also known as **Phoenix Temple**: the hall was originally designed to represent the Japanese equivalent of that mythical bird descending to earth. Marvel at the lightness and elegance of these eleventh-century buildings, which are genuinely birdlike. The temple was originally a villa for a member of the Fujiwara, the most powerful family at the court, but later it became a monastery. There is no need to buy postcards to remind yourself what this temple looks like — just look at the back of a 10-yen coin.

Byodoin is located in the town of **Uji**, just south of Kyoto, but the JTB include it in their full-day Nara itinerary.

It is a city that has clung to the past. Nara's air of antiquity is paralleled in the quaintly out-of-date fashions that the locals prefer.

Horyuji, the single most worthwhile spot in the Nara area, is also about the hardest to get to — although no harder than hopping on and off a bus, which goes from Nara-Kintetsu (Kinki Nippon) station. Note that none of the regular tours visit this beautiful and seminal temple.

When you get off the bus you will find you are out in the country, though presumably it was part of the capital in its heyday. A short walk will bring you to **Horyuji**, one of the first Buddhist temples in Japan. It was founded by Prince Shotoku, the man on the 10,000-yen note.

As the Japanese will tell you proudly, it contains some of the oldest wooden buildings in the world. A hundred years ago nobody gave two hoots. Then, with modernization in full spate, Horyuji's five-story pagoda was almost sold for firewood to the proprietor of a public bath — for quite a tidy sum, it must be said. All that prevented the deal going through was that the bath proprietor could not find any way of transporting it.

As valuable as the buildings themselves are, the Buddhist statuary they contain is some of the most beautiful in Japan. It's perhaps just as well that no tours, at least no English-speaking ones, call here, for these things deserve lingering over. Many of the best are preserved in the ferroconcrete safety of the temple's **Great Treasure Hall** (the **Daihozoden**).

Close to Horyuji, almost like an annex (though it's separate and an admission fee must be paid) is the **Chuguji** convent. This contains the oldest piece of embroidery in Japan, but the main attraction is a statue which brings the Horyuji tour to a fine conclusion, the **Miroku Bosatsu**.

This slender, youthful figure, the Buddha of the Future, head tilted forward as if listening, eyelids lowered, fingers of the right hand poised near the cheek, is meditating, we are told, on the sufferings of mankind. It is a soulful work and one full of compassion.

On the way to or from Horyuji, if you go by bus, you can visit **Yakushiji**, another famous and ancient temple. Like Horyuji, Yakushiji is noted for its beautiful statues. A booklet written in English and available at the entrance gives you all the background necessary on this old temple.

HOW TO GET THERE

As we mentioned above, the quickest and most convenient service to Nara is provided by the Kinki Nippon private line. The fastest train offered by this service from Kyoto takes about 50 minutes.

TOURING NARA

You can visit Nara on a half day tour, or as a part of a whole day tour of Kyoto and Nara.

JTB operate a **Nara Afternoon tour** daily from mid-March to mid-December. It takes in the Todaiji Temple, the deep park, Kasuga Shrine and a drive through the surrounding countryside. Cost: Adults ¥6,200, children ¥5,200.

Their **Kyoto and Nara One Day tour** adds Kyoto's Nijo Castle, Golden Pavilion, Kyoto Imperial Palace (or Higashi Honganji Temple) and the Tokyo Handicraft Center and lunch to the Nara Afternoon tour. Cost: Adults ¥12,000, children ¥9,700. For details of both these tours and others not mentioned here, contact TIC offices in Tokyo or Kyoto.

WHERE TO STAY

Room rate indications — Budget: ¥5,000 or under. Moderate: ¥5,000 to ¥11,000. Average: ¥11,000 to ¥22,000. Expensive: ¥22,000 upwards. A (*) denotes hotels offering Western and Japanese-style rooms. A (ß) denotes business hotels with mostly single rooms.

Nara Hotel ((0742) 26-3300 FAX (0742) 23-5252, 1096, Takabatake-cho. 134* rooms. Rates: average and upward.
Hotel Sun Route Nara (ß) ((0742) 22-5151 FAX (0742) 27-3759, 1110, Takabatake–Bodai-cho. 95* rooms. Rates: moderate.
Nara Youth Hostel ((0742) 22-1334, 1716 Horen-cho. 200 beds. Rates: inexpensive.
Kasuga Hotel ((0742) 22-4031 FAX (0742) 26-6966, 40, Noborioji-cho. 34 rooms. Rates: average and upward.
Ryokan Seikanso ((0742) 22-2670, 29, Higashi-Kitsuji-cho. 13 rooms. Rates: inexpensive.

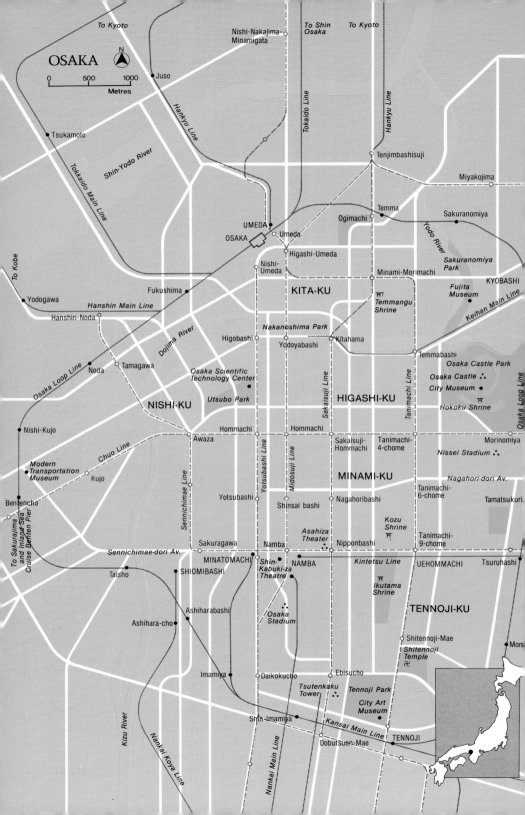

OSAKA

Kyoto is the city of temples, your guide may tell you, and Osaka the city of bridges. True enough, but more strikingly, Osaka is the city of factories: there are more than 30,000.

It is the third-biggest metropolis in the country after Tokyo and Yokohama and has roughly twice the population of Kyoto. But from the foreign visitor's point of view, it's a long way off challenging either Tokyo or Kyoto as a desirable destination. Tourist attractions are few, the crowds are dense and more aggressive than in the capital, English-language signs are rare, the labyrinthine underground train interchanges are mind-boggling, and the whole texture of the place is coarser and tackier than Tokyo.

It soon becomes clear that it's one of those places, not uncommon in Asia, which bring home to the foreign visitor, with uncomfortable clarity, the fact that they were not made with him or her in mind.

Osaka does have a number of claims to fame, however. The **Minami** downtown section puts all but Tokyo's most garish quarters in the shade. Shopping plazas are very much part of the Osaka ambiance — **Diamor Osaka,** in front of the main train station, is typical, and the central Kita district generally is characterized by extensive and lavish underground shopping centers. For innocent extravagance the decor of the underground shopping streets, for example at **Hankyu Sanbangai,** has to be seen to be believed. In the basement of the so-called "Umeda Sky Building" is Takimi Koji recreating shopping and eating as it was in Osaka in the 1930s. Shinsaibashi (at the subway station of the same name) is the city's main shopping district.

Good restaurants are innumerable, and the food is remarkable for its good value as well as its flavor. There is a new *kabuki* theater (near Namba Station on Mido-suji Boulevard, but it rarely stages *kabuki*) and a world-famous puppet theater, home of *bunraku* (see below).

In common with other major Japanese cities, Osaka has many hotels, *ryokan* and *minshuku*. See the section under WHERE TO STAY, page 184, for some recommendations.

Osaka's History

Osaka has been a settlement of importance for some 1,500 years, but it was the great sixteenth-century warlord Hideyoshi who fashioned its modern character.

He not only built his castle, Japan's greatest, on the site where imperial palaces had stood in former times, but he also induced merchants from neighboring areas to move into the city and set up shop there. As a result, during the Edo period it became

the most important distribution center in the country, and so it remains today.

Osaka enjoyed fantastic growth in the first half of this century: between 1889 and 1940 the population soared from half a million to three-and-a-quarter million. Although flattened during the war, it has more than regained its previous prosperity. Though it no longer teems in quite the way it used to, its carnal, mercantile character is unchanged.

What to See and Do

English-language literature is available from the Tourist Information Office (*Kanko*

A department store rising up from central Osaka.

Annaisho) ((06) 345-2189 in Umeda station, and at Shin-Osaka station ((06) 305-3311. But it's wiser to obtain what you can in the way of printed materials from the TIC in Tokyo or Kyoto before setting off.

Daily bus tours, conducted in Japanese, will take you round the city's sights. The booking office is underground in Osaka Umeda station and is hard to find unaided. The sights are not much except for the castle, but the ride around the city on the raised expressway at least gives you the sensation that you are coming to terms with the place. There are six half-day tours and four night tours — ring the Umeda Sightseeing Bus Information Center ((06) 311-2995 for details.

Osaka Castle

Articles have appeared in the Japanese press suggesting that **Osaka Castle** (Osaka-jo) is much smaller today than it was before: apparently the man responsible for its reconstruction copied the design from old schematics and got the scale wrong.

The castle has been destroyed twice since Hideyoshi built it, first in 1615, the second time in the civil fighting of 1868, and it was rebuilt in 1931 using ferroconcrete. The experience of visiting it is similar to that of visiting Nagoya Castle. Most impressive are the gigantic stones with which the outer walls are constructed. The castle tower was renovated in 1997 and there's a panoramic view of the city from its seventh floor. Osaka Castle is a 15-minute walk from Tanimachi-Yonchome subway station.

Unless you are really devout, don't waste your time on Osaka's temples and shrines, not even **Shitennoji Temple.** Theoretically it is the oldest in Japan, having been built in AD 593, 14 years before Horyuji (see above under NARA). But the latest rebuilding was rather recent and the temple has all the charm and atmosphere of a matchstick model. Save your legs for the real ones. Kyoto is only 32 minutes down the track.

Ethnological Museum

On the site of 1970's Osaka World Expo is the splendid **National Museum of Ethnol-**ogy. Designed by Kisho Kurokawa, one of Japan's top modern architects, it offers a vivid and enjoyable experience of different cultures around the world. A large library of short video films can be viewed in special capsules by individual visitors. An expansive garden, left over from the Expo, is nearby.

The museum is accessible by bus from Senri-Chuo (Midosuji line) or Minami-Senri (Sukaisuji line) subway stations and also from Ibaraki station, one stop from Shin-Osaka on the Tokaido line between Osaka and Kyoto.

Osaka Aquarium

This is one of the biggest aquariums in the world — the main tank is nine meters (30 ft) deep, and there are 13 others. It covers the marine life of the entire Pacific, including both poles, all of America and Australasia. **Cruises** of Osaka Bay are also available from the nearby pier. Call ((06) 576-5533 for details.

Other attractions

Osaka also has its **Fureai Minato-kan,** a museum that stages exhibitions relating to seven major sister ports around the world (San Francisco, Melbourne, Le Havre, Shanghai, Valparaiso, Pusan and Saigon), its **Museum of Oriental Ceramics** in Nakanoshima Park, specializing in Chinese and Korean work, and its **City Museum** (next to the castle) which contains among other things replicas of the items included in the time capsule buried in 1970 at the Osaka World Expo and not due to be opened for another 5,000 years.

The **Suntory Museum** ((06) 577-0001 (at Tempozan, five minutes' walk from the Osakako station on the Chuo Line subway) features a large collection of posters and art works in glass, plus an IMAX ("image maximum") 3D cinema with a 28-m (93-ft) wide, 20-m (65-ft) high screen, and a 40-m (134-ft) high Sky Lounge. Open 10 AM to 8 PM (restaurant and cinema open from 11 AM). IMAX shows last one hour.

Osaka is big on high viewing points. First there's the **WTC Tower.** This 55-story, 252 m (840 ft) high building was opened in 1995, and its observation deck is the highest point in western Japan. Next comes the 1993 **Umeda Sky Building's Floating Garden** observation deck at 170 m (570 ft), slung between two towers.

The often mundane urban architecture in Osaka, OPPOSITE, is giving way to newer cityscapes.

The favored observation point was previously the viewing deck on the **Tsutenkaku Tower** at a modest 94 m (213 ft). It's still open and is five minutes on foot from Ebisucho subway station.

The **Mint Museum** ((06) 351-5361 (open 9 AM to 5:30 PM, free entry) displays Japanese and foreign coins. More interesting would be a visit to the Mint itself, but you need to give them 10 days notice if you seriously want to take a look inside.

And the **Sakuya Konohana Kan** ((06) 912-0055 is one of the world's largest greenhouses, with plants from all the world's major climatic zones.

Takarazuka Revue

A curious theatrical experience awaits you at Takarazuka, one terminus of the private Hankyu railway, 25 km (just over 16 miles) and 34 minutes by express from Umeda station — the daily matinee performances of the all-female Takarazuka vaudeville troupe.

If you like kick lines, this is the place: Takarazuka must have the best (and longest) in the world! Typical shows consist of old-time Japanese love melodramas (pop *kabuki*), American musicals, and fast, furious and highly professional revue material. The cavernous theater holds 4,000, and most of the company's fans are teenage girls.

Takarazuka's shows have the whiff of a rather early stage in Japan's modernization, for while the company's form harks back to an earlier age — single-sex troupes (mostly male) were the norm until 80 years ago — its image is determinedly Western. The madly popular stars seem to have been picked partly for their Caucasian facial features.

For reservations ((0797) 86-7777 (10 AM to 5 PM), but a having Japanese friend on hand to speak to them would be a distinct advantage. For more information ((0797) 85-6272. The theater is closed Wednesdays "except during busy months." Tickets are from ¥800 to 4,100.

Takarazuka Family Land, in which the theater is located, has an imaginatively designed zoo, a monorail, hot-springs, a pleasant botanical garden and an "Age of the Dinosaurs" feature, among other lures. It's one of the best places in the Osaka area to give the kids a treat. It's open 9:30 AM (9 AM

on Sundays) to 5 PM, closed Wednesdays. Admission: ¥1,200.

OSAKA AT NIGHT

Downtown Osaka is divided simply into two sections, north (**Kita**) and south (**Minami**). While the best hotels and the department stores are concentrated in Kita, in the vicinity of Umeda station, Minami is the area to head towards for action at night. Namba station, on Midosuji, Sennichimae and Yotsubashi subway lines, is the best place to start from.

Walk north from Namba and, after a few of the most garishly illuminated blocks in the world, you will reach **Dotonbori**, the pedestrian street which runs east-west parallel with the river of the same name.

Dotonbori has a great concentration of worthy restaurants. The *kuidaore* was a type peculiar to Osaka, a gentleman who ate so extravagantly well that he impoverished himself in the process and Dotonbori was where he did it. Crab, blowfish, *tempura*, *nabe* (stew-like) dishes, *kushi-age* (skewered grilled food), *robatayaki* — you can tread in his footsteps.

Some 200 m (660 ft) east of where you enter the street, on the left, is a small and somewhat old building with a living tree outside, rare on both counts. It houses an *oden* establishment which has been on the premises for 200 years (the present building is just postwar) and is a good place to rest your eyes from the glare. The food is good, too, and there is a magnificent illustrated menu with captions in English.

Bunraku

Nearby is Osaka's other premier attraction, the Asahiza Theater, home of the *bunraku* puppet troupe. For a description of *bunraku*, see RELISH *BUNRAKU*, page 30 in TOP SPOTS.

having old-fashioned and often rather low-life fun. Here are the *go* and *shoji* (Japanese chess) and bingo parlors, innumerable small bars, porno cinemas and marvelously cheap restaurants specializing in dangerous delicacies like blow fish. The streets and the nearby Tennoji Zoo are littered with (fairly harmless) drunks and deadbeats, but nobody seems to mind, and on the far side of the zoo, near Tennoji Station, is a concentration of massage parlors and other soft-core cat houses. This area of town is at odds with the image of Osaka as an international city of

As they are often on tour it's wise to check with the TIC for details of performances in advance.

If you want to go to the theater directly without doing the Dotonbori promenade, Nipponbashi (Saka-suji subway line) is the nearest station.

Tsutenkaku

The authorities are not particularly keen that foreign visitors know about it, but to the north of Dobutsuen-mae station, two subway stops south of Namba, is one of the most pungent pleasure quarters in Japan.

It centers on the 103 m (335 ft) high tower, **Tsutenkaku**, a popular symbol of the city. The surrounding streets are full of people

the twenty-first century, but it has a great, if grubby, charm of its own.

HOW TO GET THERE

Hikari trains of the Tokaido Shinkansen take two hours, 53 minutes from Tokyo to Shin-Osaka. Kodama trains take four hours, 20 minutes (the price is the same). From Shin-Osaka you have to board a local train to make the five-minute journey to Osaka station.

The whole Kyoto-Osaka-Kobe area is crisscrossed with railway lines. The fastest service between Kyoto and Osaka is the Kaisoku train which takes 28 minutes nonstop.

The fabulous legs of the Takarazuka kickline.

Kansai International Airport is 60 minutes by Airport Bus from the city center. It is an attractive alternative to Tokyo's Narita for visitors heading for central Japan. Osaka also has its own domestic airport, Itami, with connections all over the country.

TOURING OSAKA

City bus tours with descriptions in Japanese are mentioned above. One English–language tour starting and finishing in Kyoto guides visitors around the city in an afternoon.

WHERE TO STAY

Room rate indications — Budget: ¥5,000 or under. Moderate: ¥5,000 to ¥11,000. Average: ¥11,000 to ¥22,000. Expensive: ¥22,000 and up. A (*) denotes hotels offering Western and Japanese-style rooms. A (ß) denotes business hotels with mostly single rooms.

Hotel New Hankyu ((06) 372-5101 FAX (06) 374-6885, 1-1-35, Shibata, Kita-ku. 922* rooms. Rates: average and upward.
Osaka Dai-ichi Hotel ((06) 341-4411 FAX (06) 341-4930, 1-9-20, Umeda, Kita-ku. 478 rooms. Rates: average and upward.

The taiko bashi (drum bridge) of Osaka's Sumiyoshi Shrine, threshold of the sacred ground.

Mitsui Urban Hotel (ß) ((06) 374-1111 FAX (06) 374-1085, 3-18-8, Toyosaki, Kita-ku. 410* rooms. Rates: moderate.
Osaka Tokyu Inn (ß) ((06) 315-0109 FAX (06) 315-6019, 2-1, Doyama-cho, Kita-ku. 402* rooms. Rates: moderate.
Osaka-Shiritsu Nagai Youth Hostel ((06) 699-5631, 1-1, Nagai-koen, Higashi-sumi-yoshi-ku. 100 beds. Rates: inexpensive.
Ebisuso Ryokan ((06) 643-4861, 1-7-33, Nihombashi-Nishi, Naniwa-ku. 10 rooms. Rates: inexpensive.

KOBE

Westward along the coast from Osaka is the city of Kobe, a port since the thirteenth century and one of Japan's largest. But just before dawn on January 17, 1995 it experienced a major earthquake which killed over 6,000 people and left very considerable physical destruction. Most of the damage has now been made good, but the old Oriental and Kobe hotels, for example, are no more.

Like Yokohama and Nagasaki, the constant sea traffic has given Kobe more of a cosmopolitan feeling than other cities, and its dramatic location, stacked up like Hong Kong on mountains rising almost directly from the sea, and its relatively balmy climate, have induced as many as 35,000 foreigners to make the city their home.

It is often said of Kobe that it's a great place to live but not much fun to visit. If you do stay for a few days you will enjoy the fine views of the harbor, the sea and the mountains of Shikoku from Mt. Rokko and Hachi-buse. **Mt. Rokko**, the highest peak at 932 m (3,057 ft), can be reached by ropeway.

Sannomiya, location (and name) of Kobe's main station, and **Motomachi** are the two principal shopping areas, while **Tor Road**, which goes north from the Daimaru store, has a number of famous restaurants. The many affluent foreign residents make loyal customers, and as a result eating out in Kobe can be a special treat. It's probably the best place to try Kobe beef: the world's most pampered cattle are raised on ranches on the other side of Mt. Rokko.

In 1981 Kobe was the site of the huge expo, Portopia, and Kobe Port Island, the man-made island in the harbor on which it was located, still features a **fairground** with the biggest, at 64 m (200 ft) high, Ferries wheel in the world and a computer-operated loop train which carries neither driver nor guard. The trains leave from Minami-koen station, which has a direct link with Sannomiya station.

Brand new at the time of writing is the **Kobe Fashion Museum** ((078) 360-4321 on another man-made reclamation, Rokko Island. It's a massive complex featuring a permanent exhibition of European costumes from the eighteenth century till now, up-to-the-moment fashion displays, an auditorium for anything from fashion shows to movies, and a resource center for fashion designers. Still partly in the construction phase, this is planned to be a major new attraction for the city, serving both workers in the fashion industry and visitors. Contact them for details. Access to Rokko Island is by the Rokko Liner, direct from Sannomiya JR Station; get off at the Island Center station.

Outside the city (40 minutes from JR Sannomiya Station) is **Suma Seaside Park**, a white-sand, pine-lined beach popular with surfers, and the Kobe young generally.

As we mentioned in the Osaka section, above, the Kobe area is richly endowed with public transport. The fastest trains from Kobe to Osaka, leaving from Sannomiya station, take about 30 minutes, while fast trains to Kyoto take about an hour.

WHERE TO STAY

Room rate indications — Budget: ¥5,000 or under. Moderate: ¥5,000 to ¥11,000. Average: ¥11,000 to ¥22,000. Expensive: ¥22,000 and up. A (*) denotes hotels offering Western and Japanese-style rooms. A (ß) denotes business hotels with mostly single rooms.

Kobe Union Hotel ((078) 222-6500 FAX (078) 242-0220, 2-1-9, Nunobiki-cho, Chuo-ku. 167* rooms. Rates: moderate.
Kobe-Tarumi Youth Hostel ((078) 707-2133, 5-58, Kai gan-dori, Tarumi-ku. 32 beds. Rates: inexpensive.
Ryokan Takayamaso ((078) 904-0744 FAX (078) 904-1823, 400-1, Arima-cho, Kita-ku. 21 rooms. Rates: average and upward.

Let's leave the hurly-burly of Kansai behind and head for open country — to be specific, for Toba, home of the cultured pearl and the Ise shrines, the mecca of Shinto. These attractions are within easy

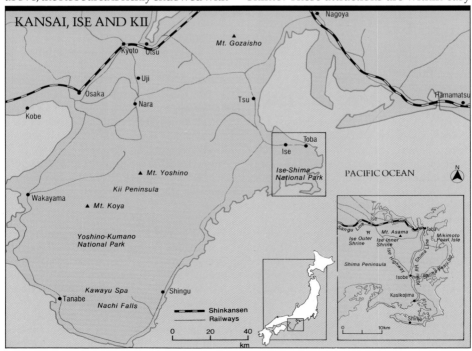

reach of each other in the pastoral Kii Peninsula, just over two hours from Kyoto (or Osaka) by Kinki Nippon Limited Express.

TOBA

Women pearl divers: the phrase, which summons up only the vaguest of images, stole into one's brain in early childhood, along with the hairy *Ainu* and the Abominable Snowman. There's something mysterious and bewitching about them: the lung power, the fishlike grace, some dis-

tant link with mermaids perhaps. One longs to know more. And here's the chance. Toba has been a center of the pearl-gathering trade for a long time, and although pearls are now only rarely dived for, there's enough demand for the many and varied sea vegetables on the sea bottom to keep about 3,500 women divers busy.

You can watch them, by an irony which seems to have passed the Japanese by, at a place called Pearl Island, a sort of shrine to the memory of Kokichi Mikimoto, the father of the cultured pearl — the man who

ABOVE: One of Tobe's women pearl divers. A young woman OPPOSITE enters the grounds of Naiku, the inner shrine at Ise, one of the five most holy shrines in Japan.

did more than anyone to put them out of business. They dive there every 40 minutes.

There's an initial disappointment: they don't live up to the disheveled geisha image of Utamaro's *ukiyo-e* print; they're well-wrapped up, middle-aged and they smile nicely. Then, leaving their wooden buckets on the surface, they double over like ducks and disappear for whole minutes, then surface again with a plaintive whistling noise. There is something uncanny and fascinating about it. Elsewhere on the island you can learn how Mikimoto made a fine art, and fortune, out of torturing oysters, and in **Pearl Hall** you can watch the whole process being enacted, with explanations in English. Some visitors will find they learn more about pearls than they ever wanted to know. But the lady pearl divers make up for it.

"She who cannot support her *tete* (husband)," runs one of their popular sayings, "cannot claim the name of *yaya* (wife)." A true pearl of wisdom from some redoubtable women.

WHERE TO STAY

Room rate indications — Budget: ¥5,000 or under. Moderate: ¥ 5,000 to ¥11,000. Average: ¥11,000 to ¥22,000. Expensive: ¥22,000 upwards. A (*) denotes hotels offering Western and Japanese-style rooms.

Kinkairo ((0599) 25-3191 FAX (0599) 25-2360, 1-13-1, Toba. 37 rooms. Rates: average and upward.
Toba Kokusai Hotel Shojitei ((0599) 25-3121 FAX (0599) 21-0054, 1-23-1, Toba. 45 rooms. Rates: average and upward.
Toba Hotel International ((0599) 25-3121 FAX (0599) 21-0054, 1-23-1, Toba. 130* rooms. Rates: average and upward.

ISE

A spectacular 40-minute scheduled bus ride over the hills from Toba (Ise-Shima Skyline bus) brings us to the two shrines of Ise, *Ise Jingu* in Japanese, and the very heart of Shinto, the native religion of Japan.

The Victoria Cross (VC) is the highest military honor which can be awarded in Britain, but the medal itself is only made of gunmetal. Similarly these two shrines, Japan's Holy of Holies, are utterly plain, unpainted and undecorated. They are built in the style which prevailed in the country before Chinese techniques of temple building were transmitted — with protruding poles, thick thatch roofs and unshaped, though perfect, knotless beams. They represent the most primitive architecture in the land, yet the workmanship is sublimely good, and the atmosphere of sanctity and harmony which blows through the forested precincts like a breeze leaves nobody unmoved.

Strangest of all to Westerners coming from the lands of Stonehenge and Chartres, is the fact that the buildings are less than 20 years old. Every 20 years since they were first built they have been reconstructed on adjacent sites. Despite the huge expense it is intended to maintain this custom indefinitely. The last time it happened was in October 1973. The slow work of gathering timber for the next version has already begun.

Two separate shrines, **Naiku** (the inner) and **Geku** (the outer), about six kilometers (four miles) apart, constitute the Ise shrines. While the outer is dedicated to Toyouke-Omikami, the goddess of farms, harvest food and sericulture, the inner is dedicated to the supreme deity of the Shinto pantheon and mythical forebear of the emperor, the sun goddess, Ameterasu-Omikami.

In both shrines the holiest spot is surrounded by four fences and the public is allowed to penetrate only the first of these. No photographs are permitted, and hats and overcoats should be removed. The area within is reserved for the emperor and shrine officials.

In the inner shrine are preserved the three sacred treasures of the imperial family — mirror, sword and jewel. The myth goes that the mirror was given by the sun goddess to her grandson when he came down to rule Japan and to father the ancestors of the present emperor.

It is evident that the Ise shrines mean a lot to the Japanese, even the very large number whose belief is faint or nonexistent. The grounds of the shrines are immaculately clean and quiet — no rubbish, no signs, no Coke machines, no candy-floss merchants. The Japanese can create a spotlessly beauti-

ful environment when they try; one only wishes they tried more often.

A small but much-loved sideshow in this area is the sight of the **wedded rocks** in the sea, a kilometer (a half mile) from Futami-no-Ura station on the JR line between Ise and Toba. They are linked by a length of sacred straw rope which is replaced in a ceremony that occurs on January 5 every year. They are taken to symbolize Izanagi and Izanami, mythological creators of Japan. They look fine with the sun rising behind them —patriotic imagery which requires no explanation.

TOURING TOBA AND ISE

A number of regular tours of Honshu include a visit to Toba and Ise in their itineraries. JTB's five-day tour starting from Tokyo and visiting Hakone and Pearl Island on the way to Kyoto and Nara involves a night and the best part of a day in the area. The JTB also offers a full-day tour of the area which starts from both Kyoto and Osaka and winds up in Osaka or Tokyo. The fare for this tour, which departs four times weekly — Mondays, Tuesdays, Wednesdays and Fridays from mid-March to the end of November — is adult ¥145,000, child ¥129,000 (four lunches included).

For information on Toba and Ise, contact the Tourism department of Ise City Hall ((0596) 23-1111. They have details of hiking courses to see wild birds, wooded areas, and into the hills, as well as details of temples and other cultural sites.

WHERE TO STAY

Ise-shima Youth Hostel ((05995) 5-0226, 1219-80, Anagawa, Isobe-cho, Shima-gun. 120 beds. Rates: inexpensive (¥5,000 and under).

HIMEJI

Another popular spot which is an easy journey from Kyoto is the old castle town of Himeji, beyond the port city of Kobe to the southwest.

Himeji is about two an a half hours by JR train from Kyoto, and its Shirasagi-jo Castle is undoubtably the finest in Japan. The name means "White Heron," for the pure white castle floats above the town as gracefully as a bird of that name.

A great many Japanese castles were "restored" in ferroconcrete during the 1950s and '60s, some of them in places where nothing but a plan of the castle remained. This was doubtless good for civic pride (and the construction industry), but it's often a little depressing for visitors, especially when the interior is decked out with lifts and air-conditioning. There are no such disappointments in store at Himeji. The eight-year repair job completed in 1964 was done with care, and the lavish lifestyle of the original sixteenth-century inhabitants can be readily imagined.

Visit in October and you may be lucky enough to catch the town's **Kenka Matsuri** (Fighting Festival). See FESTIVALS, page 117, for more details. The castle is a 15-minute walk from Himeji station. Going further west we leave the Kinki district and enter Chugoku, "the middle country" as this vitally central region is rightly named.

Here the relatively unchanged northern coast contrasts with the intensive industrial activity of the south, which faces the once-beautiful but now heavily exploited Inland Sea. Yet this southern area, fronting the northern coast of the island of Shikoku, retains a lot of beauty and history too.

WHERE TO STAY

Hotel Claire Higasa ((0792) 243421 FAX (0792) 893729, 22 Jyunishomae-cho, Himeji-shi. Rates: Moderate (¥5,000 to ¥11,000).

KURASHIKI

Kurashiki is a clean and prosperous town near the city of Okayama, 159 km (99 miles) from Kobe. One section of the town (the "Historical Area") has a strong and peculiar charm which is almost enough to justify a visit: while unmistakably Oriental, it has the atmosphere of an ideal village somewhere in rural Europe, though one can't say

quite where. Could it be mainland Greece? Spain? Or southeast England?

The reason for this is the architecture, the sturdy, handsome whitewashed granaries, with thick plaster walls and charming lattice decorations, which dominate this area. Formerly used for storing rice, they are now lived in and evidently much loved by their owners. They lend the place a coherence and harmony you don't expect to find in Japan.

Then suddenly you are stopped dead — a Greek temple, in stone! This is the **Ohara Art Gallery**, and it looks remarkably at home among the rice granaries.

Kurashiki's museums are the other reason why a visit can be highly recommended. There are three of them in this area:

The **Ohara Art Gallery** houses a fabulous collection of Western art, including works by El Greco, Rodin and Picasso. Japanese works of various types and other Oriental pieces are among recent additions.

Kurashiki Folkcraft Museum close by is housed in four granaries, and exhibits include folkcraft from Japan and elsewhere. **Kurashiki Archeological Museum** opposite the Folkcraft Museum has over 1,400 archeological relics from this area of Japan.

A pleasant stream fringed with weeping willows, excellent souvenir shops and

Himeji (White Heron) Castle seems to float above the town with the same grace as the local herons do.

friendly locals add three extra reasons for putting Kurashiki on your itinerary. The good (not cheap) souvenirs include basket-work, woodwork and pots. There is also a delicious local preserve, persimmons (*kaki*) bound tightly in rope. The locally produced *sake* is also recommended.

Only one section of Kurashiki is interest-ing, so go there directly. It's only 10 minutes on foot from the town center. Leave the sta-tion by the main exit and follow the raised walkway past the Terminal Hotel building as far as you can go. Descend, go straight ahead at the traffic lights, keep walking to the third set of lights, then turn left. You've arrived.

INFORMATION AND TOURS

There's an Information Center at Kurashiki Station ((086) 426-8681, and another in the Historical Area ((086) 422-0542. A visit to Kurashiki is included in the JTB's seven-day Japan's Highlights package tour.

WHERE TO STAY

Room rate indications — Budget: ¥5,000 or under. Moderate: ¥5,000 to ¥11,000. Average: ¥11,000 to ¥22,000. Expensive: ¥22,000 and up. A (*) denotes hotels offering Western and Japanese-style rooms.

Kurashiki Kokusai Hotel ((0864) 22-5141 FAX (0864) 422-5192, 1-1-44, Chuo. 106* rooms. Rates: average and upward.
Kurashiki Youth Hostel ((0864) 22-7355, 1537-1, Mukoyama. 70 beds. Rates: inex-pensive.

OKAYAMA

Sixteen kilometers (10 miles) east of Kura-shiki is the slightly larger city of **Okayama**, which has one of Japan's three most famous gardens. Called **Korakuen**, it's a brief one and a half kilometer (one mile)-bus ride from the station and is a celebrated example of a garden for strolling. In fact, its grassy ex-panses give it a slightly occidental feeling, but this is mitigated by the waterfalls, tea cottages and carefully tended pine, maple, plum and cherry trees. The garden was laid

out in 1700. The nearby castle, however, which heightens the picturesque mood of the place, is a reconstruction dating from 1966.

For further information on the city con-tact the Information Center ((086) 222-2912 at the JR station (main entrance).

WHERE TO STAY

Room rate indications — Budget: ¥5,000 or under. Moderate: ¥5,000 to ¥11,000. Average: ¥11,000 to ¥22,000. Expensive: ¥22,000 and up. A (*) denotes hotels offering Western and Japanese-style rooms.

Okayama Tokyu Hotel ((086) 233-2411 FAX (086) 223-8763, 3-2-18 Daiku, Okayama. 237 rooms. Rates: average.
Okayama Youth Hostel ((086) 2522-0651, 1-7-6 Tsukura-cho, Okayama. 65 beds. Rates: inexpensive.
Matsunoki Ryokan ((086) 253-4111 FAX (086) 253-4110, 19-1 Ekimotocho, Okayama-shi. 58* rooms. Rates: moderate.

HIROSHIMA

Some 150 km (93 miles) further west along this coast brings us to Hiroshima.

To people all over the world Hiroshima has come to mean far more than the sum of its parts since it was attacked with an atom bomb by the United States of America in 1945. It is one of the few places in the world to which people flock regardless of the fact that there is almost nothing to see, and that the few "attractions" are more like repulsions.

Hiroshima and Nagasaki, it could be said, are all that has kept the world straight for the past 40-odd years: two victims exhibited at the entrance to the nuclear road, whose horrible scars have deterred us from ventur-ing further. In other words there is very little for the visitor in Hiroshima, but it will and should remain a must on any tour of Japan for the indefinite future.

The salient facts are that on August 6, 1945 at 8:15 AM a single American bomber drop-ped an atomic bomb over the city. When it exploded at a height of about 500 m (1,600 ft) the temperature in the vicinity rose to 30,000°C (54,000°F). The city center was de-stroyed instantly and, of the population of

344,000 (1940 census), about 200,000 lost their lives. Many of those who survived were later to die prematurely of leukemia and other radiation-induced diseases.

These facts and many others, along with paintings, models and debris from the blast, are gathered together in the **Peace Memorial Museum** in **Peace Park (Heiwa Koen),** and this is the place for which visitors should make a beeline (take a bus or tram from the station). The entrance fee is very low, the captions are in English, and the display is vivid.

The museum building and the cenotaph outside are nothing to write home about. Far from evoking the disaster, they show the pitiful inadequacy of the vocabulary of modern architecture in the face of it. The statue in Nagasaki's Peace Park is a much braver and more powerful attempt.

Christians will want to see the **Memorial Cathedral for World Peace** near the station, constructed in 1954 as a result of the efforts of a Belgian priest who survived the blast.

And that's about all. Hiroshima is once again a large and flourishing provincial city, but there is nothing much else to see or to do. However, less than an hour away is a spot which is a balm to the soul after the rigors of Hiroshima and the Peace Museum:

Japan: The Broad Highway

Miyajima Island. You should make that your next destination.

For more on Hiroshima see CONSIDER HIROSHIMA, page 28 in TOP SPOTS.

WHERE TO STAY

Room rate indications — Budget: ¥5,000 or under. Moderate: ¥5,000 to ¥11,000. Average: ¥11,000 to ¥22,000. Expensive: ¥22,000 and up. A (*) denotes hotels offering Western and Japanese-style rooms. A (ß) denotes business hotels with mostly single rooms.

Hiroshima Tokyu Inn (ß) ((082) 244-0109 FAX (082) 245-4467. 3-17, Komachi, Naka-ku. 284* rooms. Rates: moderate.
Hiroshima Station Hotel ((082) 262-3201 FAX (082) 263-4021, 2-37, Matsubaracho, Minami-ku. 153* rooms. Rates: moderate.
Hiroshima Youth Hostel ((082) 221-5343, 1-13-6, Ushita-shin-machi, Higashi-ku. 104 beds. Rates: inexpensive.
Mitakiso ((082) 237-1402 FAX (082) 237-1403, 1-7, Mitaki 0machi, Nishi-ku. 12 rooms. Rates: average and upward.

Two views of Hiroshima's atomic bomb dome and arched cenotaph. Despite it being devoid of traditional tourist attractions, Hiroshima remains firmly on most people's itineraries, if no more than a place to contemplate the atrocities of atomic warfare.

MIYAJIMA

The easiest way to Miyajima is by JR train from Hiroshima station to Miyajima-guchi. From there to the island it is a short ferry ride. Ferries operated by both JR and a private company do the run, but the price and journey time are the same.

Miyajima is a wooded and mountainous island with more monkeys and deer than people. Its most famous feature is visible from the ferry when you embark: a large and elabo-

where they are built. Shinto works in reverse: the air of holiness comes first. It is that which often induces the building of the shrine, and such is the case here. Miyajima is a holy island.

After exploring the shrine — its *noh* stage is the oldest in Japan — wander in the park which covers the hill immediately behind it. Full of Japanese maples, this area is supremely beautiful in autumn, but at any season when it's not too crowded the meandering walks, the cries of birds and the heavy scent of flowers make it a charming place.

rate red *torii* (shrine gate) set in the sea. You will probably have seen it before in guide books or on postcards. This is the gateway to **Itsukushima Shrine**, the island's main attraction. If you pass the ferry trip to the island with your nose in this book you will miss the view popularly believed to be one of the three most beautiful in Japan. It's certainly very pretty.

The island has a strongly numinous atmosphere, like the shrines at Ise Jingu. In the West churches can, if they are beautiful enough, lend an air of holiness to the places

A ropeway takes visitors up to the highest point in the island. The base station is located near the top of the park. Ask for "ropeway" and you will be pointed in the right direction. It's not cheap — ¥1,500 — but it's worth it for the views: Hiroshima on the way up and the silvery waters of the Island Sea from the top. There's a monkey park at the top, too, while down near the harbor and the shrine deer wander freely, as at Nara.

Miyajima can be done in half a day, but if you're feeling razzled from too much city why not stay the night and take the time to unwind? There are plenty of places to stay — hotels, *ryokan* and a youth hostel. You won't find many prettier places in Japan — or anywhere else.

ABOVE: A view over the very distinctive shrine on Miyajima and back to the mainland. The famous *torii* gate OPPOSITE in the sea.

WHERE TO STAY

Room rate indications — Budget: ¥5,000 or under. Moderate: ¥5,000 to ¥11,000. Average: ¥11,000 to ¥22,000. Expensive: ¥22,000 and up. A (*) denotes hotels offering Western and Japanese-style rooms.

Hiroshima Miyajimaguchi Youth Hostel ((0829) 56-1444, 1-4-14 Miyajimaguchi, Ono-cho, Saiki-gun. 7 rooms. Rates: inexpensive. **Kamefuku** ((0829) 44-2111 FAX (075) 44-2554, 849, Miyajima-cho, Saeki-gun. 70 rooms. Rates: expensive.

TOURING HIROSHIMA AND MIYAJIMA

JTB organizes a full-day tour to Hiroshima and Miyajima which leaves from Kyoto or Osaka on the morning of every Sunday, Tuesday, Friday and Saturday between mid-March and end of November (minimum two people). These two destinations are also included in the JTB's six- and seven-day Japan's highlights tours. Adult fare for the one-day tour is ¥46,000 (child ¥38,000).

NORTH COAST

While the south coast of western Honshu has the most famous sightseeing spots, it also has a great concentration of industry. The north coast is less spectacularly endowed in both respects: placid, rural, with only a few special attractions. Traveling along the coast is simple — a JR line runs all the way from Tsuruga, north of Lake Biwa (some two hours north of Kyoto) to Shimonoseki at the southern tip of Honshu.

The noteworthy spots along the way are: **Amanohashidate**, about three hours by train from both Kyoto and Tsuruga, one of the three most scenic spots in the country, along with Miyajima (near Hiroshima) and Matsushima (near Sendai).

The attraction lies in the pine tree-dotted sandbar which stretches across the entrance of Miyazu Bay and which, when inspected upside down looking through one's legs, is indistinguishable from the sky. It's a frisson which may well be overrated. The best view is from **Kasamatsu Park** accessible from

Amanohashidate by bus and ferry. Amanohashidate means "Bridge of Heaven."

TOTTORI

Travel along the coast for another three hours and you come to **Tottori**, famous for its 16 km (10 miles) strip of sand dunes east of the city, the uncanny atmosphere of which lent such power to the classic Japanese film *Woman in the Dunes* (based on the novel by Kobo Abe, available in translation).

West of town there is bathing and surfing at Hawai Beach (accessible via JR's San-in main line; get off at Kurayoshi, then it's 20 minutes by bus). A short way further west again are Kaike Spa and Sakaimoto City, both boasting extensive marine pleasures.

Indeed, the whole region between Tottori and Sakaimoto City is a wonderful mixture of bathing beaches and dunes, hot water spa towns, and tree-covered mountains of a modest height inland. There are nine golf courses, four marinas, a dozen swimming beaches, skiing grounds for winter, and innumerable camp sites. It deserves to be better known.

Between Hawai and Kaike Spa stand a number of mountains including Mt. Daisen (1,711 m or 5,700 ft), the highest peak in the area. Other summits of prominence in the region are Mt. Hyonosen (1,510 m or 5,330 ft) near Tottori, and Mt. Mitoku (900 m or 3,000 ft).

In the Mt. Daisen area alone there is skiing in winter (at Masumizi Kogen), a whistling-swan sanctuary (at Yonago Mizutori Koen), and a winter ice-sculpture competition (Daisen Yuki-to Maturi) in late January.

More information about all these, plus details of accommodation (often in French-style "pensions" at ¥7,000 a night and under), is available from the Tourism Section of the Tottori Prefecture's Commercial and Labor Department ((0857) 26-7237.

MATSUE

Some three hours further west is the city of **Matsue**, known for its small but charming seventeenth-century castle. It's open from 8:30 AM to 5 PM, and entrance is ¥400. Nearby is the regional museum (*Matsue Kyodo Kan*).

The nineteenth-century American writer and Japanophile Lafcadio Hearn lived here, and his home and effects have been preserved in the **Lafcadio Hearn Museum** (open 8:30 AM to 5 PM, entrance ¥250). Exhibits include the tall desk he made use of to bring books and paperwork nearer to his one good eye.

There's a fairly helpful Matsue City Tourist Information Office ((0852) 21-4034 at Matsue JR Station.

Inland from the industrial town of Masuda, some two hours further on, is the station of **Tsuwano**, northern terminus of the Yamaguchi line to **Ogori** (one stop east of Shimonoseki on the *shinkansen*), one of the only two lines in the country plied by steam trains (*esu-eru* — SL — for steam locomotive in Japanese). The service operates from August to December, but not every day; check with the TIC for current details.

HAGI

Back on the coast, 90 minutes from Masuda, is the thriving pottery city of **Hagi**, renowned for the delicate gray glaze of its teaware which grows richer and deeper with use. The potteries are in the Shoin-jinja area, accessible by bus from Higashi-Hagi station. The remains of a castle and some old streets and houses add to Hagi's interest: it's probably the single most worthwhile spot along this coast.

There's good swimming at Kikugahama beach, between the harbor and Mt. Shizuki on the north side of town.

August is a good time to visit Hagi — there are five festivals during the one month. Ring the **Hagi City Tourist Bureau** on ((0838) 25-1750 for details.

Shimonoseki, at the end of the line, is the starting-point for the thrice-weekly ferry to Pusan in South Korea. It's also where most of the *fugu*, the famous poisonous blowfish, comes from. But to sample that it may be as well to cross over to Kyushu.

Where to Stay
Business Hotel Orange ((0838) 25-5880 FAX (0838) 25-7690, 370-48 Hijiwara, Hagi-shi. 32 rooms. Rates: moderate (¥ 5,000 to ¥11,000).

KYUSHU

Japan's Honshu, "Main Island," has most of the people, cities and industries which are propelling Japan at full speed into the twenty-first century. It's very exciting, but there are times when you want to escape. The best thing to do then is to jump the island.

You can go north to Hokkaido or south to Kyushu. Either place offers space, peace and country ways, but Hokkaido is Japan's new territory, with a history that goes back only a little over a century.

Kyushu on the other hand, full of splendid natural beauty, also has a long and rich history and offers some of the most rewarding sightseeing in the country. As the nearest point in Japan to the continent, it was in the early days the jumping-off point for immigrants from China and Korea. Recurrently since then it has served as the funnel through which foreign wisdom penetrated the country. At the beginning of the modern period many Kyushu men were in the vanguard of the reform movement.

Kyushu, then, is fully alive to the modern world, but particularly in the south it has so far been spared the intensity of development which marks Honshu. The cities with their colorful trams have a friendly, manageable feeling, and they don't stretch for hundreds of miles. The landscape beyond varies from the domesticated to the stupendous. Much of it is unsullied.

FUKUOKA/HAKATA

Entering Kyushu from the north, through Kitakyushu and Fukuoka, does not fill the visitor with gleeful anticipation, for this part of the island is solidly industrial. The Kitakyushu area, an agglomeration of five cities that were formerly discrete, has been known for centuries for the quality of its steel, and this tradition is upheld in the city's modern steel mills.

Fukuoka is the island's largest city and another center of industrial activity. Strictly speaking, the name Fukuoka describes the section of the city west of the Naka River, while the city on the east side is called Hakata — which is also the name of the railway station, the southwestern terminus of the Tokaido *shinkansen*.

Fukuoka is also a major port, while the airport, blessedly close to the city center, offers the cheapest and shortest air link to Pusan in South Korea.

The area's Korean connection is also manifest in the pottery-making centers near the city, Koishiwara and Onda, where Korean potters were originally employed.

Fukuoka's few sightseeing attractions need not detain you long: the rest of the island to the south offers many more sights.

But the city has two distinctive and very different features which should be mentioned before we pass on.

Fifteen minutes on foot north of Hakata station is **Shofukuji**, a temple of the Rinzai Zen sect, which is supposed to have been founded in 1195. If it was, it is the oldest Zen temple in the country. The priest who established it, Eisai, was also responsible for introducing tea into Japan from China.

On a delta about the same distance west of the station is the **Higashi-Nakasu** section of town, the main amusement quarter. As well as the usual conventional entertainment, bars and restaurants, the area has what are believed to be some of the most *risqué* clubs in the land.

Fukuoka is a major transportation center, offering ready access to all places of interest on the island.

How to Get There

The city of Fukuoka in the north of the islands is the main gateway to Kyushu for travelers from Tokyo. Flying to Fukuoka Airport takes an hour and 40 minutes from Tokyo and one hour from Osaka. The Tokaido *shinkansen* from Tokyo via Kyoto and Osaka terminates at Hakata, Fukuoka's station, and the journey from Tokyo takes about six hours. If you start from Kyoto it's possible to take a very nice boat trip through the Inland Sea from Osaka or Kobe, terminating at Beppu.

Where to Stay

Room rate indications — Budget: ¥5,000 or under. Moderate: ¥5,000 to ¥11,000. Average: ¥11,000 to ¥22,000. Expensive: ¥22,000 and up. A (*) denotes hotels offering Western and Japanese-style rooms.

Hotel New Otani Hakata ((092) 714-1111 FAX (092) 715-5658, 1-1-2 Watanaabe-dori, Chuo-ku. 414 rooms. Rates: expensive.
Hakata Green Hotel ((092) 451-4111 FAX (092) 451-4508, 4-4, Hakataeki-Chuo-gai, Hakata-ku. 783 rooms. Rates: moderate.
Mitsui Urban Hotel Fukuoka ((092) 451-5111 FAX (092) 451-51-5, 2-8, Hakata-ekimae, Hakata-ku. 310* rooms. Rates: moderate.

BEPPU

Beppu is one of the biggest hot spring resorts in Japan. Every day as much as 100,000 kiloliters (220 million gallons) of hot water bubbles up out of its 3,795 different orifices, and a large town has sprung up to take advantage of this amazing bounty.

Like women pearl divers, mixed bathing has long been one of Japan's semi-legendary attractions for the foreign male, and Beppu has it, or so the rumor goes. It's to be found at **Hoyurando**, a hotel-style resort just a few kilometers to the west of the "hells", naturally occurring pools of boiling water of various lurid colors, which are the town's most famous draw.

At Hoyurando, there are two outdoor pools, the best in Beppu, or so it's said, and both are mixed. It is not necessary to stay at the hotel to use the bath.

One hotel worth splashing out on is the enormous **Suginoi Hotel** (see contacts below under BEPPU, WHERE TO STAY), renowned for its vast baths, housed in glazed structures the size of aircraft hangars (one for each sex) and with the atmosphere of a tropical hot house in a botanical garden. There are dozens of baths of different sizes, shapes and temperatures, and ornaments include a

General Information
Beppu has a special Foreign Tourist Information Service ((0977) 23-1119, known as the "SOS". There's also an office of the City Tourist Association ((0977) 24-2838 which you'll find at the railway station.

Where to Stay
Room rate indications — Budget: ¥5,000 or under. Moderate: ¥5,000 to ¥11,000. Average: ¥11,000 to ¥22,000. Expensive: ¥22,000 and up. A (*) denotes hotels offering Western and Japanese-style rooms.

waterfall, a slide, a *torii* (gate) and a revolving image of a benignly smiling Buddha.

Also available at Beppu is the famous hot sand bath, *sunayu*. This is to be found at **Takegawa**, near Beppu station. One of the ladies at the bath digs a hole in the naturally hot sand for you. Having undressed, and not forgetting your little towel, climb in and the lady will heap more sand around you, up to the neck if you like. The unearthly feeling of relaxation as the heat penetrates to your bones has to be experienced to be believed. And, surprisingly, it's not expensive — only a few hundred yen.

(For more about baths and bath etiquette see the section under BATHS, page 121 in THE CULTURE OF JAPAN.)

Japan: The Broad Highway

Beppu Youth Hostel ((0977) 23-4116, Kankaiji-onsen. 150 beds. Rates: inexpensive.
Hotel Shin-Nogami ((0977) 23-2141, 1-8-8, Kitahama. 31 rooms. Rates: average and upward.
Shoha-so ((0977) 66-001-3, 14-32, Shohaen-machi. 10 rooms. Rates: moderate.
Suginoi Hotel ((0977) 24-1141 FAX (0977) 21-0010, 2272, Oaza Minami-Tateishi. 600* rooms. Rates: average and upward.

OPPOSITE: Fukuoka/Hakata, a major port, a central hub for exploring the island, and Japan's raunchy city. Above: Buried under the sands at Ibusuki — one of the favorite Japanese spa towns.

MOUNT ASO

The countryside between Beppu on the east and Kumamoto on the west is among the most dramatic on the island. While it can be enjoyed from the train, the trip along Yamanami Highway, which links Beppu with Kumamoto and continues to Nagasaki, is famous for its marvelous views. Whichever way you decide to go, the high point of the trip is undoubtably Mt. Aso, Japan's most dynamically active volcano.

The first thing the visitor notices on arriving in the small town of Aso is how extraordinarily flat the tops of the surrounding mountains are; and they are all of uniform height. The reason is that you are standing in the largest volcanic crater of its kind in the world, 24 km (15 miles) long, 19 km (11 miles) wide and 120 km (75 miles) in circumference. Those mountains are the crater's rim. The size of the actual volcano of which in very ancient days this was the active crater boggles the mind. Mt. Fuji would have been a mere molehill next to it.

Within this huge crater, as you can see if you take the bus from near the station up to the still-active peak, the countryside is lush and green. Beef cattle and horses graze on the rich grass (raw horsemeat, sliced thin and eaten like raw fish, is the local delicacy). A small volcano, grass-green and with an indentation in the crater which might have been made by a huge thumb, comes into view. Round a corner and beyond a lake is the **Aso Volcanic Museum**, opened in 1982. Video cameras are trained on the active crater: when an eruption takes place it is possible to watch it on screens at the museum.

The bus terminates at Aso-zan Nishi (also West station) from where it's a five-minute ropeway ride or a 15-minute walk to the edge of the crater. As you climb, the landscape grows grim, gray and lifeless. Concrete shelters with massive walls and roofs begin to appear near the road. On the rubble of the most recent eruptions wisps of grass hang tenuously. Even so, the vast size and desolation of the crater come as a shock; despite our knowledge of nuclear weapons, it is hard to comprehend power that creates and destroys on this scale. It's very impressive.

At the bottom of the crater is the bright green lake, steaming continuously. This, the largest of the mountain's five craters, is 600 m (1,964 ft) across and 160 m (524 ft) deep. Black smoke pours out of it and occasionally deep rumblings can be heard.

The volcano is as deadly as it looks. Dozens have died under the lava during the past few decades. In the 1979 eruption three died and 16 were injured. Up to that time it had been possible to approach the volcano from the west, skirt around the crater (by bus) and descend on the east side (or vice versa), and other guide books describe this possibility. However, since the last disaster, the eastern approach has been closed and there is now only one way up and down.

The chances of being done in by the volcano are of course very slight. And the views make it a worthwhile risk.

There are several places to stay in the area, both in Aso itself and in the nearby spas. For more details, obtain the TIC's mini-guide (*Kumamoto and Mt. Aso*, MG-073) to the area before setting out.

Where to Stay

Room rate indications — Budget: ¥5,000 or under. Moderate: ¥5,000 to ¥11,000. Average: ¥11,000 to ¥22,000. Expensive: ¥22,000 upwards. A (*) denotes hotels offering Western and Japanese-style rooms.

Aso Kanko Hotel ((09676) 7-0311 FAX (09676) 7-1889, Yunotani, Choyo-mura, Aso-gun. 119 rooms. Rates: average and upward.
Aso Youth Hostel ((0967) 34-0804, 922-2, Bochu, Aso-machi, Aso-gun. 60 beds. Rates: inexpensive.
Asonotsukasa ((09673) 4-0811 FAX (09673) 4-0816, 1230, Oaza Kurogawa, Aso-machi, Aso-gun. 134* rooms. Rates: average and upward.

KUMAMOTO

One hour by train from Aso is Kumamoto, the major city in the area. The castle is reconstructed, built around 1960, but is celebrated for its beauty nonetheless. To get there ride the tram (streetcar) from the train station for 20 minutes to City Hall (*Shiyakusho-mae*), then walk (five minutes). Admission is ¥500, and the castle is open from 8:30 AM to 4:30 PM (winter) and 5:30 PM (summer).

The city also boasts a lovely garden, 20 minutes by bus from Kotsu Center in the middle of town: **Suizenji Park**. It was laid out in 1632 and contains skillful reproductions of famous sights such as Mt. Fuji and Lake Biwa. There is torch-lit Noh theater at the park's Izumi Shrine on the first Saturday evening of August.

The city's most famous temple is **Honmyoji**. It's the main temple on Kyushu for Buddhism's Nichiren sect. Admission is

Kumamoto Shiritsu Youth Hostel ((096) 352-2441, 5-15-55 Shimazaki-machi. 64 beds. Rates: inexpensive.

Hotel Takeya ((096) 325-6840 FAX (096) 326-6841, 2-7-1, Kyo-machi. 12 rooms. Rates: moderate.

West of Kumamoto is an area of mountains, islands and tranquil waters known as **Unzen-Amakusa National Park**. There are several picturesque ways of negotiating it by ferry and bus, and details will be provided by the Kumamoto City Tourist Information Center on ((096) 352-3743.

¥300. To get there, take the Nº 12 bus from the downtown Kotsu Center, gate six, to Honmyoji-mae, then walk five minutes.

Where to Stay

Room rate indications — Budget: ¥5,000 or under. Moderate: ¥5,000 to ¥11,000. Average: ¥11,000 to ¥22,000. Expensive: ¥22,000 and up. A (*) denotes hotels offering Western and Japanese-style rooms.

Kumamoto Daiichi Hotel ((096) 325-5151 FAX (096) 333-7354, 3-3-85, Motoyama-machi. 84* rooms. Rates: moderate.

Kumamoto Hotel Castle ((096) 326-3311 FAX (096) 326-3324, 4-2 Joto-machi. 208 rooms. Rates: average and upward.

NAGASAKI

There is one compelling reason for passing this way: it's the road to Nagasaki. A provincial city with a richer history and with more to see than many capitals, Nagasaki is a must. It is simply one of the most fascinating places in all of Japan.

Nagasaki was the world's second A-bomb victim, but unlike Hiroshima it was not completely flattened. In fact, far more than any other Japanese city, Nagasaki is a meeting-place of peoples and cultures, a vivid, city-wide museum of the nation's interaction,

Oura Catholic Church near Glover Park, built in 1864, is the oldest Gothic-style structure in Japan.

during the last 400 years, with the outside world. The city's steep green hills bristle with spires, towers, statues and landmarks.

The city was first created as a port of entry for Western trade in the sixteenth century. It rapidly became a center of both trade and Christianity. That extrovert phase in Japan's history turned out to be a brief interlude, and among the events which brought it to an end the crucifixion of 20 Japanese and six Portuguese Christians in the city was one of the most painful. There is a relief showing the 26 saint-like martyrs outside a museum three minutes' walk up the hill opposite the station. The museum has some fascinating early European maps of Japan.

Even when the rest of Japan had severed all contact with the Western world, Nagasaki held on by a single thread. That thread was a small man-made island in the harbor called **Dejima** and here, throughout the nation's 250 years of isolation, a colony of Dutch merchants was maintained and confined.

It's hardly surprising, then, that Puccini's opera *Madame Butterfly* (1904) should have been set in Nagasaki — though not actually in Thomas Glover's house (see below) as some visitors like to believe. The English writer Rudyard Kipling was there too, in 1888, when he found the city characterized by "perfect cleanliness" and "rare taste". He went on to remark that the landscape was one of delicate pastel shades. Contemporary British novelist Kazuo Ishiguro took up this line when he called his first novel containing memories of Nagasaki (his birthplace), *A Pale View of Hills* (1983).

Dejima is no longer an island — it's just two stops on the Number One tram in the direction of Shokakuji-Shita from Nagasaki station — but reconstructions of the old buildings remain as a reminder of the stubbornness of the shogun, and the even more stubborn imperatives of trade.

Nagasaki is an exception to the rule in a country where religions habitually lie down in harmony together: not far from the martyrs' monument is a Buddhist image which clashes violently with it — on purpose, one suspects. It is a high aluminium figure of Kannon, Buddhist goddess of mercy, and it stands on a tortoise's back. It also helps to remind us that tortoiseshell is one of the city's

craft products. A shop which sells delicately crafted tortoiseshell hair clasps and sailing boats is to be found near **Megane (Spectacles) Bridge** — so called because it was Japan's first two-arched bridge.

Other figures of Kannon — tiny, these, and made of porcelain — can be found in the **Jurokuban-kan Museum** by **Glover Park**. They hold infants in their arms and their startling similarity to figures of the Virgin and Child is not accidental. These images were used by the "hidden Christians" who, in small islands south of Nagasaki, persisted in their faith throughout the 250 years of the Tokugawa period during which Christianity was proscribed.

As we have noted, Nagasaki was built for trade with the West, and the buildings which are the focus of interest in Glover Park commemorate the second great wave of foreign trading which ushered in Japan's modern age. One of the pioneers was an English entrepreneur called Thomas Blake Glover, who settled in the city. He built a pretty little house with a splendid view of Nagasaki Harbor and lived there with his Japanese wife and two children.

It was the first Western-style home in Japan and has been preserved as his shrine. Japanese visitors are impressed by the gigantic size of the rooms, while Westerners find it diminutive and charming — rather Oriental, in fact, with its delicate posts and fan-shaped rooms on the harbor side. Perhaps Glover thought he had designed a Japanese house.

Glover Park is the one place to go if there is only time to visit one place in Nagasaki — not so much because of Glover but because of the two museums. They are a treasure-trove of objects, pictures, pots and everyday things of all sorts from all phases of the city's history.

Nagasaki was the most convenient port of entry to Japan for Chinese as well as Westerners, and Chinese culture has penetrated deep into the city's customs and fabric. The bright greens, reds and golds of Chinese Ming and Ching architecture can be seen here and there. A new school of Chinese Zen Buddhism arrived in the city in the seventeenth century and its temples look interestingly garish and extravagant in Japan. There's a small **Chinatown** in the Tsukimachi district, and some of the city's festivals have a strong Chinese flavor: dragon dances, rowing races and a parade with highly decorated miniature Chinese boats on wheels, packed with musicians, which are pushed through the streets and whirled around at tremendous speed by gangs of muscular boys.

If you miss the festival itself, between October 7 and 9, console yourself with a visit to the museum in Glover Park where the boats are stored out of season. If you are lucky you may catch a film of the festival at the same place.

And if you're interested in the ancient route linking Nagasaki and Tokyo, the *Nagasaki Kaido,* you can access details on the Internet; WEBSITE http://www.edu.nagasaki-u.ac.jp/private/fukada/soft/kaidu2/ol.htm.

Nagasaki's most recent and tragic claim to fame was the disaster which occurred on August 9, 1945, three days after Hiroshima, when the second atom bomb to be used was exploded by the Americans 500 m (1,600 ft) above Matsuyama in the north of the city, "instantly mimicking the appearance of another sun in the air." Nagasaki was only chosen as a target when cloud and smoke prevented the bombing of Kokura in Kitakyushu. The city was a hapless victim, and nearly 80,000 of her citizens died.

Matsuyama is today the site of memorials to this event, the **Peace Park** with its huge statue, and the **Atomic Bomb Museum**, also known as the **International Culture Hall** (opened here in 1996). The statue is a powerful injunction not to forget and deserves to be seen. Pressures to have it replaced were resisted when the decision was made to place an alternative work, a mother and child by Tominaga Naoki, the Nagasaki-born sculptor, in another part of the restyled park in 1997.

You can get to these two places from the train station by Nº 1 tram. Nagasaki's trams (streetcars) are special — specimens have been collected from all over the country, and the varied and colorful fleet now constitutes a sort of moving museum of tram transport. Day tickets are available from any city hotel's reception desk for ¥500. You board the trams

at the back, and pay the ¥100 fare (if you don't have a day ticket) as you leave from the front. Passengers for Glover Park can use the one ticket even though they have to change trams (at Tsukimachi); ask the driver for a *norikae* (transfer ticket).

Where to Stay
Room rate indications — Budget: ¥5,000 or under. Moderate: ¥5,000 to ¥11,000. Average: ¥11,000 to ¥22,000. Expensive: ¥22,000 and up. A (*) denotes hotels offering Western and Japanese-style rooms.

Business Hotel Dejima ((0958) 24-7141 FAX (0958) 24-1603 2-13, Dejima-machi. 44* rooms. Rates: inexpensive.
Nagasaki Grand Hotel ((0958) 23-1234. FAX (0958) 22-1793, 5-3, Manzai-machi. 105* rooms. Rates: average and upward.
Hotel Ibis ((0958) 24-2171 FAX (0958) 25-5582, 8019 Kabashima-machi. Rates: moderate.
Nagasaki Oranda-Zaka Youth Hostel ((0958) 22-2730, 6 -14, Higashi-yamate-cho. 50 beds. Rates: inexpensive.
Hotel Hakuunso ((0958) 26-6307 FAX (0958) 26-4875, 6-22, Kajiya-machi. 40 rooms. Rates: moderate.

GOTO

There are various small islands easily accessible from Nagasaki which make a pleasant excursion. The largest is **Goto** just one hour, 25 minutes by highspeed jet hydrofoil (you can ((0958) 22-9151 for departure times) or three and a half hours by ferry from Nagasaki. You can also fly from Nagasaki Airport to Fukue, Goto's main town. Takahama Beach on the opposite (western) side of the island occupies a splendid situation.

Where to Stay
There is a smallish (100-bed) **Youth Hostel** ((0959) 84-3151 on the northern part of the Goto Island. Rate: inexpensive.

Huis Ten Bosch
This is a resort-cum-theme park on the lines of a seventeenth century Dutch village. It contains a hotel, restaurants, shops and a museum, not to mention canals, boats and windmills. It's an hour and a half by rail from

Nagasaki (or an hour and five minutes by bus), and trains also run there direct from Fukuoka/Hakata.

And of course the Dutch presence in the Nagasaki area is, as we've said, very old. A 30-m (100-ft) flagpole at Dejima, for instance, for centuries regularly flew the Netherlands flag on various important occasions, even during Japan's closed period. During the few years when the Netherlands was annexed by France during the Napoleonic Wars this was thought to be the only site in the world where the Dutch flag was still being publicly

are shameless imitations of popular spots in Hawaii — and the weather's so good they almost pull it off.

Following the east coast of Kyushu south from Beppu, some 150 km (95 miles) you reach the city of Miyazaki. This was one of the semi-legendary centers of Japan's earliest culture and in **Heiwadai Park**, about two kilometers (just over a mile) from the city center, are to be found many *haniwa*, clay figures which have been excavated from nearby burial mounds. Miyazaki has great beaches, too. The **Nichinan Kaigan** area

flown. A reconstruction of the flagpole was erected on the original site in 1997.

General Information

Maps and advice about the city and the adjacent prefecture is available from the Information Center on the left side of the station forecourt. Further information can also be had from the Nagasaki Prefectural Tourist Federation ((0958) 26-9407 or (0958) 28-7875.

MIYAZAKI

The further south you go in Kyushu the brighter and balmier it becomes. The landscape starts to glitter. Palm trees line the streets. Some of the tourist traps around here

stretches for about 100 km (62 miles) south of the city and is one of the best in Japan.

Where to Stay

Room rate indications — Budget: ¥5,000 or under. Moderate: ¥ 5,000 to ¥11,000. Average: ¥11,000 to ¥22,000. Expensive: ¥22,000 upwards. A (*) denotes hotels offering Western and Japanese-style rooms.

Sun Hotel Phoenix ((0985) 39-3131 FAX (0985) 38-1147, 3083, Hamayama, Shioji, Miyazaki 880-01. 296* rooms. Rates: average.
Aoshima Youth Hostel ((0985) 65-1657, 130 Umizoi, Oryuzako. 130 beds. Rates: inexpensive.

KAGOSHIMA

Satsuma oranges come from here—Satsuma was the old name of this region. Many of the samurai who ousted the shogun at the start of Japan's modern period came from this city, the most famous being Saigo Takamori, a giant of a man who committed *seppuku* (*harakiri*) with his comrades in a cave in one of the city's parks when his rebellion against the government failed.

The chief attraction at Kagoshima is the active volcano a brief ferry ride from the city on the island of **Sakurajima**, luring visitors while it threatens the populace. On account of the volcanic dust which frequently spews forth from the crater, Kagoshima people are renowned for carrying umbrellas in all weather. You can't get as close to the active peak, **Minami-dake**, as the bravest might wish: too dangerous, they say.

Where to Stay
Room rate indications — Budget: ¥5,000 or under. Moderate: ¥5,000 to ¥11,000. Average: ¥11,000 to ¥22,000. Expensive: ¥22,000 upwards. A (*) denotes hotels offering Western and Japanese-style rooms. A (ß) denotes business hotels with mostly single rooms.

Kagoshima Daiichi Hotel (ß) ℂ (0992) 55-7591 FAX (0992) 55-0256, 1-4-1, Takashi. 68 rooms. Rates: moderate.
Sakurajima Youth Hostel ℂ (0992) 93-2150, Yokohama, Sakurajima-cho, Kagoshima-gun. 95 beds. Rates: inexpensive.

IBUSUKI

An hour or so down the coast from Kagoshima — trains, buses and hovercraft make the trip — is the popular hot springs resort of Ibusuki. The town is famous for its hot sand baths (see BEPPU, above, for details) and like other similar places is a center for the sybaritic pleasures of the Japanese, with geishas, cabaret shows and plenty of booze to augment the hot bathing.

There is a "Jungle bath" at Ibusuki's enormous **Kanko Hotel**, which is mixed — in theory. There is a ladies' entrance but it doesn't seem to be used much. A number of

foreign visitors have soaked themselves into a stupor waiting for it to open.

There is pretty country in the vicinity of the town, as there is all over southern Kyushu. Volcanic **Mt. Kaimon** lodges in the memory: perfectly shaped, it sits on the coast like a cone of green incense.

Where to Stay
Room rate indications — Budget: ¥5,000 or under. Moderate: ¥5,000 to ¥11,000. Average: ¥11,000 to ¥22,000. Expensive: ¥22,000 and up. A (*) denotes hotels offering Western and Japanese-style rooms.

Ibusuki Iwasaki Hotel ℂ (0993) 22-2131 FAX (0993) 24-3215, 3755, Juni-cho. 428* rooms. Rates: average and upward.
Ibusuki Youth Hostel ℂ (0993) 22-2758, 2-1-20, Yunohama. 96 beds. Rates: inexpensive.
Ibusuki Kanko Hotel ℂ (0993) 22-2131 FAX (0993) 24-3215, 3755, Juni-cho. 200* rooms. Rates: average and upward.

TOURING KYUSHU

The JTB offers four regular tours to Kyushu.

The first two are only really flights from Tokyo plus accommodation (in Kanazawa or Nagasaki); assistance at the airport appears to be the only extra thing you get for your money. It's probably better to fix these sorts of trips up on your own, perhaps with the help of your hotel in Tokyo.

There are, however, sight-seeing tours of half a day that can be booked in addition to these "Fly and Stay" tours. Of course you have to pay again, ¥12,500 for Kanazawa, ¥10,000 for Nagasaki. No lunch is included.

The Dutch presence in Nagasaki dates back a long while. Building on this foreign culture, a resort-cum-theme park, Huis Ten Bosch, has been developed along the lines of a seventeenth-century Dutch village OPPOSITE. It is an excursion which is, probably, more interesting to the Japanese or Asian visitor who may never have encountered the Dutch culture but nevertheless is worth a visit if you are staying in the Goto area.

Japan: Off the Beaten Track

IF YOU FEEL LIKE GETTING out of the tourist rut you are following a great tradition. One hundred years ago Western diplomats delighted in being lugged around the backside of Japan in palanquin. The first person to climb Japan's highest mountain range was an Englishman – the Japanese had never tried it, believing mountains to be infested with goblins — and they've been known as the Japan Alps ever since. The chief pleasure in the life of Chicago University Professor Frederick Starr was storming up Mt. Fuji dressed like a native pilgrim in a white tunic, gaiters and straw sandals and carrying a sunshade, crying *"Rokkon Shojo!"* ("May our senses be purified!") and *"Oyama wa seiten!"* ("May the weather in the mountains be good!").

More recently, British writer Alan Booth took a summer off to walk the entire length of the country from Hokkaido to Kyushu, raising bewildered eyebrows all the way.

The truth that all these pioneers acted on is that there is as much or more of the real Japan to be found outside the tourist traps as in. There are holy mountains (home of crows, kites and mountain ascetics), pretty towns and villages and farms and festivals, carrying on in much the same way as they always have.

Then there are whole regions like Hokkaido which lack historical interest but display facets of the Japanese landscape and character that are almost unknown outside the country.

A hundred years ago there was the fascination of the totally unknown, the absolutely alien — but there was the inconvenience of the unknown to contend with as well. Nowadays, even in the remotest hamlet, there are reminders of Japan's white-hot technology; the microchip factory nestling in the mountains, the robot helping out in the village workshop. But in compensation there is the ease of getting there. Japan's transportation system is among the best in the world, and though the places described below are off the foreign tourist track, the roads leading to them have been well-tramped by the Japanese.

Learning to use this system efficiently takes patience and some basic information. Read TRAVELERS' TIPS before setting out.

TRIPS FROM TOKYO

You've been in Tokyo a few weeks and you're craving greenery. You've seen Nikko, hiked round Hakone, you've paced out every last meter of Yoyogi and Ueno Parks. Where next?

CHICHIBU-TAMA NATIONAL PARK

This park contains bona-fide mountains, it's not hard to get to, and if you set off early it makes a good one-day outing. Several million

other people know this too, so the area is not totally deserted. Beware of sunny Sundays and national holidays.

How to Get There
Take the Chuo line *Tokubetsu Kaisoku* (special express) from Tokyo or Shinjuku to Tachikawa. Change at Tachikawa to the Ome line. Board the Ome line train. Tachikawa is the terminus of only a few Chuo trains.

The Ome line which runs alongside the pretty valley of the River Tama offers two attractive possibilities:
Exploring Mt. Mitake. Get off at Mitake station and either walk or take a bus or taxi to the base of Mt. Mitake. (It takes the best part of an hour to walk it.) From the base you can either walk to the top or take the cable car. There's an old shrine at the top and very pleasant gentle hiking, as well as several *minshuku*, including one which is thatched.

LEFT: Tranquillity in Takamatsu, Shikoku.
ABOVE: The crowded waterfront of Yokohama, one of the world's largest ports.

Idyllic weekends have been idled away on this mountain top.

Nippara Shonyu-do. No, this is not a countrified nude show but a terrific complex of icy caves full of stalactites. Take the Ome line to Okutama, the terminus, then the bus to Shonyu-do. Good hiking around here, too, and places to stay.

Ask the Tokyo TIC for their mini-guide to *Chichibu-Tama National Park* (MG-033) for more detailed information on this area.

Mt. Takao. Though not strictly in this park, 600 m (2,000 ft) high Mt. Takao is also very

accessible. Its attractions are comparable to Mt. Mitake's, with a cable car running to the summit and varied hiking possibilities once you've got there. Convenient stations for the mountain are Takao on JR's Chuo Line, and Takaosan-guchi on the private Keio Line which runs from Shinjuku. The latter is right at the foot of the mountain. Yakuo-in, the temple at the mountain's summit, is said to have been founded in the eighth century.

IZU PENINSULA

Want to swim in the sea? It's lovely and warm but can be mucky (June to September) — in Tokyo Bay the water looks like *miso* (or oxtail) soup. Some of the closest clean beaches are

in the Izu Peninsula, part of the **Fuji-Hakone-Izu National Park**.

Take the *shinkansen* Kodama (not Hikari) from Tokyo to Atami (about 55 minutes). JR and private trains run from Atami via Ito to Shimoda, the peninsula's principal town.

There are noted beaches near Ito in the north of the peninsula, including Usami and Ito itself, and also in the south, near Shimoda: check out **Shirahama** and **Sotoura**.

The railway terminates at Shimoda, but buses will take you round to the pleasantly rustic west coast. If you are lucky your bus

conductress may be wearing a kimono and straw sandals. **Matsuzaki** and **Toi** beaches are known for their bathing.

Atami, at the very top of the peninsula, is one of the nation's most popular hot spring resorts and also boasts an art gallery, the **Museum of Art ℂ** (0557) 84-2511, (MOA) 25 minutes on foot from Atami, 10 minutes by bus. It is run by a religious organization called the Church of World Messianity and apparently has a fine collection of Japanese works of art, including wood block prints and ceramics, many of which are National Treasures and Important Cultural Properties. How and why they found their way into the hands of the Church of World Messianity is for the reader to discover.

There is a fair bit to do here so it's worth asking at the TIC for their mini-guide (MG-037), *The Izu Peninsula*, before setting out. It has comprehensive information on the area.

Where to Stay

Room rate indications — Budget: ¥5,000 or under. Moderate: ¥5,000 to ¥11,000. Average: ¥11,000 to ¥22,000. Expensive: ¥22,000 and up.

Ito Youth Hostel (90557) 45-0224, 1260-125 Kanawa, Ito. Beds: 100. Rates: inexpensive.

Yokohama's **Sankei-en Park** is a landscaped garden on a large scale, and has an excellent collection of old buildings, including tea-ceremony cottages, an aristocrat's villa, a three-story pagoda and a gigantic eighteenth-century farm house. Industrial Yokohama is all around but quite out of sight, until you reach the far end of the park and see huge pink gas tanks.

Also notable is the **Yokohama Doll Museum** (Yokohama-Ningo-no-ie). It's near the Marine Tower containing over 1,700 dolls from all over the world. And the city's **Land-**

Kawana Hotel ((0557) 45-1111 FAX (0557) 45-3834, 1459 Kawana, Ito. 140 rooms. Rates: expensive.
Shimoda Tokyu Hotel ((0558) 22-2411 FAX (0558) 23-2419, 5-12-1, Shimoda City. 117 rooms. Rates: average to expensive.

YOKOHAMA

Yokohama, 30 minutes by train from Tokyo, is the port where a community of Western merchants grew up in the last century. A few of their original houses have been preserved in a place called **The Bluff**. Not far away is Yokohama's **Chinatown**, the largest Chinese community in Japan, boasting many excellent Chinese restaurants.

mark Yokohama, an office tower is, at 296 m (989 ft), the highest building in Japan.

General Information

The Yokohama International Tourist Association has several offices; the most convenient is probably the one at Yokohama Station ((045) 441-7300, open from 10 AM to 4 PM weekdays. An office open at weekends and public holidays can be contacted on ((045) 211-0111.

OPPOSITE LEFT: Watering the pigeons in central Yokohama and OPPOSITE RIGHT pampering the poodle. ABOVE: Testament to an industrialized nation. The port and refinery at Yokohama.

How to Get There

The Tokaido line from Tokyo station takes just 30 minutes to Yokohama. Transport within Yokohama is a bit fussy. A N° 8 bus from the east side of Yokohama station will take you to Marine Tower, a short walk either to The Bluff or to Chinatown, and on to Sankei-en. For the latter get off at Sankei-en-mae bus stop.

In the bus, position yourself close to one of the loud speakers so you can hear when the stop is announced, then press one of the buzzers.

Where to Stay

Room rate indications — Budget: ¥5,000 or under. Moderate: ¥5,000 to ¥11,000. Average: ¥11,000 to ¥22,000. Expensive: ¥22,000 upwards. A (*) denotes hotels offering Western and Japanese-style rooms.

Bund Hotel ((045) 621-1101 FAX (045) 621-1104, 1-2-14, Shin-Yamashita, Naka-ku. 50* rooms. Rates: average and upward.
Hotel Aster ((045) 651-0141 FAX (045) 651-2064, 87, Yamashitacho, Naka-ku. 72* rooms. Rates: average and upward.

ABOVE: Dusk in Yokohama's Sankei-en Park. The perfectly conical peak OPPOSITE of Mt. Fuji.

Sannai Yokohama Hotel ((045) 242-4411 FAX (045) 242-7485, 3-95, Hanasakicho, Naka-ku. 81 rooms. Rates: moderate.
Yamashiroya Ryokan ((045) 231-1146, 2-159, Hinode-cho, Naka-ku. 10 rooms. Rates: moderate.

KAWASAKI

Another collection of interesting old buildings is located on the outskirts of Kawasaki, an industrial city sandwiched between Tokyo and Yokohama. It's called **Niho Minka-en** or Japan Farmhouse Park. In the quiet, wooded grounds are some 20 old thatched farmhouses which have been brought here from various parts of the country. The interiors of many of them may be explored, and upstairs in one is a museum of old farming tools and other equipment.

How to Get There

Take the Odakyu line from Shinjuku to Muko-ga-oka Yuen station, about 30 minutes by express (*kyuko*). Ask a friendly face, "*Nihon Minka-en, doko des' ka?*" ("Where is the Nihon Minka-en?") when you arrive and you will be pointed in the right direction.

Where to Stay

We suggest that you visit the above on a half day trip from your hotel or hostel in either Yokohama or Tokyo.

TSUCHIURA AND TSUKUBA

Approximately an hour on the Joban Line from Tokyo's Ueno Station are the twin conurbations of Tsuchiura City and Tsukuba Science City. Not exactly green, these two venues nevertheless offer a change of air, and besides they have natural attractions — a lake and a mountain — very close by. Between them they embrace several different attractions (scientific, aquatic, pastoral) enabling a group to divide according to their interests and reunite for the journey back to Tokyo in the evening.

Tsuchiura City stands on the shore of **Lake Kasumigaura**, Japan's second largest lake. Its traditional sailing boats, each with one huge rectangular sail, are striking objects and justly famous.

Adjacent, Tsukuba is a scientific center of world standing and a major venue for international scientific conferences. It's home to a **National Laboratory for High Energy Physics** ("striving towards the discovery of unknown particles"), a 14-hectare **Botanical Garden**, the National Space Development Agency's **Space Center**, an Automobile Research Institute, an Expo Center, and much more.

Both cities are overlooked by Mt. Tsukuba which is accessible by cable car and ropeway. Tsuchiura's Tourist Information Cen-

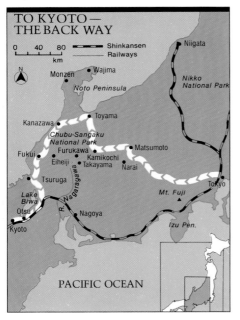

TO KYOTO —
THE BACK WAY

ter is on ((0298) 21-4166, while Tsukuba's is on ((0298) 55-8155.

LONGER TRIPS FROM TOKYO

The following trips can be as long or as short as you like, within reason, but you will need to spend at least one night and usually more on the road. If you are anxious about this, enlist the help of Japanese friends (or the TIC if they're not too busy) to book hotels, *ryokan* or *minshuku* before you leave Tokyo.

This is a necessity if you are traveling in mid-August (the O-bon holiday season) or over other national holiday periods such as Golden Week (end of April/beginning of May). At such times of year it is also imperative to book train seats well in advance.

If you are traveling off-peak, however, advance. As soon as you arrive at the station in the town where you have decided to spend the night, seek out the Kanko Annaisho Tourist Information Office, and have them book a hotel, *ryokan* or *minshuku* for you. They will speak enough English to be able to help you satisfactorily.

CLIMBING MOUNT FUJI

Mt. Fuji is the highest mountain in Japan and by far the most splendid, but during July and August (the open season) it is not a dauntingly hard climb. An athlete, it is said, could leave home in Tokyo in the morning, reach the peak and be home in time for dinner. Most people prefer to take it at a more leisurely pace, spending a night at the top and greeting the morning sun with a cry of *"Banzai!"*

Here's how to tackle it. Either find your way to Go-gome (Fifth station) on the north side of the mountain or Shin-go-gome (New Fifth station) on the south side. Shin-go-gome is the more convenient. Quite a number of buses travel there from Gotemba, Mishima and Fujinomiya stations on the Tokaido line from Tokyo.

From Fifth or New Fifth stations it takes five hours or more to the top. Although all sorts of people do the climb, including the blind and the extremely aged, the mountain demands respect. It's bitterly cold at the top, the wind can be fierce, part of the climb requires hauling oneself along by chains, while part of the descent is a sandy slide.

So warm protective clothes, including gloves, are a necessity. Take water along unless you want to buy it on the mountain; take easy-to-carry food such as nuts and raisins, too — food and drink are available but they're not cheap.

At the top there are primitive stone shelters where a space on *tatami* mats may be rented for about ¥3,000 a night. Alternatively, you can take a tent. It gets too cold at the top to stay in the open all night.

To avoid having to sleep at the top, many people have taken to setting off long after dark and climbing through the night, arriving at the peak or at one of the higher stations — the eighth has been recommended — in time to greet the sun. Sunrise on the peak at the start of the midsummer open season is at around 3:40 AM, becoming later as the season advances.

Where to Stay

Room rate indications — Budget: ¥5,000 or under. Moderate: ¥5,000 to ¥11,000. Average: ¥11,000 to ¥22,000. Expensive: ¥22,000 and up.

Hotel Bugaku-so ((0555) 62-1100, 508, Hirano, Yamana-kako-mura, Minami-Tsuru-gun. 24 rooms. Rates: moderate.
Kawaguchiko Club ((05557) 2-0554 FAX (05557) 2-0939 51-1, Azagawa, Kawaguchiko-machi, Minami-Tsuru-gun. 16 rooms. Rates: moderate.

TO KYOTO — THE BACK WAY

Route: Tokyo – Matsumoto and Kamikochi – Takayama – Toyama – Kanazawa – Noto Peninsula – Kanazawa – Eiheiji – Kyoto.

This leisurely route to Kyoto passes through several of the most charming and well-preserved towns and cities in Japan.

MATSUMOTO

Two and a half hours from Shinjuku by the hourly Azusa Express, has one of Japan's finest castles. Painted black, it is known as **Crow Castle** in contrast to White Egret Castle at Himeji. The original castle on this site was built in 1504. The present building is not as old as that but is fully authentic.

Once you get inside it's rather like being below deck in an old man-of-war sailing ship: the impression is of massive beams and very

little else. Certainly there are no display cases and no lifts, so it's a longish trudge up the six stories to the top for little reward.

The historical relics which would, if this were a concrete reconstruction like Nagoya's or Osaka's, be on display in the castle are here stored in the **Japan Folklore Library** in the castle's compound. The ticket to the castle admits you to this, too.

Matsumoto is where the late Mr. Suzuki developed an unique method of teaching youngsters to play musical instruments. It also hosts a brand new museum designed by

In contrast to the light and airy castle at Himeji, the black yet equally ornate castle at Matsumoto is called the Crow Castle. ABOVE: Two views of this old and authentic building.

Kazuo Shinohara, one of Japan's most original architect, devoted entirely to *ukiyo-e* prints.

From the footbridge above the tracks in Matsumoto station a famous panoramic view of the Japan Alps can be enjoyed, weather permitting.

Where to Stay

Enjyoh Bekkan ((0263) 33-7233 FAX (0263) 36-2084, 110, Utsukushigahara-onsen, Matsumoto City. Good views of the Alps. 19 Japanese-style rooms. Rates: moderate.

minute walking section). Sections of this latter can, of course, be used to gain access to the high mountain country, and serious hikes can then be undertaken from the vantage points so reached.

Note that both Kamikochi and most of the Tateyama–Kurobe Route are closed from November to late April except to intrepid travelers equipped with cross-country skis.

TAKAYAMA

Takayama, accessible without much diffi-

KAMIKOCHI

Two hours by train and bus from Matsumoto is Kamikochi, center of the **Chubu-Sangaku National Park** and one of the most attractive parts of the northern Alps. Take the train from Platform № 7 at Matsumoto to Shin-Shimashima (half an hour), and from there by bus to Kamikochi. There narrow basin is surrounded by high peaks and the resort is as a result a popular base for climbing them. See CLIMB A SMALL MOUNTAIN, page 16 and CROSS THE ALPS, page 32 in TOP SPOTS for more information on Kamikochi and on the Tateyama-Kurobe Route, a dramatic way to cross the whole range by a combination of various forms of public transport (with a ten-

culty both from Matsumoto (some 50 km or 31 miles away), and from the villages of Narai, Tsumago or Magome, is an elegant and prosperous city, a "little Kyoto" (like Kanazawa, described below) with a number of strong and unique attractions.

The street of shops and workshops parallel to the river and just east of it (the further side coming from the station) called **Kami-san-no-machi** is beautiful in the severe, classical Edo manner, and an excellent place to find souvenirs: *sake* (from the brewery), *miso* (from the factory), fine textiles, wooden objects, antiques. The town is dotted with small *sake* factories, and if you approach them nicely (and ideally in Japanese) the owners of some of them may be willing to show you around — a fascinating experience.

The city has plenty of *ryokan* and hotels, and if you stay overnight you can catch the outdoor vegetable and flower market in the morning. Or rather markets, for there are two locations: one by the river and one in front of a historic building called **Takayama Jinya**.

Takayama Jinya, the town's administrative office from about 1700 to 1868, is a must for anybody interested in Japanese history. Shrines, temples and castles; these are the three types of ancient structures which are readily encountered in Japan. Takayama Jinya is a great rarity, being the only one of 60 administrative offices of the Edo period still standing.

It's a large, rambling building with a garden full of trees swathed in straw bandages (in winter). Admire the roof of cypress bark, the storerooms for rice (the unit of currency and taxation), the large *tatami*-matted reception rooms. Takayama was directly under the domain of the Tokugawa shogun, which was one of the prime reasons for the city's prosperity: this building was the seat of his delegate's authority.

Takayama is an ideal size for exploring by bicycle. There are bike rental shops near the station — prices: ¥300 for the first hour, ¥200 for subsequent hours — and the Tourist Information people in the station will point you in the right direction. With the help of their map you will also be able to find the **Hida Old House Reservation**, 15 minutes southwest of the station by bike (five minutes by bus or taxi).

This is one of the biggest such parks in the country and may well be the best, with houses of many different types and several different social strata. It's permitted to poke around inside the houses, so vivid impressions of rural life in the old days can be obtained. The **Wakayama House**, one of the smaller group of houses near the ticket office, has a collection of old spinning, weaving and cooking equipment. The house itself has a steeply pitched thatched roof in the *gass-hozukuri* ("praying hands") style.

One has only two reservations about the Reservation: first, the friendly jumble of houses of different types can give a

confusing impression of old-time social realities. In fact all the houses come from very different sections of different towns and villages; no real village ever looked like this.

Second, the place is as phony as Disneyland because no one lives here. The atmosphere is dead. The old streets in the middle of Takayama, or a village like Narai, give a much stronger sense of living tradition.

There is a shrine in this phony old village. A question for the proprietors: when you move a shrine bodily to an old house reser-

vation, does the enshrined god oblige by tagging along too?

Entrance to the reservation is ¥300 (children half-price). The English pamphlet is informative.

Magnificent festivals are held in Takayama every April and October. See FESTIVALS, page 118, for more details. Four of the huge and gorgeously decorated festival wagons (*yatai*) are on permanent display in the **Takayama Yatai Kaikan** in the grounds of **Hachiman Shrine**, close to the center of town.

OPPOSITE: The snow capped peaks of the Japanese Alps near Kamikochi. ABOVE: A vermilion bridge in Takayama.

Some 15 km (just over nine miles) north of Takayama on the road to Toyama, is the small city of **Furukawa** which shares some of Takayama's antique charms: old atmospheric streets, richly ornamented wagons and a fine festival (April 19 to 20) during which they are displayed.

The city of **Toyama**, north of Takayama, need not detain you long, but deep in the mountains, 90 minutes by bus west of the city, an amazing (for a place so off the main route) institution has been started up: a festival of international theater, based on two

¥11,000 to ¥22,000. Expensive: ¥22,000 upwards. A (*) denotes hotels offering Western and Japanese-style rooms.

Hida Hotel Plaza ((0577) 33-4600 FAX (0577) 33-4602, 2-60, Hanaokacho, Takayama. 152* rooms. Rates: average and up.
Hishuya ((0577) 33-4001 FAX (0577) 34-5065, 1-464 Kamiokamoto-machi. 13 rooms. Rates: average and up.
Ryokan Seiryu ((0577) 32-0448 FAX (0577) 32-2345, 6, Hanakawa-machi, Takayama. 22 rooms. Rates: moderate.

new theaters in the village of **Togamura**, one inside an old *gasshozukuri* farmhouse, the other an outdoor stage of the Greek type. The first festival, featuring some of the world's most eminent fringe theater groups, took place in summer 1982. The following years the presence of eminent director Tadashi Suzuki ensured theater-lovers of a worthwhile experience.

Check with TIC for up-to-date details and dates. To get there, take the train from Toyama to Etchu-Yatsuo, then a bus to Togamura.

Where to Stay
Room rate indications — Budget: ¥5,000 or under. Moderate: ¥5,000 to ¥11,000. Average:

NARAI, TSUMAGO AND MAGOME

A detour in a southwesterly direction, halfway to Nagoya, brings us to three of Japan's best-preserved villages where, perhaps much more than in cities like Kyoto, it is possible to imagine what life was like in the old days.

The closest to Matsumoto, 50 minutes away by the stopping train, is **Narai**. The other, **Tsumago** and **Magome**, entail nearly a two-hour express train ride to Nagiso and then a brief bus ride. All three are located along the Nakasendo, the old alternative

An area noted for the brewing of fine quality *sake*, visitors can visit the breweries and see its production OPPOSITE then buy attractive souvenir bottles, or kegs, ABOVE directly from the brewery.

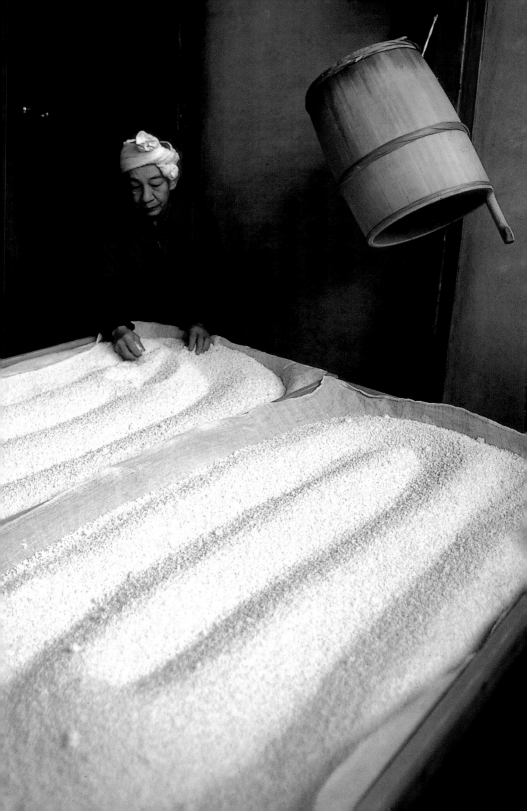

route between Edo and Kyoto, and the *raison d'être* for all three was to provide accommodation for travelers along the road.

As many of the travelers were of high caste, including the *daimyo* (feudal lords) and their retinues doing the obligatory commuting between their home province and the shogun's capital, the standard of some of the inns was very high. Interspersed among the various inns were small craft workshops turning out exquisite souvenirs as well as everyday articles, and teahouses. In fact, the villages were quite different from the typi-

cal farmer's villages in the countryside and more like fragments of the metropolis set down in the wilds.

The villagers have rather miraculously managed a smooth transition from feudal days to the present. Their economic activity remains almost exactly what it was — inns, crafts and tea (and now coffee) — but today the clients are ordinary modern Japanese in search of one of modern Japan's strongest reminders of the past.

Some wise souls have realized that the survival of the villages depends on their maintaining their historical appearance, and this is what they have done. Modern-look-

ing structures are very few, and when a new building goes up — a post office in Narai, for example — it's in the traditional style and traditional materials. And very charming it is, too.

A night in a *minshuku* or *ryokan* in one of these villages is perfect time travel. After a hot dip in one of the tiny bathrooms, in which everything is made of *hinoki* (Japanese cypress), there may be time for a stroll before supper. Array yourself in the *yukata* (cotton kimono), *haori* (half-coat) and *geta* (wooden shoes) provided by the *ryokan* (take a parasol if it's raining) and explore the village's single street. Note how narrow the houses are at the front, but how deep: houses were taxed according to the width of their frontage. Note also the small front doors covered with *shoji* paper and the narrow wooden bars on the upper windows.

You can deepen your understanding of the place the following morning by dropping into one of several *shiryokan*, houses typical of the village whose antique appearance has been preserved inside as well as out. The kettle hangs over the hearth, the abacus is ready by the desk, the second floor is full of silk-weaving equipment.

Craftsmen, including makers of lacquered vessels and combs, are still at work in the villages.

While Narai is out on its own, Tsumago and Magome are connected by the old Nakasendo road. The walk between them takes about three hours and is pleasant, particularly if you go from Tsumago to Magome, as that way the road is largely downhill.

KANAZAWA

Like Takayama, **Kanazawa**, 50 km (31 miles) west of Toyama, is often compared with Kyoto. But this sizable city has a special atmosphere of its own.

It's an old castle town still intact, with many narrow streets and blind alleys designed to deceive and trap invaders. For centuries it was the seat of the Maeda clan who ruled the city with a light and civilized hand, encouraging literature, silk-dyeing and other cultured pursuits. Their influence lingers on. Though in "the back of Japan" there is no sense here of being stuck in the sticks.

ABOVE: The stark fluidity of a Japanese character. A restaurant OPPOSITE in the post town of Narai.

Off the Beaten Track

Kenroku-en is a large and exquisite landscaped garden near the city center. With its ponds and streams, grotesque pines, charming views and tea cottages, it is arguably the most beautiful garden of its type in Japan. Many other people think so, too. If you go expecting peace and quiet you will be scandalized by the crowds and the hubbub. Go expecting Shinjuku station and you may be impressed by how nicely everyone behaves.

In one corner of the garden is *seison-kaku*, a ravishingly beautiful traditional villa, well

worth the admission fee. Wander through its rooms, admire the bold decorative scheme upstairs, sit on the veranda and enjoy the placid garden: the lifestyle of the aristocrats who used to live here is quite easy to imagine — and quite enviable.

Outdoor nighttime performances of Noh drama illuminated by torchlight take place in the garden in early summer.

Bits of Kanazawa Castle survive close by, but more interesting is the small but very well-defined area of old samurai houses called **Nagamachi**.

This area is easily recognized by the long, high walls of packed earth which enclose the houses. There are old tea shops in this small section and a silk-dyeing workshop. You can watch the craftsmen and craftswomen at work.

There are several other things worth seeing and doing in Kanazawa. Crafts generally are prominent; yuzen silk dyeing, for example, and ceramics in the village of Kutani, south of Kanazawa. The city has recently published an excellent English-

language guidebook, entitled *Kanazawa — The Other Side of Japan*, and Tokyo TIC have a mini-guide to the area (MG-043) as well.

You can also obtain brochures and other information from Ishikawa Prefecture's Tourism Division in Kanazawa ((0762) 23-9197 FAX (0762) 23-9498.

Kanazawa is the gateway to the placid and rural **Noto Peninsula.** The train from Kanazawa to Hakui and the bus from there northwards will bring you to **Monzen**, a small town with a beautiful and urbane Zen temple, **Sojiji**.

Much of the way there the bus runs along the coast. The fantastic rock formations – phalluses, doughnuts, pinnacles joined by holy rope — the old-fashioned prosperity of the little villages with their shiny black roofs, the *wakame* (seaweed) drying by the roadside, the sleek-prowed fishing boats, all help to make the journey a memorable one.

Where to Stay

Room rate indications — Budget: ¥5,000 or under. Moderate: ¥ 5,000 to ¥11,000. Average: ¥11,000 to ¥22,000. Expensive: ¥22,000 and up. A (ß) denotes business hotels with mostly single rooms.

Castle Inn Kanazawa (ß) ((0762) 23-6300 FAX (0762) 65-6365, 10-17, Konohana-machi. 96 rooms. Rates: moderate.
Kanazawa Youth Hostel ((0762) 52-3414, 37, Suehiro-cho. 120 beds. Rates: inexpensive.
Chaya Ryokan ((0762) 31-2225 FAX (0762) 31-2227, 2-17-21, Hommachi. 22 rooms. Rates: moderate.
Mitakeya ((0762) 31-1177 FAX (0762) 31-1179, 8 Gaiku, 102 Sainen-machi. 10 rooms. Rates: average and upward.

ECHIZEN

Wajima, a small city north of Monzen, is noted for its pretty lacquerware. From there express trains will take you back to Kanazawa and on to **Fukui**.

Fukui is the center of the Echizen area, celebrated far and wide for its many crafts. Lacquerware (*Echizen-Shikhi),* handmade paper *(Echizen-Washi)*, pottery *(Echizen-Yaki)* and a range of high-quality cutlery (*Echizen-Uchihamono)* are all made nearby.

Awara Town, on the coast half an hour to the north by the Keifuku Railway, is a hot spring resort. Stay on the train another six minutes and get off at Mikuni station to visit the coastal rock columns at Tojinbo. (From Mikuni take a 15-minute bus ride to Tojinbo; from there it's a three minute walk). Boat trips round the 25-m (80-ft) high rocks are available.

EIHEIJI

From Fukui take a train, or taxi after 3 PM or so, to **Eiheiji**, the main temple of the Soto Zen sect. It was founded by Zen Master Dogen who brought the teachings of Soto Zen to Japan.

> *The landscape of the mountains –*
> *The sound of streams –*
> *All are the body and voice of Buddha*

is one of Dogen's famous sayings. He's one of Japan's authentic saints.

The temple's location among great cryptomeria trees is awe-inspiring; the only pity is that its fame has turned it into something of a machine for tourists. If you are interested in Zen, try engaging the young monk who hands you the English-language pamphlet in conversation. He may be friendly and eager to talk.

Where to Stay

Room rate indications — Budget: ¥5,000 or under. Moderate: ¥5,000 to ¥11,000. Average: ¥11,000 to ¥22,000. Expensive: ¥22,000 and up.

Eiheiji Monzen Youth Hostel ((0776) 63-3123, 22-3, Shihi, Eiheiji-machi, Yoshida-gun, Fukuiken. 46 beds. Rates: inexpensive.
Yours Hotel Fukui ((0776) 25-3200 FAX (0776) 25-3458, 1-4-8, Chuo, Fukui. 74 rooms. Rates: average.

There: you've done it. Returning to Fukui you are poised for the descent to Kyoto, going by way of Tsuruga and Lake Biwa.

The track described above may well be on the way to becoming beaten: in 1982 the JTB offered for the first time a tour which visits several of the places mentioned. The four-day tour doesn't happen very often (not much more than once a month) so enquire for departure dates. It starts from Tokyo and visits Matsumoto, Takayama, Kanazawa and other places of interest on the road to Kyoto. The adult fare is ¥159,000, ¥152,000 for a child, and 15 days advance reservation is required.

THE NARROW ROAD TO THE DEEP NORTH

Broken in health and dressed in the robes of a monk, the great lyric poet Matsuo Basho

set off from Edo (Tokyo) in 1689, with one disciple, for the perilous regions of the north.

He was on the road for five months. The book — poems and prose travel sketches — which resulted was first published in English in the 1960s as *The Narrow Road to the Deep North*. Since then that phrase has entered the language; it seems to encapsulate one aspect of the Orient, conjuring up images of high cliffs, deep gorges and tiny figures toiling up winding mountain paths.

Well, where is that narrow road? Where does it lead? What is it like?

It starts, conveniently enough, from Tokyo and goes north some 400 km (250 miles)

Takayama's morning market OPPOSITE and ABOVE a roadside stall in Kyoto.

as far as present-day Akita Prefecture. Many of the spots that charmed Basho have disappeared under a blanket of industry. Some survive practically unchanged, however. Others have sprung into existence since Basho's day.

Taking his map as our text and leapfrogging and making detours at will, we can put together a fine tour of **Tohoku**, Honshu's northern quarter, an all but undiscovered country for the foreign tourist. At the same time we can enjoy the thoroughly modern pleasures of the green-and-white Shinkansen

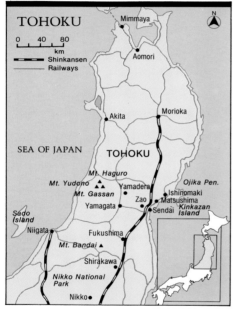

which runs from Ueno in central Tokyo (the platforms are underground) to Morioka in Iwate Prefecture.

Nikko (see also page 151 in JAPAN: THE BROAD HIGHWAY and SEE NIKKO, page 18 in TOP SPOTS) was one of his early stops. Going north from Nikko there is nothing much to detain us before Fukushima (other than Tsuchiura and Tsukuba — see TRIPS FROM TOKYO, page 207). Fukushima Prefecture is the most industrialized part of Tohoku. But at Haramachi, on the coast east of the city, spectacular ritual contests are held every summer in which mounted warriors compete for supremacy, fighting for banners shot into the air by fireworks. It's called Soma Nomaoi, and takes place July 23 to 25.

East of Fukushima and accessible by bus is a spectacular area Basho knew nothing of — for it didn't exist.

In 1888 the volcanic Mt. Bandai exploded with stupendous violence, destroying 11 villages and killing hundreds of people. The discharged rock blocked the courses of local rivers, creating an area of ponds and marshes. This is of peculiar beauty because the water of each of the ponds is a different color. A pretty nature course runs around and between five of them.

This area, called **Goshikinuma**, some 270 km (168 miles) from Tokyo, is very popular with Japanese tourists and should be avoided at weekends and national holidays.

The Bandai-Azuma Skyline toll-road which covers the distance between Goshikinuma and Fukushima features some spectacular scenery.

SENDAI

Sendai is the next stop going north, about 350 km (220 miles), two hours by JR Tohoku super-express from Tokyo. It's a historic city some of whose interest disappeared under wartime bombs. Rinnoji Temple, for example, is largely reconstructed (though the gate is original). But its garden setting is very fine. To get there, take a bus from Stand № 24 at Sendai station and get off at Rinnoji-mae.

Two other historical locations are the site of Sendai Castle (bus stand № 9 from the station to Sendai-shi Hakubutsukan) and the reconstructed Zuihoden Mausoleum (bus stand № 11 to Otamayabashi, then a 10-minute walk).

The seventeenth century black-lacquered **Osaki Hachiman Shrine** near the river, however, is a National Treasure. To get there, take a bus from stand № 25 or № 29 at the station, alighting at Hachiman Jinja-mae.

Today Sendai is vigorous and prosperous and looking good, tackling the modern age with confidence. A splendid example of this is the entirely covered-in Ichiban-cho Shopping Mall (10 minutes' walk from the station), with a good choice of restaurants and bars as well as boutiques and department stores.

Where to Stay

Room rate indications — Budget: ¥5,000 or

under. Moderate: ¥5,000 to ¥11,000. Average: ¥11,000 to ¥22,000. Expensive: ¥22,000 and up. A (ß) denotes business hotels with mostly single rooms. An (*) denotes hotels offering Western and Japanese-style rooms.

Sendai Chitose Youth Hostel ((022) 222-6329, 6-3-8, Odawara, Aoba-ku. 50 beds. Rates: inexpensive.
Hotel Sendai Plaza ((022) 262-7111 FAX (022) 262-8169, 2-20-1 Honcho. 186 rooms. Rates: moderate.
Sendai Royal Hotel (ß) ((022) 227-6131, 4-10-11, Chuo. 70* rooms. Rates: moderate.

MATSUSHIMA

Only 40 minutes by train from Sendai is **Matsushima**, one of the "three most scenic spots in Japan" (Miyajima near Hiroshima, details on page 192, is another). Basho visited Matsushima, and so should you.

The calm waters of the bay are dotted for miles with islands and islets, and each one is crowned with pine trees. It is indeed beautiful and rather other-worldly. You can take a pleasure boat around the bay to inspect the islands more closely. The jetty is five minutes walk from Matsushima-kaigan JR station.

Matsushima also boasts a **Music Box Museum** housing over a hundred specimens in working order, some of which are played every day. It's a 10-minute walk from the station, as is the Michinoku Date Masumune History Museum where 200 wax figures depict the life and times of Lord Date Matsumune, the seventeenth century power in the area. (Sendai's Zuihoden Mausoleum contains his ashes, and the Asaki Hachiman Shrine, also in Sendai, was built at his command).

Where to Stay

Room rate indications—Budget: ¥5,000 or under. Moderate: ¥ 5,000 to ¥11,000. Average: ¥11,000 to ¥22,000. Expensive: ¥22,000 and up. An (*) denotes hotels offering Western and Japanese-style rooms

Matsushima Youth Hostel ((0225) 88-2220, 89-48, Minamiakasaki, Mobiru, Naruse-cho. 90 beds. Rates: inexpensive.

Matsushima Century Hotel ((022) 354-4111 FAX (022) 354-4191, 8 Senzui, Matsushima-aza, Matsushimacho. 150* rooms. Rates: expensive.

KINKAZAN

Some two hours by train, and half an hour by ferry north of Sendai, is the small island of **Kinkazan**, at the tip of the Ojika Peninsula. It's a tranquil place of forests, with monkeys and deer running free. There's a large shrine, **Koganeyama-jinja**, which attracts many visitors, and the whole island has a slightly uncanny, numinous atmosphere like that of Miyajima, near Hiroshima. The island's youth hostel is near the shrine. The island makes an excellent retreat for anybody wanting a weekend away from urban frenzy. *Kinkazan* means "Gold Flower Mountain", probably a reference to the fragments of mica which sparkle in the island's rock.

The best ferry service to Kinkazan is from the port of Ayukawa, reached by bus from Ishinomaki, terminus of JR's Senseki line from Sendai. One ferry per day also sails from Ishinomaki itself.

YAMAGATA PREFECTURE

From Sendai the Senzan line takes you due west into neighboring Yamagata Prefecture. The stop to watch for is **Yamadera**, which means "Mountain Temple", and the temple is the attraction. It is perched on a spectacular hill of massive boulders covered with moss from which ancient pines and cypresses sprout at crazy angles. It is one of the most curious sites for a temple in the country, and it is also the place where Basho wrote one of his famous *haiku*:

> *So silent!*
> *The cicada's cry*
> *Penetrates the rocks.*

The western part of Yamagata Prefecture is a tranquil area, greatly depopulated and full of natural beauty. The tour ends here, with the three holy mountains which Basho climbed. All three still attract surprisingly large numbers of pilgrims and one of them,

Mt. Haguro (419 m or 1,397 ft), is a treat for anybody.

Of the first two **Mt. Yudono** (1,504 m or 5,002 ft) is really an extrusion of **Mt. Gassan** (1,980 m or 6,600 ft). Both are bitterly cold places of fierce wind and driving rain, even in summer.

Mt. Haguro, some 20 km (12 miles) to the north, is by contrast a placid, gentle peak, though possessing that atmosphere of spirituality that was earlier noted at Ise Jingu and Miyajima. A high pagoda, unpainted, stands in forested isolation at the foot of the peak. A stairway of shallow, aged steps makes for a pleasant climb to the top, and halfway there, if you break away from the path and walk for a short distance, is the site of the Southern Valley Temple, where Basho stayed overnight. It's a pleasant spot for a picnic. Nearby a stone tablet bears the words of the *haiku* he wrote when he was there:

> *The summer breeze*
> *in this blessed southern valley*
> *bears the fragrance of snow.*

Upon reaching the top of the mountain your eyes are greeted by a multitude of shrines-cum-temples, the chief of which has a roof of incredibly thick thatch. Relax in this, one of the most pleasant spots in northern Japan, and listen to the plaintive music of the holy mountain as an old mountain ascetic, dressed all in white, blows on a huge conch.

AOMORI

This is the topmost prefecture of Honshu, facing north to Hokkaido. It's rich in natural peace and in apples, though bleak enough in winter. It has two Quasi National Parks on the west coast, and one of these — Tsugaru Quasi National Park — contains Mt. Iwaki (1,625 m or 5,750 ft). To the south of the park are the Shirakami Mountains and the world's largest virgin beech forest, now declared a World Heritage Site by UNESCO.

Inland, meanwhile, is the popular Towada Hachimantai National Park. This contains Lake Towada, celebrated for the deep blue of its water and as a result it is frequently crowded with tourists, especially in autumn.

The most developed place along the shore is Yasumya.

How to Get There

Tohoku has long had the reputation of being in the back of beyond. Even today it is the place to go in search of shamanistic survivals into the modern era (associated with the Shugendo Buddhists, the sect for which the mountains of Haguro, Yudono and Gassan are sacred). Impoverished, remote, in recent times losing much of its population to the cities further south, there may appear little in Tohoku to make a visit imperative. But its very remoteness and strangeness will be an attraction for the intrepid.

Not that access is hard these days. *Shinkanzen* trains run as far as Morioka, approximately an hour north of Sendai, and Sendai, as we have said, is only two hours by the fastest trains from Tokyo. You can fly to Sendai from Osaka and Nagoya (70 minutes), Fukuoka (one hour, 40 minutes) or Sapporo (70 minutes). Sendai airport is 50 minutes from the center of the city. Another *shinkansen* runs between Tokyo and Niigata, the city on the Japan Sea opposite Sado Island, mentioned in OTHER ISLANDS, below. You can also get here via Nagano, site of the 1998 Winter Olympics. This train, the Joetsu *shinkansen*, cuts the journey time to Niigata from three hours, 55 minutes to less than two hours. As the jet foil from Niigata to Sado takes only one hour, this picturesque island to which political dissidents were formerly exiled has suddenly become accessible for summer weekend trips.

Where to Stay

Room rate indications — Budget: ¥5,000 or under. Moderate: ¥5,000 to ¥11,000. Average: ¥11,000 to ¥22,000. Expensive: ¥22,000 and up. An (*) denotes hotels offering Western and Japanese-style rooms.

Okura Hotel Niigata ((025) 224-6111 FAX (025) 224-7060, 6-53, Kawabatacho, Niigata. 303* rooms. Rates: average and upward.
Onoya Ryokan ((0252) 29-2951 FAX (0252) 29-3199, 981, Rokuban-cho, Furumachi-dori, Niigata. 24 rooms. Rates: average and upward.

As getting around in these parts requires more detailed information than can be encompassed in a book of this size, it would be a good idea for the visitor to arm himself with a copy of *Exploring Tohoku* by Jan Brown. Tohoku's biggest attractions are undoubtedly the three great summer festivals, held in Sendai, Akita and Aomori (see FESTIVALS, page 119).

HOKKAIDO

Hokkaido (Ezo in former times) is really a

only remaining tribal activity appears to be that laid on for tourists.

Hokkaido's lack of historical interest is made up for by its spaciousness and relative emptiness — it has 22 percent of the nation's total land area but only five percent of the population — and its pleasant reminders, for Westerners, of home: rolling green meadows spotted with cows and waving fields of grain. The towns seem as American-inspired as the agriculture: they spread on and on.

Due partly to the spaciousness, the people of Hokkaido enjoy a reputation for being

destination in its own right. Japan's most northerly large island, it has only been developed in earnest since the onset of modernization and is very different from the rest of the country. Huge, wild, thinly populated, it is a summer paradise and a winter challenge.

It is also the home of the *Ainu*, the Japanese archipelago's aborigines whose domain in prehistoric times covered much of Honshu. Almost are all now integrated more or less happily into mainstream society. In the eyes of some, however, they have suffered the fate currently being handed out to the Tibetans: dilution by immersion in the large-scale immigration of the numerically much larger neighboring ethnic group. Either way, the

looser and franker than other Japanese. Another reason for this is that, as the population is drawn from all parts of Japan, the old-fashioned, soil-rooted clannishness prevalent elsewhere has been unable to survive.

The island is great for hiking and camping holidays, particularly in summer when the weather is pleasantly cool compared to the rest of the country. In winter, though, it's cold. Temperatures can go down to minus 15°C in Sapporo, below minus 20°C inland, and ice-flows stand off the east coast (i.e. in

Tokaido Line *shinkansens* ABOVE zip between Tokyo and Hakata. The ones traveling north are painted green and white. Trains to Sapporo take 16 hours and provide a scenic ride halfway across Japan.

the Sea of Ouhotsk) every winter. But skiers flock here. Sapporo, the capital, was the site of the Winter Olympics in 1972, and its 90-m (300-ft) Okurayama Jump Hill is one of the longest ski-jumps in Japan.

And Hokkaido is in places very wild, in so far as anywhere in Japan is ever permitted to be wild. Seventy percent of its surface is covered by forest — an astonishing figure. Dangerous Hokkaido brown bears can be found, especially in Daisetsuzan National Park, swans migrate from nearby Siberia to the east coast, Japanese cranes arrive in villages in the Akan and Kusharo lake areas, and sea-eagles fish off the ice-flows.

SAPPORO

Sapporo charmingly announces its symbolic tree to be the lilac, its flower the lily of the valley, and its bird the cuckoo. Official statistics for 1996 put heinous crimes at 101 (and arrests for heinous crimes at 90), books lent from its nine municipal libraries at 4,400,000 (with a total population, including babes in arms, of 1,770,569), with the total number of visitors as 10,340,000 (this figure for 1995).

The actuality is that, laid out in a grid pattern like Nagoya and traversed by a subway system, Sapporo is superficially an unlovely city which nonetheless has quite a lot going for it. The nightlife, centered in the **Susukino** district, is said to be the hottest north of Tokyo, and the city has more than 3,500 bars and cabarets.

Also like Nagoya, the city's central park, **Odori Park,** is a block-wide strip, stretching from east to west. At the east end is the 147-m (481-ft) high TV tower from which there is a fine view of the city and the mountains beyond. You can also get a fine panorama by driving or riding the gondola up 531-m (1,800-ft) Mt. Moiwa (*Moiwa Yama*).

A notable feature of shopping in Sapporo are the heated all-weather arcades around the Sapporo Factory: no pushing through snow and slush for these northern sophisticates. Instead, winter conditions are turned to advantage in the February Ice Festival (see FESTIVALS, page 120 in THE CULTURE OF JAPAN), the most common reason for visiting the city. There's even a **Museum of Winter Sports**, adjacent to Nakajima Park (*Nakajima Koen*),

open 10 AM to 5:30 PM, closed Mondays and December 29 to January 3.

Sapporo is also the name of one of Japan's best-known beers, and the **Sapporo Beer Garden and Museum** (*Sapporo Biruen* and *Biru Hakubutsukan*) (731-4368, is a nineteenth century brick building with an all-you-can-eat-and-drink menu. The beer garden (742-1531) is open from 11:30 AM to 9 PM, and closed on December 31 and January 1. The museum, for which "reservation is required" (phone and check on this) is open from 9 AM to 5 PM (8:40 AM to 6 PM June to August); it's closed December 29 to January 5.

Sapporo's Chitose Airport is 35 minutes by rail from the city center courtesy of JR's Chitose Airport Station.

Where to Stay
Room rate indications — Budget: ¥5,000 or under. Moderate: ¥ 5,000 to ¥11,000. Average: ¥11,000 to ¥22,000. Expensive: ¥22,000 and up. An (*) denotes hotels offering Western and Japanese-style rooms

Sapporo Prince Hotel ((011) 241-1111 FAX (011) 231-5994, 11, Nishi, Minami-Nijo Chuo-ku. 322* rooms. Rates: average and upward.
Sapporo House Youth Hostel ((011) 726-4235, 3-1, Nishi 6-chome, Kita Rokujo, Kita-ku. 120 beds. Rates: inexpensive.
ANA Hotel Sapporo ((011) 221-4411 FAX (011) 222-7624, Nishi 1-chome, kita Roku jo, Chuo-ku. 460 rooms. Rates: moderate.
Nakamuraya ((011) 241-2111 FAX (011) 241-2118, 1, Nishi-7-chome, Kita-Sanjo, Chuo-ku. 29 rooms. Rates: moderate.

GREAT CREATING NATURE

What would the world be, once bereft
Of wet and of wildness? Let them be left,
O let them be left, wildness and wet;
Long live the weeds and the wilderness yet.
Gerard Manley Hopkins, *Inversnaid* (1881)

There are six designated national parks in Hokkaido, all sites of large tracts of unspoiled and dramatic nature.

In the southwest is **Shikotsu-Toya National Park**. The two lakes, Shikotsu and Toya, are the attraction here, plus the spa town of **Noboribetsu**. Noboribetsu is famous for the mixed bathing which is to be enjoyed at **Dai-ichi Takimoto Hotel** ((0143) 84-2111. It is one of the very few mixed baths in the country which is operational and in full swing. The bath is enormous and has nearly 20 large pools.

Daisetsuzan National Park, right in the center of the island, offers mile after mile of fairly undemanding and very enjoyable hiking. **Asahikawa**, Hokkaido's second city and one hour 34 minutes from Sapporo by Japan Rail, is the gateway to the magnificent area.

Two mountains in the more accessible northern part of the park are **Asahi-dake** (2,290 m or 7,634 ft) making it the highest summit on Hokkaido) and Kuro-dake (1,984 m or 6,614 ft).

To climb Asahi-dake, take an Asahikawa Denki Kido bus from Asahikawa JR Station to Asahikawa Ropeway bus stop (it's about 90 minutes), take the cable car to Sugatami Station, and then walk, two hours, to the summit.

Going up Kuro-dake is easier. From Kamikawa JR station (a short distance east of Asahikawa), take a Dohoku bus to Sounkyo, and then a cable car or lift to the peak. Sounyo, incidentally, in the Sounyo Gorge, is the place to stay in this more frequented part of the park. Daisetsuzan (sometimes spelt Taisetsuzan) is very popular with young Japanese, and hostels are often crowded in summer. Skiing, of course, is a favorite winter pastime.

The dramatic remains of past volcanic activity dominate the area around Kutcharo in the north of **Akan National Park** in east Hokkaido. This park features three main lakes, Kusshro, Mashu and Akan, and two smouldering volcanoes, Mt. Meakan at 1,499 m (4,995 ft) and Mt. Oakan at 1,371 m (4,570 ft). The town of **Akankohan** to the west of Lake Akan features an *Ainu* village where tribespeople can be observed doing tribal things — phony, but perhaps interesting anyway. The park is usually approached from Kushiro on Hokkaido's south coast, four and a half hours by train from Sapporo; the park itself is two hours by bus, or JR's Semmo Line, to the north.

Shiretoko National Park, in the extreme east, is a narrow but mountainous penin-

sula. **Mt. Rausu** rises to 1,661 m (5,570 ft), and **Rausu** is the resort (hot springs) at its foot. But there are other peaks — **Io** (1,560 m or 5,200 ft), **Omnebetsu** (1,331 m or 4,438 ft) and **Shiretoko** (1,254 m or 4,180 ft), as well as other spas — **Utoro**, for example. Boat trips can be taken to see the fine coastline.

The **Rishiri-Rebun-Sarobetsu National Park** is on the northernmost tip of Hokkaido. Rishiri and Rebun are islands off the coast, while Sarobetsu is a haven for wetland flowers on the mainland nearby. Alpine flowers are a feature of Rebun, while on Rishiri stands the 1,718-m (5,728-ft) mountain of the same name.

Lastly, the **Kushiro Marshlands National Park** is what it says it is. Situated on the southeast coast of Hokkaido, it is home to the rare Japanese White Red-crested Crane.

Hakodate

This town in the far southwest of the island is the first important place you come to on the main JR line from Honshu. It's overlooked by Mt. Hakodate (335 m or 1,120 ft, accessible by cablecar) and contains an Orthodox Church and a Trappist convent. **Yunokawa Spa** is on the coast close to the town.

Nearby Hakodate is what the Japanese quaintly call a Quasi National Park, at **Onuma**. There are facilities for tennis, golf, cycling and hiking.

Yubari

Situated east of Sapporo, Yubari is a former coal-mining village that has been preserved and developed as a tourist attraction. Neighboring Mt. Yubari (1,668 m or 5,560 ft) attracts many skiers in winter. That is the time, too, when a fringe offshoot of the annual Tokyo Film Festival takes place in the town, specializing in fantasy films, and this regularly attracts a number of celebrities, either as members of the jury or as special guests of the festival.

HOW TO GET THERE

Planes, trains and boats all go to Hokkaido from Tokyo. The air service, 35 flights a day from Haneda, is quickest (one hour, 30 minutes) but is expensive at ¥48,000 the round trip. Your JR Pass will allow you to go all the way by train, via the 24-km (14-mile) Seikan Tunnel that connects Hokkaido with Honshu; the total traveling time from Tokyo to Sapporo is 16 hours.

An interesting alternative for those with time to spare is the ferry service which, leaving from Tokyo Bay at 11:30 PM, arrives in Tomakomai at 5:30 AM, 30 hours later. The service only operates in summer. When the present writer made this trip he did so in the company of several tattooed gangsters and a party of Alaskan Indians. We all enjoyed a game of bingo together in the evening.

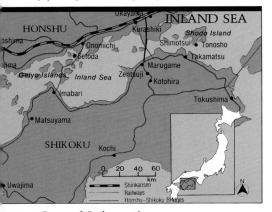

General Information

Further details of this large area can be had from the Hokkaido Tourist Association on ((011) 231-0941 or the International Information Corner at Sapporo's International Communication Plaza on ((011) 211-3678 FAX (011) 0020. This latter organization has another Information Corner. It is at Sapporo JR Station, open daily from 9 AM to 5 PM.

Where to Stay

This area (out of Sapporo) is too large to give specific hotel and hostel recommendations for but there are various of youth hostels around the island and plenty of hotels and *ryokan*. You can find details of these in the excellent Hokkaido Hotel List, produced by the Office of Tourism, Sapporo, or in one of the other publications mentioned in ACCOMMODATION, page 240 in TRAVELERS' TIPS.

Three "graces" resplendent in their best kimonos and fine makeup OPPOSITE.

SHIKOKU

Shikoku is the smallest of the four main islands of the archipelago and is separated from southern Honshu by the picturesque but much-exploited Inland Sea (Seto Naikai). It is a placid, unhurried island with a beautiful south coast, which is popular with divers, and some marvelous festivals. There are not as many tourist draws as in Honshu or Kyushu which means that, like the northern coast of southern Honshu, it is an ideal place for the traveler who wishes to become familiar with the texture of every day rural life. Shikoku is far from being an unspoiled paradise, however, and the light industrial skirts of the towns and cities sprawl as badly as anywhere else.

Takamatsu is the island's principal city, with a population above 250,000. The large, walled park two kilometers (just over one mile) south of the station **Ritsurin Koen** is the best thing to see in the city. There are tea cottages, grassy lawns and ponds with ornamental fowl, all wrought into pleasing harmony with pine-dotted rocks in the background.

Near the station and facing the Inland Sea is **Tamamo Park**, where what's left of the city's castle stands—which is not much. But admission is nominal so it's good value.

One hour and 20 minutes distant to the southeast by the fastest train is **Tokushima**, a city a little smaller than Takamatsu, rightly renowned for its summer festival (see FESTIVALS under THE CULTURE OF JAPAN). It is also the starting point of the island's famous pilgrimage course, which takes in 88 of the island's temples. A pilgrimage to each of these in turn is a popular folk-cure for all sorts of problems and a good way of endearing oneself to the gods in general.

People usually embark on such a pilgrimage after retirement. In the old days pilgrims used to hike from temple to temple and the whole course would take some two months. Now most of them go by bus and it takes about a week. They still dress completely in white. Spring and autumn are the most likely seasons in which to spot pilgrims (*o-henro san* in Japanese).

The major city in the south of the is land, capital of the prefecture of the same name, is **Kochi**. It's about two and a half hours from Takamatsu by the fastest train. The best thing in the city is the small but perfect castle, built in 1753, perched at the top of a steep slope about two kilometers (just over one mile) from the station. Some of the castle's interesting exhibits include some wobbly attempts at Roman calligraphy, pre-modern toys (wooden whales on wheels) and impressive photos, blown up to an enormous size, of the castle's nineteenth century samurai proprietors, looking as fierce and noble as American Indians.

Stretching from the castle gate one kilometer (just over half a mile) east of the castle is a large open-air market, held every Sunday, with a history going back 300 years.

Thirteen kilometers (eight miles) southeast of Kochi, accessible by bus from Kochi station, is **Katsurahama beach**. With its pine trees, white sand and excellent swimming, it is a typical section of the agreeable coastline of southern Shikoku.

On the route between Takamatsu and Kochi are several temples and shrines worth knowing about. **Zentsuji Temple**, just over a kilometer (three-quarters of a mile) from Zentsuji station, unusually spacious and with a fine five-story pagoda, is known as the birthplace of Kobo Daishi, one of Japan's greatest teachers of Buddhism. The temple was founded in AD 813.

Kotohira, just five kilometers (three miles) south of Zentsuji, is famous for its shrine of the same name, one of the most revered in the country, which is reached by a one-hour ascent of granite steps.

Uwajima, at the western extreme of the island and accessible by rail from the north or south, is famous for its bloodless bullfighting, in which two of the beasts lock horns and strive to push each other backwards in the sumo style. The sport takes place six times a year: check with the TIC for details.

Where to Stay
Room rate indications — Budget: ¥5,000 or under. Moderate: ¥5,000 to ¥11,000. Average: ¥11,000 to ¥22,000. Expensive: ¥22,000 and up.

Takamatsu Kokusai Hotel ((0878) 31-1511 FAX (0878) 61-0293, 2191-1, Kitacho. 103* rooms. Rates: average and upward.
Tokiwa Honkan ((0878) 61-5577 FAX (0878) 61-5584, 1-8-2, Tokiwacho. 24 rooms. Rates: average and upward.

MATSUYAMA

Shikoku's most populous city is Matsuyama. Two hours and 45 minutes by limited express from Takamatsu, and three hours by ferry from Hiroshima, it has two main attractions.

One is **Matsuyama Castle** with its three-story *donjon* in the center of the city. It is one of Japan's best-preserved, and, set as it is on a hilltop among trees, it provides framed views east to the Inland Sea and west to the Ishizuchi mountains. The other is **Dogo Onsen**, an ancient spa housed in an old wooden building. It's 15 minutes from the station by bus or tram to the stop of the same name, and then along a street of souvenir shops.

Also of interest is **Ishite-ji**, the best-known of the city's eight temples. Located in the same area as Dogo Onsen, its Kamakura-period gate has been designated a National Treasure.

Matsuyama is the capital of Ehime Prefecture, an area which contains some wonderful scenery, notably the indented coast and offshore islands of west Shikoku known as the Ashizuri-Uwakai National Park.

Further information on both the city and its region can be obtained from the Tourism Association of Ehime Prefecture ((0899) 43-5416, or the International Association of Ehime Prefecture ((0899) 43-6688, both located in Matsuyama.

Where to Stay
Room rate indications — Budget: ¥5,000 or under. Moderate: ¥5,000 to ¥11,000. Average: ¥11,000 to ¥22,000. Expensive: ¥22,000 and up.

Matsuyama Youth Hostel ((0899) 33-6366, 22-3 Dogohimezukaotsu, Matsuyama. 70 rooms. Rates: inexpensive.
ANA Hotel Matsuyama ((0899) 33-5511

FAX (0899) 21-6053, 3-2-1, Ichibancho, Matsuyama. 333 rooms. Rates: moderate to expensive.

THE INLAND SEA

The sea which divides Honshu, Shikoku and Kyushu is the birthplace, they say, of the Japanese sense of beauty. And in the scaly seas, the mists, the fishing boats, the shifting perspective of pine tree-prickly islets and islands, there is certainly something quintessentially Japanese, something

There are two principal ways to enjoy the Inland Sea: by spying on it from a height, and by traveling through it by ship.

High spots with excellent views are **Miyajima** (see HIROSHIMA, page 190 in JAPAN: THE BROAD HIGHWAY), Onomichi and Washuzan Hill.

Onomichi is halfway between Okayama and Hiroshima. A 20-minute bus ride to Nagaeguchi followed by a cable car ride brings you to the observatory in **Senkoji Park**, from which there is a great view of the Geiyo Islands.

which invites depiction in *sumie* ink rather than oils.

But, as Donald Richie lamented in his marvelous book *The Inland Sea*, (see FURTHER READING page 257) much of the area's beauty is vanishing under a slick of industry. Nothing has happened in the past 10 years to reverse that trend.

Vast suspension bridges now straddle the sea, linking Honshu and Shikoku, and even more are planned: the last in the series, scheduled for completion in 1998, will be the longest in the world at 1,990 m (6,630 ft). Although they may help to revive the economy in this backwater of Japan, but they will not help to restore the Inland Sea's lost tranquillity.

Washuzan Hill is on the eastern edge of Shimotsui, south of Kurashiki (see JAPAN: THE BROAD HIGHWAY). Buses run directly from Kurashiki, taking approximately 80 minutes. Shimotsui is itself a pleasant fishing village, from which frequent ferries run to Marugame on Shikoku.

Many ferries ply between various points on the sea's coasts, and details are to be found in the TIC's mini-guide to the Inland Sea. Three of the long-distance ferries which pass through many of the pretty spots during daylight hours (in summer — and you may have to get up early!) are as follows:

The classic, clean lines of Japanese architecture and the surrounding garden.

Osaka/Kobe – Beppu
Hiuga (in Kyushu) – Kobe
Shibushi (in southern Kyushu) – Osaka

Shorter trips which are recommended include the following:
Shimotsui – Tomari – Marugame
Onomichi – Setoda – Imabari
Hiroshima – Imabari
Onomichi – Matsuyama

For times of all these ferries check the comprehensive train/bus/ferry timetable published monthly and titled *Jikokuhyo* (unfortunately available only in Japanese).

A third way of getting acquainted with the Inland Sea is by spending time on one of its many islands. **Shodo-shima** (Shodo Island) is a good place to start: it has a dramatic gorge, lovely countryside, a monkey park and convenient buses to haul visitors between these attractions. It also has olive groves, one of many similarities between the Inland Sea and the comparably myth-steeped Aegean.

Ferries call at three ports on Shodo-shima — Tonosho, Ikeda and Fukuda — linking the island with major cities in Shikoku and Honshu, including Takamatsu and Kobe.

WHERE TO STAY

Room rate indications are as follows: Inexpensive: ¥5,000 and under. Moderate: ¥ 5,000 to 11,000. Average and upward: ¥11,000 to 22,000. Expensive: ¥22,000 and upward. An (*) denotes hotels offering both Western, and Japanese-style, rooms

Shodoshima Olive Youth Hostel ((0879) 82-6161, Olive-mura, Uchiumi-cho. 123 rooms. Rates: inexpensive.
Shodoshima Kokusai Hotel ((0879) 62-2111 FAX (0879) 62-1444, Ginpaura, Tonoshocho, Shozu-gun. 105 rooms. Rates: average to expensive.

OKINAWA

Japan has four distinct seasons, which inevitably means that approximately half the time the weather is too wet or humid or cold for total comfort. This is no southern California.

At the extreme southwestern end of the archipelago, however, hanging on as it were

by a thread, is a group of islands which is largely exempt from Japan's climatic vagaries. Okinawa, the name both of the main island and of the prefecture of which it is the hub, is halfway between Kyushu and Taiwan. It's Japan's very own tropical paradise. The average annual temperature is over 21°C (70°F); in January the average only goes down to 16.1°C (61°F). Rainfall is so slight it's a problem, though not for the visitor. The islands are fringed by numerous deliciously clean, white sandy beaches, most of them deserted. For all these reasons, it is possible in Okinawa to do numerous things which are enormously difficult in the rest of Japan: to lose the crowds, to relax and soak up the sun in splendid isolation, to snorkel and dive in crystalline waters of cobalt blue, to drive along spectacular coast roads without seeing another car for mile after mile.

As if all this were not enough, Okinawa is also a fascinating place in its own right. For centuries it was an independent kingdom, **Liu-Chiu**, "the Land of Propriety" as the Chinese condescended to describe it. The

Okinawan kings sponsored a rich and distinctive culture whose flavor can still be found in the weaving and dyeing traditions unique to the island. **Naha** the capital was an important entrepôt for silk, medicines and metals from China, swords, armor and gold from Japan, and spices and textiles from elsewhere in Asia. Okinawan seamen were known and respected throughout the Far East.

This golden age of prosperity and independence came to an end when the expansionist Japanese shogun Hideyoshi invaded the island in 1609 and brought it under Japanese control. From then on the Okinawan kings, reduced to the status of puppets, were obliged to pay tribute both to Japan and China. The entrepôt trade dwindled and profits from sugar, the island's most important crop, were siphoned off by the Japanese.

Relations with the Japanese big brother have been complicated ever since. Ethnically and linguistically Japan and Okinawa are very close, and it is believed that the islands were originally populated by Japanese drift-ing south. But through centuries of separation clear differences developed — the Okinawan dialect, for example, as spoken by the older generation, is incomprehensible to mainland Japanese — and when the islands were brought within Japanese domain, the Japanese decided that the Okinawans were an inferior breed and treated them accordingly.

Much the worst trauma in Okinawa's history occurred in the spring of 1945. Peaceable throughout its history, Okinawa was suddenly forced to arm in a hurry; young and old, fit and feeble were pressed into service. When the United States invaded, the Japanese fought to the last man, as was their custom: some 244,000 Japanese soldiers perished, as against 12,500 Americans. In the process, however, a vast number of innocent Okinawan civilians were slaughtered as well. More than 120,000 lost their lives.

Islands emerging from the mist in a sea of beaten bronze — the Inland Sea. Many foreign tourists never get this far south in Japan. It's a pity for here there is a different aspect of the country's culture to discover.

The island's towns and villages were reduced to piles of rubble.

The bloody final stages of the Battle of Okinawa took place in the extreme south of the island and the cliffs here are dotted with various monuments to the fallen. The most moving and interesting to visit is the Okinawa Prefectural **Peace Memorial Museum** (*Heiwa Kinen Shiryokan*) in which the savage facts and pitiful leavings of the conflict are displayed with eloquent simplicity.

After the war Okinawa became one of America's biggest military bases in the Far East, and America retained administrative control long after the main islands of Japan had been returned to Japanese control. Reversion to Japan finally occurred, after intense political agitation, in 1972. The United States still has large bases in the island, a perennial source of tension with the civilian population.

WHERE TO STAY

There are a number of youth hostels on these remote islands and a couple of decent hotels in Ishigaki. Prices are, because of the remoteness of the isles, on the high end of moderate to expensive side. However, they are probably worth it for the tranquillity and unspoiled beauty of the area.

NAHA

The capital of Okinawa Prefecture, Naha is a largely undistinguished modern city of more than 300,000 people which looks like a slice of Tokyo and sprawls across much of the southern half of the island. The airport is fairly close to the city center. *Kokusai O-dori*, "International Avenue," is a long, broad street in the middle of the city lined with shops, many of them oriented towards young visitors on vacation from the mainland. Unusual souvenirs available here include army surplus hand grenades and bullets (novelty key rings), extract of snake venom (used medicinally) and *wamori*, the fragrant and fiery local hooch.

Shuri is the only part of Naha which retains some of its antique, prewar atmosphere and charm, and it is worth exploring. A narrow stone-paved lane threads between the modest houses and voluptuous gardens of the capital's old ruling class up to *Shurei-no-mon*, the reconstructed gate of the old castle. The castle itself, the **Seiden**, which commands panoramic views, was reopened after total restoration in 1992.

Also in the vicinity are workshops turning out kimono and other fabrics dyed gloriously colors using the traditional *bingata* techniques. These are among Okinawa's most attractive and distinctive traditional products; the artisans in this area used to supply the needs of the court.

Out-of-town attractions are the **Ryuku-no-Kaze** theme park reproducing the life and culture of the Ryuku Kingdom (80 minutes by bus from Naha), and the **Gyokusendo Stalactite Cave** (*Gyokusendo Bunkamura*), the largest limestone cave in East Asia containing almost a million stalactites, stalagmites and connected pillars. It's 50 minutes by bus from central Naha.

Cycling is a good idea too. You can rent bikes in many places. Try Rent-a-Bike Naha ((098) 861-0040, Rent-a-Bike's Trade ((098) 863-0908 or Rental Bike ((098) 864-5116.

Where to Stay

Room rate indications — Budget: ¥5,000 or under. Moderate: ¥5,000 to ¥11,000. Average: ¥11,000 to ¥22,000. Expensive: ¥22,000 upwards. An (*) denotes hotels offering Western and Japanese-style rooms

Naha Youth Hostel ((0988) 57-0073, 51, Onoyamacho. 84 beds. Rates: Inexpensive.
Okinawa Hotel ((0988) 84-3191 FAX (0988) 85-2102, 35, Daido. 78* rooms. Rates: average and upward.
Okinawa Miyako Hotel ((0988) 87-1111 FAX (0988) 86-5591, 40, Matsugawa. 318 rooms. Rates: average and upward.
Okinawa Hotel ((0988) 84-3191 FAX (0988) 85-2102, 35, Daido. 18 rooms (plus 60 rooms in Western style). Rates: average and upward.

Further Afield

The principle lure of Okinawa, however, has to be its beaches. These are to be found in all parts of the island that lie beyond Naha's sprawl, and the most convenient way to get to them is by rented car. (See THE OPEN ROAD, page 46 in YOUR CHOICE for where to rent cars in Okinawa).

Try **Moon Beach, Tiger Beach, Manza Beach** or **Inbu Beach** on the west coast north of Naha, or **Nibara Beach** on the south coast. The less visited east coast has long stretches of pristine sand undefiled by so much as a solitary sunbather. If Japan's crowds are getting to you, this is the place to leave them behind. Beyond the Motobu Peninsula, the northern part of the island is densely wooded and scantily populated, and offers little for the vacationer besides some well-preserved villages and a delightful coast road.

A pleasant alternative to the main island's beaches is the island of **Tokashiki** in the Kerama Archipelago, reached in just an hour and a half by ship from Naha's Tomari harbor. From Tokashiki's uninteresting little harbor microbuses zip over to the island's best beach in the south, where beach umbrellas, snorkel equipment, etc. may be rented. At 3 PM the microbuses return and the ferry leaves Tokashiki for Naha at 4 PM. If the tranquillity of the beaches and forested hills seems worth enjoying in a more leisurely manner, there are several reasonably priced *minshuku* (simple Japanese inns) on the island.

Tokashiki is only one of numerous islands near Okinawa that repay the effort of visiting them. Some are in the Ryukyu Islands group of which Okinawa is the largest member, others in other groupings.

Ishigaki and **Iriomote** are the two principal Yaeyama Islands, and both belong to the area that became a national park in 1972. Ishigaki is accessible by air from Miyako Island. The town has several traditional buildings redolent of the old lifestyle of the island's nobility. Iriomote, one hour from Ishigaki by boat, contains Japan's most unspoiled tropical forest and is popular with serious hikers on that account. Deep in its shade dwell the last of the *yamaneko*, the rare Iriomote Wildcats.

Miyako Island itself, one hour by plane from Naha, was undamaged in the war and retains more of the look of old Okinawa than Okinawa itself. Many old houses survive here, their roofs of brown, semicircular ceramic tiles so all-embracing that there is hardly any house to be seen, huddled against the earth to avoid damage from the typhoons that frequently ravage this part of the world.

How to Get There

Several carriers operate frequent flight to Naha from Tokyo's Haneda Airport. The flight are frequent and take two and a half hours. You can also fly from Nagoya, Osaka, Fukuoka and other important Japanese cities. For those with more time, ferries leave Tokyo for Naha roughly once a week. The one-way trip takes two days and two nights.

General Information

For more information contact the Tourist Promotion Division of Okinawa Prefecture

((098) 866-2763 FAX (098) 866-2767, or the Naha City Tourist Association ((098) 868-4889.

OTHER ISLANDS

There is almost no end to the islands of Japan. **Sado**, the fifth largest, though much smaller than Shikoku and located off the coast of Niigata in the north of Honshu, is a delightful backwater, renowned for folk dancing, puppet plays and cuttlefish. It also offers excellent hiking. **Oshimac** and the other, smaller islands of the Izu chain are close enough to Tokyo to be viable for weekend escapes. There are two live volcanoes and a number of good beaches on them.

A lone fishing vessel plies the Inland Sea.

Travelers'
Tips

ARRIVING

Most visitors enter Honshu, Japan's main island, by one of two international airports: the New Tokyo International Airport (Narita) and Kansai International Airport (for Osaka and Kyoto). Tokyo's Narita, however, is the premier port of entry. Haneda, Tokyo's old international airport, is now only used by VIPs and Taiwan's China Airlines (so as not to annoy Beijing). It is much missed: it was only a 15-minute monorail ride from the center of town; Narita is 66 km (40 miles) out in the country.

There is a 500-room **Holiday Inn Narita** hotel ((0476) 32-1234 FAX (0476) 32-0617 at Narita Airport which may be of interest to travelers connecting flights or taking very early flights out of Japan.

VISAS AND WHATNOT

A visa is not required for the citizens of the following countries who do not engage in any remunerative activity in Japan through a Reciprocal Visa Exemption arrangement.

For six months or less: Austria, Germany, Ireland, Liechtenstein, Mexico, Switzerland, and the United Kingdom except where the passport was originally issued in British colonial territories.

For three months or less: Argentina, Bahamas, Barbados, Belgium, Canada, Chile, Colombia, Costa Rica, Croatia, Cyprus, Denmark, Dominica, El Salvador, Finland, France, Greece, Guatemala, Honduras, Iceland, Israel, Italy, Lesotho, Luxembourg, Malta, Mauritius, Netherlands, New Zealand, Norway, Portugal (except where passport originally issued in present or former Portuguese colonial territories), San Marino, Singapore, Slovenia, Spain, Surinam, Sweden, Tunisia, Turkey, Uraguay and the United States.

Malaysia and Peru are also included in this category, but securing a visa before arrival is officially recommended.

Iran and Pakistan are also included in this category, but in their cases the reciprocal visa exemption treaty is at the time of writing suspended.

For a stay of up to 14 days: Brunei.

If in any doubt, check with the Japanese Embassy about how best to proceed.

Immigration will stamp your passport and give you a status of residence which specifies how long you can stay. For tourists this is in practice normally three months. If you want to extend your period of stay you must go to an Immigration Office (*Nyukoku Kanri Jimusho*) and fill in a form stating your reason. If the application is accepted you pay a modest fee.

The address of Tokyo's Regional Immigration Bureau, Tokyo ((03) 3213-8111 is 2nd floor, Otemachi Godo Chosha Ichi-Go-Kan Building, 1–3–1, Otemachi, Chiyoda–ku. Opening hours 9 AM to 5 PM weekdays, 9 AM to noon on Saturdays.

If your country is not covered by a visa exemption agreement, obtain a visa from the Japanese Embassy before you set out. Without a visa, you will not be able granted permission to enter the country.

Commercial visas are also available for those conducting businesses involving a short stay. Apply as for a tourist visa, but with in addition two copies of a letter from the firm assigning you to visit Japan.

If you plan to stay in Japan for more than three months you should go to the local municipal office well in advance with two 5 cm x 5 cm (2 in x 2 in) mug shots and fill in two copies of the Application for Alien Registration form. You will generally be issued with your Alien Registration Certificate (colloquially known as the *gaijin* card) on the spot. You should carry it with you at all times. Not doing so can mean spending several hours at a police station and writing an apology.

CUSTOMS ALLOWANCES

You may bring three bottles of alcoholic beverages (760 cc each) into Japan with you; also 400 cigarettes or 100 cigars or 500 gm (8.75 oz) of tobacco, and 56 ml (2 oz) of perfume. In total, goods worth up to ¥200,000 (including watches, jewelry, etc.) may be brought in.

Don't try to bring marijuana or other illegal narcotics into the country; the last famous person who tried was Paul McCartney; he spent the whole of his stay behind bars. The Japanese authorities are very strict about drugs. Firearms, too, are strictly controlled.

The Japanese pornography law is curiously tight: don't be too shocked if your copy of *Playboy* or a similar magazine, is confiscated on arrival.

Complex rules apply to the import (and export) of dogs. Get in touch with your nearest Japanese embassy or consulate for details. No regulations apply to the import or export of domestic cats.

CURRENCY

You can and should buy some yen as soon as you are through Customs. The rate against the US dollar fluctuated dramatically in the mid-1990s, and may do so again. At the time of going to press, the rate is around US$1 = ¥120.

Yen come in 1-yen, 5-yen, 10-yen, 50-yen, 100-yen and 500-yen coins, and 1,000-yen, 5,000-yen and 10,000-yen notes.

Credit cards are almost universally accepted without surcharge.

Note that the opening hours of banks are 9 AM to 3 PM, Mondays to Fridays.

ELECTRICITY

The electric current in Japan is mostly 100 volts AC, but two different cycles are used: 50 in Eastern Japan (including Tokyo) and 60 in Western Japan (including Nagoya, Kyoto and Osaka). At major hotels two outlets for both 110 and 220 volts are installed for hair driers, electric razors, irons etc.

LOST AND FOUND

The Japanese are both meticulously honest with regard to lost items, and scrupulously efficient in dealing with them. Follow these instructions and there is an excellent chance anything you lose in the Tokyo area will be recovered.

If items are lost in taxis, go to the Tokyo Taxi Kindaika Center ((03) 3648-0300, 7-3-3 Minamisuna, Koto-ku, Tokyo.

If items are lost on JR trains, go to the JR Lost and Found Office, either at JR Tokyo Station ((03) 3231-1880 or at JR Ueno Station ((03) 3841-8069.

If items are lost on Eidan subways, go to the Lost and Found Office ((03) 3834-5577

of the Teito Rapid Transit Authority at subway station Ueno on the Hibiya Line.

If items are lost on Tokyo Metropolitan buses and subways, go to the Lost and Found Section ((03) 3431-1515 of the Tokyo Metropolitan Government at 2-3-29 Hamamatsu-cho, Minato-ku, Tokyo.

A Japanese friend should be with you when you phone as English will in all probability not be spoken. Finally, after three or four months all items found in Tokyo are sent to the Central Lost and Found Office of the Tokyo Metropolitan Police Department.

IN FROM THE AIRPORT

All agree that Narita is a ludicrous distance from the center of town. There are several ways to get into Tokyo from there.

For many travelers the best way is by the service called Narita Express (NEX), operated by Japan Rail, from inside Narita Airport Terminal to Tokyo Station. There are 23 trains a day. Fares: Single, ¥2,890; Green Car, ¥4,890; there are private compartments (for four) which cost slightly more. Time: Tokyo–Narita, 53 minutes. Japan Rail Passes are valid on this train, and you can change

Interior of a large shopping mall, Kyoto.

your exchange voucher for an actual pass at either of two offices at Narita, one at Terminal One, the other serving Terminals Two and Three. They're open daily from 7 AM to 11 PM.

If you don't have a JR Pass an alternative is the Keisei Railway's Skyliner train. All seats are reserved and tickets can be bought in the airport, opposite the Arrivals gate. A shuttle bus will take you from the airport to Narita Kuko station from where the trains leave. The trains travel nonstop between Narita and Ueno, a few stations north of Tokyo. The journey takes exactly one hour and trains

leave every 30 minutes on the hour and half-hour. The fare is ¥1,880.

There are limousine services between the airport and the Tokyo City Air Terminal. The comfortable journey takes about 55 minutes, though if traffic is heavy this may be as long as two hours. The fare is ¥2,700. The main drawback is that the terminal is located in Hakozaki and you have to take another bus, of which there are plenty, to Tokyo station.

A fourth alternative is the bus service which runs between the airport and Tokyo's major hotels. There is a special counter with information about this on the airport's ground floor. This is much the most convenient option for visitors who have made hotel reservations before arrival. Fares: ¥2,500 to

3,500, depending on the hotel; most hotels are ¥2,900. Call in at the TIC office on Narita's ground floor, between North and South Wings, for details.

In from Haneda

If these complexities incline you to postpone your Japan trip indefinitely, you could consider flying China Airlines to Haneda. Not surprisingly, they are well booked up in advance. From Haneda there is a monorail service (fare: ¥470) to Hamamatsucho subway station. A bus will take you to the monorail station from the forecourt outside arrivals.

In from Kansai

You can change your Japan Rail Pass exchange voucher for an actual pass at the Japan Rail West Information Counter in the International Arrivals Lobby (1st floor; open 8 AM to 9 PM), or at the green-colored Midori-no-madoguchi Reservations Ticket Office (open 5:30 AM to midnight).

JR trains run to Osaka (fare ¥1,160, one hour, five minutes) and Shin-Osaka (via Tennoji; fare ¥2,270, 45 minutes, or ¥1,320, 70 minutes); also to Kyoto (via Tennoji and Shin-Osaka; ¥3,490, 75 minutes, or ¥1,830, 95 minutes). The airport bus to Osaka takes 60 minutes and costs ¥1,030. JR also run a train service to Kobe; it takes 80 minutes and the fare is ¥1,660. The airport bus takes 70 minutes and the fare is ¥1,800.

ACCOMMODATION

Speaking very broadly, there are four basic types of accommodation in Japan: *ryokan*, major hotels, *bijinesu* (business) hotels and hostels. Prices vary widely. The most expensive *ryokan* in Kyoto may set you back about ¥40,000 per night, while the cheapest *ryokan* in the same city may not even cost ¥4,000. There are many choices available between those extremes, but however much or little you choose to fork out you can be almost certain of cleanliness, honest and prompt service and fine plumbing.

Most of Japan's internationally renowned hotels are concentrated in the capital, and include the **Akasaka Prince**, the **Takanawa Prince**, and the famous **Okura**, which is aging very elegantly. Outside Tokyo the **Miyako** in Kyoto and the **Hakone Prince** in Hakone are rightly respected around the world.

Business hotels, marked with a (ß) in the listings, are a peculiarly Japanese category aimed principally at the many Japanese businessmen traveling around the country on tight budgets. They offer decent, no-frills accommodation often in extremely compact rooms, a large proportion of which are singles (usually charged at no more than half the price of twins). Though not aimed at foreigners they present no cultural problems — unless you really feel like sprawling.

but often the simpler ones are just as nice; simplicity, after all, is what so much of the Japanese aesthetic sense is about.

Before gasping at the prices charged by some of the *ryokan*, remember that supper and breakfast are as a rule included in the overnight charge. Food is indeed often one of the best things about staying in a *ryokan*; your supper may consist of as many as twenty side dishes in addition to rice and soup.

Also, there is a useful organization called the Japanese Inn Group that links together over 80 small and economic *ryokan*, often in

A special feature is the tiny moulded fiberglass bathroom unit each room in a *bijinesu* is fitted with.

Hotels rooms followed by an asterisk (*) indicate that the hotel offers both Western and Japanese-style rooms. Even if a hotel is categorized as Western and we don't show an asterisk, and you'd fancy Japanese-style accommodation, you can always enquire when booking. You'll find that even in the most Westernized hotels, there are usually a handful of Japanese-style rooms available.

Ryokan are described in STAY IN A *RYOKAN*, page 24 in TOP SPOTS , and in THE PLEASURE OF JAPAN, page 120. A good *ryokan* is undoubtedly the most pleasant way of getting close to Japan. The most opulent ones will amaze,

little-visited parts of the country. Their directory of these places is available from TICs and contains a booking form. Prices range from ¥5,000 to ¥8,000 a night.

Minshuku are family houses where rooms are let out to visitors. They therefore offer the chance to get to know something of Japanese life from the inside. The Japan National Tourist Office has a list of recommendations — ask at their TICs.

Japanese youth hostels are like youth hostels all over the world: cheap, well-located, rough-and-ready, overorganized and segregated by sex. There are two types: Japan

OPPOSITE: Store sign in Takayama. ABOVE: Inside the Osaka Capsule Inn. Cheap accommodation like this can now be found in nearly every Japanese city.

Youth Hostels, Inc. hostels and public hostels run by local authorities. The latter have no membership requirement, and even with the ones where membership is required you can pay ¥600 at reception for a Welcome Stamp, and six stamps within a year entitle you to an International Card without further payment.

As there are over 500 hostels nationwide, many located in remote and picturesque spots, and some occupying the spare rooms of old temples, they are one of the best bets for the intrepid. If that means you, don't leave Tokyo without copies of *Youth Hostels Map of Japan* and *Public Youth Hostels*. Together they contains the addresses and phone numbers of all the country's youth hostels and are available at the TICs. Remember to book well in advance for holiday periods.

We have proposed in this guide, a limited list of accommodation which covers the major destinations throughout Japan. You'll find this shown under WHERE TO STAY in each area or destination. Western-style establishments are listed first, followed by *ryokan*. Many Western-style hotels also have some *ryokan*-style rooms; this is indicated by an (*).

TOURIST INFORMATION

Phone numbers of Japan's four **Tourist Information Centers** (TICs) are as follows:
Tokyo: ((03) 3201-3331, B1F, Tokyo International Forum, 3-5-1 Marunouchi. Chiyodaku; near Yurakuco JR station.
Narita Airport: ((0476) 34-6251.
Kyoto: ((075) 371-5649 Kyoto Tower Building, near Kyoto station.
Kansai Tourist Information Center: ((0724) 65-6025, Kansai International Airport.

The Tokyo and Kyoto offices are open from 9 AM to 5 PM Monday to Friday and 9 AM to noon on Saturdays, closed on Sundays and national holidays. The office at Narita Airport is open every day of the year from 9 AM to 8 PM, the one at Kansai Airport every day of the year from 9 AM to 9 PM.

The TIC's staff are well aware that there are not nearly enough branches to deal with the large numbers of foreign tourists coming to Japan these days, but they work hard to make up for it and go to a lot of trouble to be helpful. They will give you maps, leaflets,

guides and help you with travel schedules. One of the best things they've done is to prepare a series of mini-guides, leaflets full of detailed, practical and up-to-date information about how to get the most out of your trip to a large number of popular destinations in the country. These are not on the shelves in TIC offices; you have to ask for the particular guide or guides you need.

The following is a list of mini-guides currently available:

HOKKAIDO
011	*Sapporo & Vicinity*
012	*Southern Hokkaido*

TOHOKU
021-1	*Towada-Hachimantai National Park*
021-2	*Kakunodate & Lake Tazawa, Akita & Oga Peninsula*
022	*Morioka & Rikuchu Kaigan (Coast) National Park*
023	*Sendai, Matsushima & Hiraizumi*
024	*Aizu-Wakamatsu & Bandai*

KANTO
025	*Tsuchiura & Tsukuba*
031	*Nikko*
032	*Narita*
033	*Chichibu-Tama National Park*
034	*Hakone & Kamakura*
036	*Walking Tour Courses in Tokyo*

CHUBU
035-2	*Mt. Fuji & Fuji Five Lakes*
037	*The Izu Peninsula*
038	*Tateyama, Kurobe & Toyama*
041	*Niigata & Sado Island*
042	*Matsumoto & Kamikochi*
043	*Kanazawa*
044	*Takayama & Shirakawago*
045	*Nagoya & Vicinity*
046	*Karuizawa Heights*
047	*Kiso Valley*
049	*Noto Peninsula*

KINKI
048	*Lake Biwa, Otsu & Hikone*
051	*Ise-Shima*
052	*Walking Tour Courses in Kyoto*
053	*Walking Tour Courses in Nara*
054	*Shirahama & Wakayama Prefecture*
066	*Kobe, Himeji & Takarazuka*

CHUGOKU, SHIKOKU

055   *Fukuyama, Mihara & Onomichi*
061   *Okayama & Kurashiki*
062   *Matsue & Izumo-Taisha Shrine*
063   *Hiroshima & Miyajima*
064   *Hagi, Tsuwano & Akiyoshi-do Cave*
065   *Inland Sea*
067   *Shikoku*

KYUSHU, OKINAWA

068   *Saga & Vicinity*
071   *Fukuoka*
072   *Beppu & Vicinity*

If you need travel advice in English and you can't get to a TIC office, call them. Outside Tokyo and Kyoto you can take advantage of the free Japan Travel-Phone service. For queries (0120-44-4800 or 0088-22-4800. The same service is available in Tokyo and Kyoto, but you have to pay the usual local phone charges. The numbers to dial are as above: in Tokyo (3201-3331, in Kyoto (371-5649. The TIC will help you in any way they can, but they make the point that they are not a travel agency. So don't expect them to make, for example, hotel reservations for you.

073   *Kumamoto & Mt. Aso*
074   *Nagasaki & Unzen*
075   *Miyazaki & Vicinity*
076   *Kagoshima & Vicinity*
077   *Okinawa*

OTHERS

(By themes)

081   *Museums & Art Galleries*
082   *Skiing in Japan*
083   *Industrial Japan*
084   *Camping in Japan*
086   *Annual Events in Japan*
087   *Ceramic Arts & Crafts in Japan*
088   *Traditional Sports*
089   *Japanese Gardens*
090   *Japanese Hotsprings*

If they are not too busy, however, and if it is likely that the person on the other end won't understand English, they will go with you to a public phone in the office and help you out with your call.

The Japan National Tourist Organization operates a homepage on the Internet called **Japan Travel Updates.** The address (URL) is http://www.jnto.go.jp.

In addition, there is a national Information System that operates 91 centers in some 60 cities. They are usually situated at the train stations, with a second center sometimes in the city center. They can be

Stepping stones through the water gardens at the Heian Shrine, Kyoto.

recognized by their logo, a red question mark with the word "Information" below it.

MEASUREMENTS

In Japan, it's metric: centigrade, kilograms, liters, kilometers and meters. A few old measures (*i-sho*, about half a gallon, used for *sake*, and *tsubo*, the area of two *tatami* mats, used for measuring the area of land) add some spice.

COMMUNICATIONS

TELEPHONES

You will probably be startled by the number of public telephones in Japan, both in Tokyo and elsewhere. Many of them are just there on the street, quite unprotected; almost all of them work. They come in five colors: pink, red, blue, yellow and green. Pink ones take only 10-yen coins. Some red and blue and all yellow and green ones take 100-yen coins as well. Many also accept phone cards.

They're easy to use. Lift the receiver, insert one or more coins and dial. Have the number handy and dial promptly or you will have to start all over again. To avoid being cut off in midstream it is a good idea to put a few coins in at the start: some red phones will accept six 10-yen coins, others will accept five 10-yen and four 100-yen coins, and when you've finished they will return coins which have not been used. They will not, however, return fractions of 100-yen coins unused. Within the city you get one minutes' talking time for 10 yen. When dialing a Tokyo number from outside the city, prefix the number with 03.

International calls

To make an international call via IDD, the prefix is 001. If you use the prefix 002, however, you will be called back after the call and told what it cost. To speak to an international operator dial 0051.

Economy, and the even cheaper Discount, IDD rates are available at the following times:
Discount: 11 PM to 8 AM every day.
Economy: 7 to 11 PM weekdays, 8 AM to 11 PM Saturdays, Sundays and Public Holidays.

Rates are reasonable. They are charged in six-second units, at one rate is for the first minute you are connected, and then a second rate is applied during all subsequent minutes. Some examples of the most frequently called destinations are given below:
United States — rate per six seconds during first minute: Standard ¥33, Economy ¥26, Discount ¥20; rate per six seconds during subsequent minutes: Standard ¥17, Economy ¥14 and Discount ¥10.
United Kingdom, France and Germany — rate per six seconds during first minute: Standard ¥41, Economy ¥33 and Discount ¥26; rate per six seconds during subsequent minutes: Standard ¥30, Economy ¥24 and Discount ¥18.
Netherlands — rate per six seconds during first minute: Standard ¥43, Economy ¥34, Discount ¥26; rate per six seconds during subsequent minutes: Standard ¥30, Economy ¥24 and Discount ¥18.
Switzerland, Spain and Italy — rate per six seconds during first minute: Standard ¥43, Economy ¥34 and Discount ¥26; rate per six seconds during subsequent minutes: Standard ¥30, Economy ¥24, Discount ¥18.
Australia and Canada — rate per six seconds during first minute: Standard ¥37, Economy ¥30 and Discount ¥22; rate per six seconds during subsequent minutes: Standard ¥22, Economy ¥18 and Discount ¥13.

Directory Enquiries

For Directory Enquiries (in English):
Tokyo ((03) 3277-1010
Yokohama ((045) 322-1010
Narita Airport ((0476) 28-1010
Of priceless value is the English Telephone Directory, entitled **TOWN PAGE.** It contains ordinary and classified (Yellow Pages) listings, and comes in two volumes, East Japan (which includes Tokyo area) and West Japan.

Emergencies

In an emergency, dial 110 for Police, and 119 for Fire or Ambulance services. From a public call box you will not need a coin for these calls, but you must press the red button before dialing the number. If no one speaks English (0120-461-997. It's the Japan Helpline, and it's open 24 hours.

POST OFFICES

They are called *yubin-kyoku* and function in the normal manner. The symbol of the post office is (〒). Airmail rates around the world are as follows:

Letter up to 25 g (¹/₂ oz)
Asia: ¥90; Australasia, North and Central America, Europe and the Middle East: ¥110
South America and Africa: ¥130
Postcard: all countries : ¥70

NEWSPAPERS ETC.

As many as four daily English-language newspapers are published in Tokyo, which is extraordinary considering that native English speakers constitute a very minority.

The *Japan Times* (¥160), the oldest and most famous newspaper, is somewhat staid, however it is wonderful, nonetheless, to get such excellent news coverage in English in Asia. Several columns of news analysis are

A **braille letter** can be sent anywhere in the world free of charge.
International Letax (*Kokusai Denshi-yubin*) combining fax with the postal service (in other words, sending faxes to people without fax machines) — South America and Africa — first page ¥1,850, subsequent pages ¥800. All other countries — first page ¥1,350, subsequent pages ¥450. International Mini-Letax (with A5 writing space): all countries ¥1,000.

While many post offices are closed on Saturdays and Sundays, certain offices are open in the mornings on both days, and some others on Saturday afternoons. None of the post offices in Okinawa are open on Sunday mornings.

also reprinted from British and American publications.

The *Mainichi Daily News* (¥120), and the *Asahi Evening News* (¥120), both offshoots of Japanese-language papers, are absorbing and print translations of articles from the vernacular press that can be interesting. The *Daily Yomiuri*, also ¥120, is somewhat thin.

The monthly *Tokyo Journal*, ¥600, is the best source of information in English about what's on in town, including concerts and out-of-the-way cinemas and theaters.

The weekly *Tokyo Weekender*, free, also has film listings and the odd amusing article.

ABOVE: A typical restaurant frontage in the heart of Takayama, Honshu. OVERLEAF: An imported goods shop in Yokohama's Chinatown.

Every month sees a new edition of the considerably less bulky *Tokyo Finder,* another listings magazine, selling at ¥300. And even slimmer is *City Life News,* again monthly, selling at ¥220.

International magazines and papers are to be found at bookstores in major hotels. These are also the best places to find English-language books about Japan. The Imperial Hotel and New Otani Hotel are among those with good bookstores, and the bookstore at Tower Records in Shibuya is excellent.

LIBRARIES

Or, you may prefer to borrow a book. There are a few good libraries in town where you can borrow books, free:

American Center ((03) 3436-0901, ABC Kaikan, 2-6-3 Shiba-koen, Minato-ku, Tokyo.

This library is stronger on American periodicals than books. Three minutes from Shiba-koen subway station, Toei-Mita line. Open noon to 6 PM; closed Saturdays, Sundays, and Japanese and American public holidays.

British Council ((03) 3235-8035 Kenkyusha Eigo Center Building, 1-2 Kagurazaka, Shinjuku-ku, Tokyo.

A large library with a British emphasis. Three minutes' walk from Iidabashi JR Station (West Exit) and subway station (Exit B3) towards Yotsuya. Open 9 AM to 12:30 PM, and 1:30 to 5 PM. Closed Saturdays and Sundays. Readers must be 18 years old.
The Japan Foundation ((03) 5562-3527 **(** (03) 3263-4505, Akasaka 1-12-32, Ark Mori Building, 20th floor, Tokyo.

The Japan Foundation is Japan's culture-exporting body, modeled on the British Council. It has a good library of books on many Japanese subjects, a selection of local

newspapers and magazines, and a quiet reading-room. When you apply for a card it may be as well to say you are studying some aspect of the culture, however informally. The Foundation is 10 minutes from Kamiyacho subway station.

TELEVISION AND RADIO

Then, of course, there's the tube. There are seven regular TV channels available in Tokyo. Almost all broadcasting is in Japanese and most films are dubbed; one of the piquant pleasures of Japan is listening to John Wayne or Charles Bronson speaking fluent Japanese. However, if you can lay hands on a set with **multiplex** you can listen to certain programs, including several news broadcasts and some American soap operas, in English. Details are in the daily papers.

Major hotels have cable and satellite TV.

As for radio, an English language station, broadcasting largely popular music, is InterFM. It can be heard on 76.1 MHz in the metropolitan area. Another, FM-Cocolo, on broadcasts on 76.5 MHz in the Kansai area. Both stations feature some programs in languages other than Japanese and English — Mandarin Chinese, Portuguese, Hindi and Korean, for example.

An excellent music station, broadcasting a mixture of Western classical music, Japanese music (both pop and traditional), and much else, is NHK-FM. It broadcasts on 82.5 MHz in Tokyo, 88.1 MHz in Osaka, 82.5 MHz in Nagoya, 84.8 MHz in Fukuoka and 85.2 MHz in Sapporo.

TIME

Japan is 17 hours ahead of Los Angeles, 14 hours ahead of New York, nine hours ahead of London, eight hours ahead of Paris, Frankfurt, Rome and Amsterdam, six hours ahead of Moscow, one hour ahead of Beijing and Hong Kong, one hour behind Sydney, and three hours behind Auckland.

EMBASSIES

Tokyo's embassies are open five days a week. The following are their telephone numbers:

Afghanistan ((03) 3407-7900
Algeria ((03) 3711-2661
Argentina ((03) 5420-7101
Australia ((03) 5232-4111
Austria ((03) 3451-8281
Bangladesh ((03) 5704-0216
Belgium ((03) 3262-0191
Bolivia ((03) 3499-5441
Brazil ((03) 3404-5211
Bulgaria ((03) 3465-1021
Canada ((03) 3408-2101
China ((03) 3403-3380
Chile ((03) 3452-7561
Colombia ((03) 3440-6451
Costa Rica ((03) 3486-1812
Cuba ((03) 3716-3112
Czech Republic ((03) 3400-8122

Denmark ((03) 3496-3001
Dominican Republic ((03) 3499-6020
Ecuador ((03) 3499-2800
Egypt ((03) 3770-8022
El Salvador ((03) 3499-4461
Ethiopia ((03) 3718-1003
Finland ((03) 3442-2231
France ((03) 5420-8800
Gabon ((03) 3488-9540
Germany ((03) 3473-0151
Greece ((03) 3403-0871
Guatemala ((03) 3400-1830
Guinea ((03) 3443-8211

Haiti ((03) 3486-7070
Holy See ((03) 3263-6851
Honduras ((03) 3409-1150
Hungary ((03) 3798-8801
Iceland ((03) 5493-8776
India ((03) 3262-2391
Indonesia ((03) 3441-4201
Iran ((03) 3446-8011
Iraq ((03) 3423-1727
Ireland ((03) 3263-0695
Israel ((03) 3264-0911
Italy ((03) 3453-5291
Jordan ((03) 3580-5856

OPPOSITE: Souvenirs on sale including bright fans and ceramic *tunuki* (raccoon dogs).
ABOVE: Colorfully clad street sweepers ensure Yokohama's cleanliness.

Kenya ((03) 3723-4006
Republic of Korea ((03) 3452-7611
Kuwait ((03) 3455-0361
Laos ((03) 5411-2291
Lebanon ((03) 3580-1227
Libya ((03) 3477-0701
Madagascar ((03) 3446-7252
Malaysia ((03) 3476-3840
Mexico ((03) 3581-1131
Mongolia ((03) 3469-2088
Morocco ((03) 3478-3271
Myanmar (Burma) ((03) 3441-9291
Nepal ((03) 3705-5558

South Africa ((03) 3265-3366
Spain ((03) 3583-8531
Sri Lanka ((03) 3585-7431
Sudan ((03) 3476-0811
Sweden ((03) 5562-5050
Switzerland ((03) 3473-0121
Syria ((03) 3586-8977
Tanzania ((03) 3425-4531
Thailand ((03) 3441-7352
Tunisia ((03) 3353-4111
Turkey ((03) 3470-5131
Uganda ((03) 5493-5690 (consulate)
United Arab Emirates ((03) 5489-0804
United Kingdom ((03) 3265-5511
United States ((03) 3224-5000
Uruguay ((03) 3486-1888
Venezuela ((03) 3409-1501
Vietnam ((03) 3466-3311
Yemen ((03) 3499-7151
Zaire ((03) 3423-3981
Zambia ((03) 3491-0121
Zimbabwe ((03) 3280-0331
European Union Delegation ((03) 3239-0441

RELIGION

Check weekend issues of the *Japan Times* and back pages of the weekly *Tokyo Weekender* for details of Christian and other regular services. Tokyo has a mosque and a synagogue as well as a large number of churches.

HEALTH

Avoid getting sick in Japan if you can. And come with a travel insurance policy if you are holidaying for a week or few. Foreigners can join the health insurance system but it's only worthwhile if you are staying a longish time. And if you're not insured you must pay the full cost of pretty hefty medical charges.

Medical treatment is a problem in Japan. Doctors and hospitals with conditions of immaculate hygiene are plentiful, but many doctors are in thrall to their machines, and many others are strikingly greedy, loading their patients up with as many drugs as they can get away with. Dentists are also expensive.

If you need help, one place you could try is the **International Clinic** ((03) 3582-2646 FAX (03) 3583-8199, in Roppongi. English, French, Chinese, Greek and Japanese are

Netherlands ((03) 5401-0411
New Zealand ((03) 3467-2271
Nicaragua ((03) 3499-0400
Nigeria ((03) 5721-5391
Norway ((03) 3440-2611
Oman ((03) 3402-0877
Pakistan ((03) 3454-4861
Panama ((03) 3499-3741
Papua New Guinea ((03) 3454-7801
Paraguay ((03) 5485-3101
Peru ((03) 3406-4240
Philippines ((03) 3496-2731
Portugal ((03) 3400-7907
Romania ((03) 3479-0311
Russia ((03) 3583-4224
Rwanda ((03) 3486-7800
Saudi Arabia ((03) 3589-5241
Senegal ((03) 3464-8451
Singapore ((03) 3586-9111
Slovakia ((03) 3400-8122
Slovenia ((03) 5570-6275

ABOVE: Modern Yokohama department store. OPPOSITE: Kamakura *okonomiyaki* house, with the ingredients displayed outside.

among the languages spoken by its small team of doctors. The place's appearance may not inspire confidence (the waiting-room resembles the staff room of an English prep school that has seen better times) but the treatment is reliable and unhurried, and charges moderate by Japanese standards.

Then you might try the hospitals. In Tokyo the following may prove helpful:

International Catholic Hospital (Seibo Byoin) ((03) 3951-1111, 2-5-1 Naka-Ochiai Shinjuku-ku, Tokyo 161.

Japanese Red Cross Medical Center (Nihon Sekijujisha Iryo Center) ((03) 3400-1311, 4-1-22 Hiroo, Shibuya-ku, Tokyo 150.

St. Luke's International Hospital (Seiroka Byoin) ((03) 3541-5151, 9-1 Akashicho, Chuo-ku, Tokyo 104.

Tokyo Adventist Hospital (Tokyo Eisi Byoin) ((03) 3392-6151, 3-17-3 Amanuma, Suginami-ku, Tokyo 167. Note that in Japan medicines are dispensed at the same clinic or hospital where you see your doctor, as well as at pharmacists' (drug stores).

If none of these meets your needs, you can contact the TIC for advice about other English-speaking doctors.

If you need help at once, shout *"Tas'kete kur!"* ("Help!") at the top of your voice.

Chinese herbal medicine is very popular among Japanese and can be remarkably efficacious for minor problems. Many ordinary-looking drug stores specialize in Chinese medicine, called *kanpo- yaku*. Acupuncture (*hari*) and finger-massage (*shiatsu*) are other Chinese-derived treatments which are popular. Practitioners are all licensed but far from cheap. The TIC may be able to help you find a good one.

Western medicines and drugs are available from the **American Pharmacy**, in the same district as Tokyo's TIC.

CLOTHING

Short sleeves and cotton clothes for summer. Nobody likes wearing jackets in summer but most "salarymen" still do, and if you are on business so should you. Casual wear is acceptable in all but a very few nightspots in the capital. Bring sweaters and a warm coat for winter. If you wear your souvenir happi coat you will cause great mirth, unless you

are at a festival. Likewise with kimonos, though at a *ryokan* it's all right to slop around in the *yukata* (informal kimono, also used for nightwear) you are issued with. Remember the left-hand panel goes over the right for both men and women; the opposite way is only for corpses. Split-toed socks (*tabi*) are useful for *ryokan* in winter and go with the split-toed sandals. They make good souvenirs, too. Slip-on shoes — no laces — make life much easier at *ryokan* and private houses, where you are always taking them off and putting them on.

TRAVELING IN JAPAN

BY AIR

The three major operators of domestic air services are Japan Air Lines, All Nippon Airways and Toa Domestic Airlines. Call the numbers listed below among the other airlines' numbers for details of their services.

The following are the phone numbers of Tokyo's airline offices:

Aeroflot ((03) 3434-9671
Air Canada ((03) 3586-3891
Air China ((03) 5251-0711
Air France ((03) 3475-2211
Air India ((03) 3214-1981
Air Lanka ((03) 3573-4261
Air New Zealand ((03) 3287-1641
Air Nippon ((03) 5489-8668
Air Pacific ((03) 3435-1371
Alitalia ((03) 3580-2242
All Nippon Airways
    international flight reservations
    (0120-029333

domestic flight reservations
(0120-029222
American Airlines ((03) 3214-2111
Ansett Australia ((03) 5210-0791
Asiana Airlines ((03) 3582-6600
Austrian Airlines ((03) 3597-6100
Biman Bangladesh Airlines ((03) 3502-7922
British Airways ((03) 3593-8811
Canadian Airlines International
((03) 3281-7426
Cathay Pacific Airways ((03) 3504-1531
China Airlines ((03) 3436-1661
China Southern Airlines ((06) 448-6655

Korean Airlines ((03) 5443-3311
Lot Polish Airlines ((03) 3437-5741
Lufthansa German Airlines ((03) 3578-6700
Malaysian Airlines ((03) 3503-5961
MIAT—Mongolian Airlines ((03) 3237-1852
Northwest Airlines ((03) 3533-6000
Olympic Airways ((03) 3201-0611
Pakistan International ((03) 3216-6511
Philippine Airlines ((03) 3593-2421
Qantas ((03) 3593-7000
Royal Brunei ((06) 343-1567
Royal Nepal Airlines ((03) 3369-3317
Sabena World Airlines ((03) 3585-6151

Continental Micronesia ((03) 3508-4611
Delta Air Lines ((03) 5275-7000
Egypt Air ((03) 3211-4521
EVA Airways ((03) 3281-7001
Finnair (0120-700915
Garuda Indonesia ((03) 3593-1181
Iberia Airlines of Spain ((03) 3578-3555
Iran Air ((03) 3586-2101
Japan Air Lines (0120-255931
Japan Air System (0120-7-11283
Japan Asia Airways ((03) 5489-5411
KLM Royal Dutch Airlines ((03) 3216-0771

Scandinavia Airlines System ((03) 3503-8101
Singapore Airlines ((03) 3213-3431
South African Airways ((03) 3470-1901
Swissair ((03) 3212-1016
Thai Airways International ((03) 3503-3311
Trans World Airlines ((03) 3212-1477
Turkish Airlines ((03) 3543-9781
United Airlines ((03) 3817-4411
Varig Brazilian Airlines ((03) 3211-6751
VASP Brazilian Airlines ((06) 444-4441
Vietnam Airlines ((03) 3258-5255
Virgin Atlantic Airways ((03) 3499-881

ABOVE: If you plan on hiring a motorbike be aware
that road signs are sometimes rather bewildering.
OPPOSITE: The famous *shinkansen* (bullet train)
speeds passengers through the country in comfort.

By Rail

The Japanese railway network is one of the
best and most comprehensive in the world.

The privatized national system, known simply as JR, is expensive to use, but the trains are fast, clean and very punctual. As the land area of Japan is not very large, and as roads are frequently clogged with cars, rail travel is the most attractive way for most visitors to see Japan.

JR Services

The *shinkansen* runs at maximum speeds of 210 kph (130 mph) between Tokyo and Hakata (a.k.a. Fukuoka), by way of Nagoya, Kyoto, Osaka and Hiroshima. Two other

A few representative *shinkansen* fares:
Tokyo — Odawara: fare ¥1,420; surcharge for *shinkansen*: ¥2,150.
Tokyo – Kyoto: fare ¥7,830; surcharge ¥5,140.
Tokyo — Hiroshima: fare ¥11,120; surcharge ¥6,580.
Tokyo — Hakata: fare ¥13,180; surcharge ¥8,120.
Tokyo — Niigata: fare ¥5,360; surcharge ¥4,720.

The surcharges shown above are for reserved seats. If an unreserved seat is

services run north of the capital, one to Morioka in Iwate Prefecture and one to Niigata on the Japan Sea Coast.

Tokkyu special express trains are the fastest trains apart from the *shinkansen* and are used for long-distance travel on other lines.

Kyuko ordinary express trains make a limited number of stops.

Futsu ordinary trains stop at all stations. Fares are calculated according to distance. If you travel by any train other than a Futsu you also have to pay a surcharge; extra is also charged for reserved seats. The Green Window (Midori-no-mado guchi) and Travel Service Centers at JR stations sell these surcharge tickets, as well as berths for sleeping cars.

used all the way, then the charge is ¥500 less.

Phone calls using a phone card can be made on most *shinkansen* trains.

The surcharge for Tokkyu trains is cheaper than for the *shinkansen*, but the trip of course takes longer, and on lines that run parallel with *shinkansen* services there are not many trains. A very few Kyuko and Futsu trains cover long distances overnight with no sleeping cars. It may be hard to sleep but these, along with JR's bus service from Tokyo to Kyoto, are the cheapest ways of crossing the country.

Japan Rail Pass

A Japan Rail Pass is highly recommended. It

is vital to note that they can only be bought outside Japan. They are in two classes, Green or Ordinary. Green passes entitle the holder to travel in Green Cars, a euphemism for First Class. (As Japan's Ordinary Class is equal in comfort to most other countries' First Class, there would seem to be little point in paying the extra). The passes run for seven, 14 or 21 days, and constitute an immense saving if you plan to travel a lot. A seven-day ordinary pass currently costs ¥28,300; a 14-day ordinary costs ¥45,100; and a 21-day ordinary, ¥57,000. Children are half-price.

These are for Ordinary Class; Green Car passes are some 35 percent more. Payment is in your local currency at that day's official exchange rate.

The procedure for obtaining a JR Pass is as follows. Before leaving home, go to one of the agents appointed to sell you an Exchange Order. Japan Travel Bureau, Nippon Travel Agency, Kinki Nippon Tourist, Tokyu Tourist Corporation, and Japan Airlines should all be able to do this; the nearest office of the Japan National Tourist Organization will advise you in case of difficulty.

LEFT: A Nara temple restaurant offering warming winter fare including thick *oden* noodles. An Osaka restaurant RIGHT advertises its seafood.

On arrival in Japan you hand in the Exchange Order at any JR station that has a Japan Rail Pass exchange office and in return receive your pass. There are two such offices at Narita (Tokyo's main international airport), one for Terminal One, the other for Terminals Two and Three. They are open from 7 AM to 11 PM. In Tokyo itself there are such offices at Tokyo, Ueno, Shinjuku, Ikebukuro and Shibuya JR stations.

One small point — you must arrive in Japan on a "temporary visitor" status. Almost every tourist occupies this category. But if you are, for instance, coming in on "trainee" entry status, then you will unfortunately not be eligible for a Rail Pass.

Once in Tokyo, remember you can use your Pass on the Yamanote Line (that circles the city), as well as all the other JR lines that radiate out of Tokyo.

The only JR trains you cannot use your pass on without paying a supplement are the ones called *nozomi*, the fastest of the many long-distance *shinkansen* (bullet trains). For trips on all other long-distance *shinkansen*, or any other trains, go to the ticket office, present your Pass, and you will be given a reserved seat ticket free of charge, unless of course the train you choose is fully booked. But there are so many *shinkansen* and other departures it is usually possible (holidays apart) to get a seat a few minutes before departure. Several coaches are reserved, anyway, for passengers without reservations.

An example of the saving available from possessing a Japan Rail Pass is that the return fare from Tokyo's Shinjuku Station to Matsumoto, gateway to the Japan Alps, is ¥14,600, over half the seven-day rate for a rail pass. The trip, by the way, takes on average two and three quarter hours in each direction.

Excursion tickets and timetables

Excursion tickets, called the *shuyuken*, can be economical if you plan to travel from Tokyo to a particular area, for example Kyushu, and travel around in that area for some days. The details of these tickets are complicated; ask the TIC to help, or take a Japanese-speaking friend to the station with you.

The TIC have a Condensed Railway Timetable in English which gives details of all *shinkansen* and some other mainline services and gives a good rundown on fares, facilities and other details.

The ambitious traveler, however, who plans to travel extensively in the country alone should arm himself with a copy of *Jikokuhyo*, the book of timetables, published monthly, which covers all the trains, buses, planes and ferries in the country. It's published in various editions, available at station kiosks, at a price of about ¥600. The drawback? It's all in Japanese!

However, with a good English-language map of Japan to compare with the maps in the front of *Jikokuhyo*, and with a lot of patience, it's possible to use this volume without any knowledge of the language. The numbers on the train and ferry lines marked on the map refer to the page on which the timetable for that particular service starts; the arrow next to the number shows the direction. You may spend an inordinate amount of the journey with your head buried in the timetable, but the feeling of satisfaction when you sort it out is immense!

By Bus

Local buses are hard to use because destinations are not written in arabic numerals.

If you do use one, note that you take a ticket when you board the vehicle which registers at which stop you got on; you then pay the fare appropriate for the distance you've traveled when you leave (at the front of the bus). The fare will be displayed on an electronic board on the driver's left.

There are three overnight "Dream" buses from Tokyo, one each to Nagoya, Kyoto (plus Nara) and Osaka. They are operated by JR.
Nagoya bus: departs Tokyo 11:20 PM, arrives Nagoya 6:00 AM; or departs Tokyo 11:40 PM, arrives Nagoya 6:20 AM. Cost: ¥6,420.
Kyoto bus: departs Tokyo 10 PM, arrives Kyoto 6:00 AM; or departs Tokyo 11:00 PM, arrives Kyoto 6:50 AM. Cost: ¥8,180. The 10 PM bus goes on to Nara, arriving at 7:30 AM. Cost: ¥8,400.
Osaka bus: departs Tokyo 9:40 PM, arrives Osaka 6:03 AM; or departs Tokyo 10:20 PM, arrives Osaka 6:53 AM; or departs Tokyo 23 PM arrives Osaka 7:43 AM. Cost: ¥8,610.

These buses leave from the Yaesu side of Tokyo station, near the south entrance. Tickets can be bought from the Travel Service Center nearby.

By Taxi

A taxi with a red light in the window is cruising for a fare. The door at the back on the left-hand side will open and close automatically (it is operated by the driver). Minimum fare is ¥660 at the moment, though it rises frequently. This flag-fall fare is advertised on the nearside rear seat window; some cars do advertise lower fares, but the difference in your bill will not be great if you travel at all far). If you are stuck in traffic you pay for the time you spend there too. The fare which registers on the meter is the total charge. Fares are 30 percent higher between 11 PM and 5 AM. Before using an express way in Tokyo the driver will normally ask your permission as the toll, ¥600, will go on your bill. Tipping is neither necessary nor expected.

The days when it was common, early in the morning in Ginza, to come across taxis upside down with their wheels gently spinning, are fortunately over. Your driver still believes himself to be king of the road, however. If he's going too fast yell *"Yukkuri!"* ("Take it easy!")

THE LAST WORD

Two thousand years of alien history — the crowds, the typhoons, the earthquakes — you can't take it any more!

If you're in Tokyo, phone **Tokyo English Life Line (TELL)** and talk to them about it. 9 AM to 4 PM and 7 to 11 PM, seven days a week. ((03) 5721-4347. They offer everything from Samaritans-like advice in emergencies to simple about-town information; but essentially they're a listening service. For professional counselling they have another number ((03) 5721-4455.

INSTANT JAPANESE

Japanese is difficult for westerners to speak, but it's not hard to pronounce. So let's start with the easy bit.

Say the sentence, "Pass me two egg rolls". You have now spoken all the vowels of Japanese, and in the right order: a-i-u-e-o. The only modification we might make is to cut off the "lls" of "rolls" so the "o" sound is short, as in the word "hot".

Consonants are easy too, roughly the same as English except for "g" which is always hard and "r" which is somewhere between "r" and "l". The Japanese cannot in fact distinguish between the two sounds, which causes endless problems with words like "pray", "clap" and "rice".

A bar over a vowel lengthens it: "kyu" (abrupt) becomes "kyuuu", for example; "hot" becomes "ho-o-ot" (not "hoot").

Most Japanese words end with a vowel. This is why borrowed words sound strange. "Beer" becomes *"beer-u"*, "base ball" becomes *"baseboor-u"*, "hot" becomes *"hot-to"* and so on.

A few basic phrases will delight the Japanese because it means you are trying hard. Soon you will hear that great word *"jozu!"* ("skillful!") ringing in your ears.

Good morning. *O-ha-yo go-za-i-mas.*
Good afternoon. *Kon-ni-chi-wa.*
Good evening. *Kon-ban-wa.*
Good night. *O-ya-su-mi-na-sai.*
Goodbye. *Sayonara.*
Yes. *Hai.*
No. *Ie.*

Beer, please. *Beeru ku-da-sai.*
Coffee, please. *Kohi ku-da-sai.*
Menu, please. *Menu ku-da-sai.*
Thanks. *A-ri-ga-to.*
Thank you very much. *Do-mo a-ri-ga-to.*
That's all right. *Do i-ta-shi-ma-sh'te.*
It's wrong. *Chi-ga-i-ma-su.*
That's right. *So des'.*
I don't understand. *Wa-ka-ri-ma-sen.*
I understand. *Wa-ka-ri-ma-shi-ta.*
Please wait a minute. *Chot-to-mat-te ku-da-sai.*
I'm sorry. *Su-mi-ma-sen.*
Please (requesting something). *O-ne-gai-shi-ma-s'.*
Please (offering something). *Doe-zoh*
Please take me to Tokyo station. *To-kyo eki ma-de o-ne-gai-shi-mas.*
Where is… ? … *wa doe-koh des ka?*
How much? *E-ku-rah- des ka?*
Please show me a cheaper one. *Motto yasui-no-wo- me-se-teh ku-dah-sai.*
Where is the restroom? *O teh-a-rai wa doe-koh des ka?*

The most important point to bear in mind is that you should enunciate each syllable separately and distinctly, without slurring. We don't do this in English so it takes some practice. But relish the satisfaction of getting your point across!

If you want to study the language formally, schools advertise in the back of the *Japan Times.* One such in Tokyo, Kanda Gai Go Career College ((03) 3504-1356, claims that it can teach you to handle yourself in "just about any daily situation" in 22 weeks.

Further Reading

KOBO ABE, *The Woman in the Dues*, New York, Random House, 1972. Translated by E. Dale Saunders.

JAN BROWN, *Exploring Tohoku*, Tokyo, Weatherhill, 1983.

JAMES CLAVELL, *Shogun*, London, Hodder & Stoughton, 1975.

EUGENE HERRIGAL, *Zen in the Art of Archery*, London, Routledge & Kegan Paul, 1953.

MASUJI IBUSE, *Black Rain*, Tokyo, Kodansha International, 1969. Translated by John Bester.

MATSUO BASHO, *The Narrow Road to the Deep North and Other Travel Sketches*, London, Penguin Books, 1966. Translated by Yuasa Nobuyuki.

MATSUO BASHO, *A Haiku Journey—Basho's Narrow Road to a Far Province*, Tokyo, Kodansha International, 1974. Translated and introduced by Dorothy Britton.

YUKIO MISHIMA, *Five Modern Noh Plays*, New York, Alfred A. Knopf, 1957. Translated by Donald Keene.

MURASAKI SHIIKUBU, *The Tale of Genji*, New York, Alfred A. Knopf, 1966. Translated by Edward G. Seidensticker.

DONALD RICHIE, *The Inland Sea*, Tokyo, Weatherhill, 1971.

R. STEVENS, *Kanazawa: The Other Side of Japan*, Kanazawa, Society to Introduce Kanazawa to the World, Kanazawa Chamber of Commerce, 1979.

ROBER MARCH, *Reading the Japanese Mind*, Tokyo, Kodansha, 1996.

HARRY GUEST (Ed.) *Travellers' Literary Companion: Japan* Lincolnwood, Passport Books, 1995.

IAN BURUMA, *A Japanese Mirror*, London, Penguin Books, 1984.

DAVID PRICE *Travels in Japan*, London, Olive Press, 1986.

PETER POPHAM, *Tokyo: The City at the End of the World*, Tokyo, Kodansha, 1985.

FREDERIK L. SCHODT, (author of *Manga! Manga! The World of Japanese Comics*) *Dreamland Japan: Writings on Modern Manga*, Berkeley, Stone Bridge Press, 1997.

ALAN BOOTH, *The Roads to Sata*, London, Penguin, 1985.

JAMES R. BRANDON, (Ed.) *The Cambridge Guide to Asian Theatre*, Cambridge, Cambridge University Press, 1993.

Photo credits

All photos in this book are by Nik Wheeler except those listed below:

ROBERT HOLMES pages 12, 13, 15, 37, 48 left and right, 49 left and right, 64, 67, 68, 71, 81, 87, 94, 96 left, 100, 111, 121, 124, 126, 139, 144, 151, 153, 169, 172, 211, 216 and 229.

CHRIS TAYLOR pages 4, 11, 38, 55, 125, 79 and 202.

ADINA TOVY pages 7, 23, 57, 75, 89, 164-5, 170, 189, 193 and 253.

BRADLEY WINTERTON pages 16, 17, 32, 35, 40, 69, 152, 167 and 214.

Quick Reference A–Z Guide
to Places and Topics of Interest with
Listed Accommodation Restaurants and
Useful Telephone Numbers